LOAN SHARKS

THE GRANGERS' DREAM OF CHEAP MONEY.

LOAN SHARKS

THE BIRTH
OF
PREDATORY
LENDING

CHARLES R. GEISST

BROOKINGS INSTITUTION PRESS

Washington, D.C.

Library of Congress Cataloging-in-Publication data

Names: Geisst, Charles R., author.
Title: Loan Sharks : The Birth of Predatory Lending / Charles R. Geisst.
Description: Washington, D.C. : Brookings Institution Press, [2017] |
    Includes bibliographical references and index.
Identifiers: LCCN 2016017493 (print) | LCCN 2016028749 (ebook) |
    ISBN 9780815729006 (hardcover : alk. paper) | ISBN 9780815729013
    (ebook)
Subjects: LCSH: Usury—United States—History. | Consumer credit—
    United States—History. | Finance—United States—History.
Classification: LCC HG3756.U54 G453 2016 (print) | LCC HG3756.
    U54 (ebook) | DDC 332.8/3097309041—dc23
LC record available at https://lccn.loc.gov/2016017493

9 8 7 6 5 4 3 2 1

Typeset in Garamond

Composition by Westchester Publishing Services

CONTENTS

PREFACE

BEFORE WORLD WAR I, A MOVEMENT BEGAN IN THE UNITED States that has been all but forgotten today. It addressed a problem that reformers thought they could defeat in the name of economic efficiency and social justice. The problem was loan sharking, and the proposed remedy was legislation designed to put loan sharks out of business while replacing regulatory laws that were routinely evaded. The movement was a coordinated attack on loan sharks and their practices.

Memories of that movement lasted for about thirty years before fading, but it left a curious legacy. In the 1940s, cartoonist and satirist Al Capp named one of his best-known characters, Fearless Fosdick, after one of the movement's leaders, a New Yorker named Raymond Fosdick. On the other end of the political spectrum, the founding fathers of the contemporary Islamic finance phenomenon in the developing world cited another of the movement's leaders, Arthur Ham, also a New Yorker, as a crusader against what they considered to be the epitome of social and religious injustice: charging interest, or *riba*. Not just excessive interest, but any interest. The original Fearless Fosdick attacked interest as a menace to New York City, while Muslims attacked it more broadly as a menace to humankind.

At the heart of the problem was the practice of usury, or high-interest lending, in the United States. Usury has been public enemy number one in most societies since antiquity. Despite a three thousand year history, it is still discussed in policy circles as an economic problem, overlooking the social problems it causes in favor of often-antiseptic discussions about market rates of interest and financial intermediation. Few economic and social issues have the distinction of appearing, in one guise or other, in the Old Testament, canon law, English common law, and the Dodd–Frank Act of 2010 as a difficult problem doing harm to society.

The primary reason usury has been at the center of so many moral and social debates is fairly simple. Since antiquity, legislators have fixed the maximum rate of interest. In Rome it was 12 percent, in Elizabethan England 6 percent, and in the United States, it has ranged from 6 percent to 40 percent. But as soon as a rate was set, it became inflexible and out of date. Naturally, exceeding the maximum by lenders became an art, and then a science. In modern times lenders are aided by free market advocates who maintain that such rates are outdated and symptomatic of simple-minded adherence to an unattainable ideal. The market should decide how much the poor and the hard-put should pay the lenders of last resort, like loan sharks, for example. Maximum interest rate ceilings are one of the earliest examples of laws passed in one era that do not travel well to another.

The result was an attempt to circumvent old rates with newer ones that, while usurious by most standards, sought to strike a balance between borrower and lender. Borrowers get funds that may be unobtainable otherwise, while lenders are compensated for the risks involved in lending. But the argument does not finish there. If the rate is too high at 25 to 40 percent, the financially distressed borrower may never adequately get out of the debt cycle. The old moral arguments about excessive interest lost that battle because the fairness part was defeated by the notions that lenders must be compensated for the risks they incur and the market should decide how much that compensation should be. Usually, the "market" has been what lenders say it is and they have gone mostly unchallenged.

Loan sharking has always been closely related to other social problems. As the chapters that follow show, the American debate has spilled over to labor practices, Prohibition, and federal–state clashes over banking jurisdiction. Al Capp's Fearless Fosdick, like his namesake, was a crusader against many social issues at the same time, and not much has changed. Today, usury problems manifest themselves in credit card lending, subprime lending, payday lending, antitrust issues, truth-in-lending, access to higher education, and the residential housing market.

The early history of high-interest lending in the United States that *Loan Sharks* examines demonstrates this connection between interest rates and related social issues. Loan sharking in its many forms has caused stock market panics, structural banking problems, and often has impeded economic recovery after severe economic downturns. It is frequently ignored as an antiquated problem, but remains very much alive today.

CHAPTER ONE
A POPULIST ISSUE

IN THE THREE DECADES FOLLOWING THE CIVIL WAR, THE United States underwent more social and economic change than at any time since independence. In addition to the social upheaval caused by the war itself, the country was expanding west at a rapid pace. States and the federal government granted hundreds of millions of acres to the railroads so they could reach the West Coast, providing infrastructure to a country with extremely poor roads. But the country was experiencing other momentous changes that at first went unnoticed.

The United States had begun to develop its financial economy. The war had seen an explosion in the demand for life insurance, speculation and investing in common stock, and commodities trading. As a result, a growing class of well-to-do entrepreneurs emerged quickly, and investing in intangibles became more important in the get-rich-quick environment than working at a profession or in manufacturing or farming. These trends occurred about the same time, causing further upheaval and widespread suspicion among those on the lower rungs of the social ladder. At first, the rapidly emerging financial economy made sensational headlines. During the Civil War, gold traded actively on the New York market, and prices fluctuated wildly.

When Abraham Lincoln visited the gold exchange, he was appalled to discover that traders would buy or sell depending on news from the battlefront. When the North won a victory they would whistle the "Battle Hymn of the Republic." When the South won a battle, they whistled "Dixie." Lincoln was infuriated. Results did not seem to matter—only trading profits. Similar events continued after Appomattox. In 1869 the already infamous speculator Jay Gould and cohorts had attempted to corner the U.S. gold supply by bidding up prices on the New York gold market and selling out before prices eventually crashed. The day they did so became known as Black Friday, and the reported $10 million profit made by the speculators did not go unnoticed on the farms and in the factories, where the annual wage was well below a thousand dollars a year. Adding to the intrigue were rumors that Gould had persuaded President Ulysses S. Grant, elected the year before, to provide unwitting assistance in driving up the price of gold.

The result of the corner was a severe recession and a banking crisis—disruptions in the economy were felt all the way to the factory floor and the distant farm. But the allure of the financial economy proved too great to be resisted. The West proved a great attraction to the financial economy as well; not as a place to farm, but as a vast area requiring financial services. Initially, banking was concentrated in the big cities, mostly on the East Coast, and did not accommodate the needs of farmers and small businessmen, especially those in faraway states and territories. Many entrepreneurs packed their bags and moved west to open small banks and financial service companies to deal with individuals and small businesses. They soon realized that, by setting up shop west of the Ohio River, they had also escaped any sort of regulatory oversight imposed by Eastern states.

By the 1890s, loan sharking—as the practice of high-interest lending came to be called—had become a large cottage industry, especially west of the Ohio River. Merchants, businessmen, and even clergymen with a few thousand dollars to invest eagerly became high-interest lenders. They filled a large vacuum not yet occupied by banks and other small financial institutions. The practice had profound implications for economic policy from the 1870s to the beginning of the Great Depression. The overwhelming dominance of banks and the general reluctance of the federal government to intervene in economic affairs except in times of emergency set a precedent that became embedded in the financial system. Banks were given free rein in most states to charge interest as they saw fit, and usurious lending was attacked on a local or state level if it was challenged at all. Interest rates were set by businessmen, and complaints about excessive interest charges were regarded as nothing more than an annoyance. Litigation against predatory lenders was rare and, before long, the precedent became institutionalized. Lenders charged what the market would bear and borrowers seldom complained publicly. The rewards were plentiful; lending for mortgages and consumption loans could earn returns from a relatively modest 10 percent to well over 500 percent per year or more.

The term "loan shark" quickly became the preferred term for high-interest lenders in the American vernacular, replacing the much older term "usurer." The word "shark" was a popular epithet throughout the nineteenth century for describing anyone who was predatory in his chosen profession, whether it was playing billiards or selling snake oil. By contrast, the word "usurer" was derived from Latin and made the practice sound archaic and alien. Ironically, the term loan shark actually softened the image of the usurer, who had often been depicted as a moral scourge in popular art and newspaper cartoons. The loan shark was nothing more than a marginal businessman who provided a vital service for a price (albeit a high price). Later in the nineteenth century some loan sharks would acquire an even softer image, being depicted as "aunties and uncles" (although they, too, provided loans at unavuncular rates). When the filmmaker D. W. Griffith depicted the nationwide lending problem in his 1910 film *The Usurer*, he opted to use the harsher term.

Usury, Arguments For and Against

Many states had begun to look critically at their own usury laws even before the Civil War. The focus on usury laws in mid-nineteenth-century America came on the heels of their official repeal in Britain in 1854. England's usury laws dated back to the eleventh century, and over the centuries the country had, at times, made usury a crime and at other times, it had experimented with different maximum lending rates. In the decades before the repeal of the official usury laws English economists, from Jeremy Bentham to David Ricardo, had expressed misgivings about the laws in varying degrees, and their arguments on both sides of the issue were well known to Americans. The English movement was strongly influenced by a free market outlook that favored few restraints on economic activity. Ironically, Adam Smith, the father of free market economics, did not favor abolishing usury laws across the board. He recommended a band, or collar, of interest rates with a maximum and a minimum lending rate, using the market as a guide.

Usury laws occupied an unusual place in American society well before 1776. Georgia, founded in 1733 by James Oglethorpe, a member of the British Parliament, had the distinction of being the only colony that provided a haven for debtors. Each of the original thirteen states enacted laws on maximum rates of interest on real property loans, usually fixing a maximum of 6 to 8 percent as the highest rate lenders could charge. These limitations were written into their original colonial charters from Britain and into their first constitutions. The 8 percent rate remained in force in Massachusetts until 1692, when it was lowered to 6 percent. The Maryland legislature set the maximum rate at 6 percent, allowing for an 8 percent rate for trade-related transactions. New York introduced an original maximum rate of 6 percent for a five-year period; this was subsequently raised to 8 percent, only to be reduced again to the original rate in 1737.

Between the Revolution and the Civil War, lenders ignored usury laws with varying degrees of impunity. The fragmented nature of banking and the lack of a central bank meant that credit allocation originated with the large New York banks. There was little flexibility when the supply of credit and money became a problem unless those banks decided to act. If the banks perceived risky conditions they would curtail the amount of loans in circulation, often exacerbating already tight credit conditions. The large banks provided services to merchants and wealthier individuals but were not in the habit of making small loans to consumers. But even merchants relied on the judgment of the banks in tough times.

In any event, commercial loans of $250,000 were exempt from usury laws in most states. Small borrowers—generally those borrowing $300 or less—had to rely on private lenders or small institutions. Lenders did not overtly advertise rates in violation of local usury laws; instead, they hid them in the details of the loan agreement. This allowed lenders to appear to operate within the confines of the usury laws while exacting much higher effective rates of interest.

Following trends in England, many states begin to experiment with abolishing their often-abused usury ceilings or, at least, raising the maximum allowable rate of interest. This movement, which extended from the 1830s through the Civil War, drew heated debate on both sides. The arguments ran from defending usury ceilings on grounds of moral justice to economic arguments couched in the theory of money as a commodity that should fetch a market rate for its use.

Both sides provided compelling arguments but poor evidence. Adherents of usury ceilings could point to the short-lived attempts before the Civil War by some states to abolish ceilings. Despite those attempts, all states but one had usury laws back on their books by the mid-1850s. The lone exception was California; the state was reported to have ruinously high borrowing rates, fueled in part by the gold rush that created a borrowing frenzy for land and equipment and everything else tied to gold.

The repeal of usury laws in Eastern states met with varying degrees of success. New York's usury ceiling of 7 percent was maintained better than other states. The movement toward abolition of ceilings, interrupted by the Civil War, continued shortly thereafter. In early 1873, however, as repeal was being considered in neighboring Massachusetts, New York Governor John Adams Dix announced that his state should consider repealing its usury ceiling. The matter centered on whether the ceiling was economically viable for Wall Street. "It is quite clear that in the City of New York," Dix said, "that for scruples on the one hand and fears on the other by which conscientious and timid capitalists are restrained from lending at prohibitive rates, the enormous interest paid under the pressure of extraordinary demands for the use of money could not be maintained for a single day."[1] Dix recognized the enforcement problem that the ceiling created. Nevertheless, his plan to abolish New York's usury ceiling went nowhere.

Different laws in different states often created interstate tensions. Courts usually took the location of lenders into consideration when deciding charges of usury. In one case in 1862 a New York court rejected the suit brought by a borrower who had signed for a loan at 26 percent interest in Minnesota then claimed that the rate under the laws of New York, where he now lived, was usurious. The court acknowledged that the rate would be usurious under New York law but considered the matter to be governed by Minnesota law.[2] The U.S. Supreme Court would not definitively decide the location issue for another 100 years.

The patchwork of state usury laws was complemented by one usury prohibition at the federal level, but even that left the states' prerogatives intact. The National Bank Act of 1864 contained a usury provision seeking to restrain the national banks—a designation Congress had created for banks that would submit to oversight and regulation by the new Comptroller of the Currency—from overcharging customers on loans. Many banks originally sought the designation "national" during the Civil War as a matter of loyalty to Washington, D.C. The law explicitly stated that national banks had to observe the usury laws of the states in which they resided. If the state did not have one, then the maximum rate was set at 7 percent. This rate, like that for most states, was for real property loans, and even when local usury laws were abolished most mortgage rates never exceeded 8 percent legally. The rates for chattel loans (consumption loans) usually were much higher. Borrowers who claimed they were charged too much had two years from the beginning of the loan to seek redress. If they were successful, the damages awarded were typically twice the amount of interest originally charged.

There was only one problem. Most of the entities that loaned money to consumers were not banks and, thus, did not fall under the act's usury limits. The language of the act created a gray area that would unwittingly produce a whole generation of entrepreneurs attracted to usury because of its high returns. Specifically, the act stated that national banks were limited in the amount of interest they could charge, but "natural persons" were not.[3] Individuals, therefore, could charge interest on loans at any agreed-upon rate of interest. State banks—those that did not apply for national designation—fell under state laws and, therefore, were exempt from the National Bank Act of 1864. New York and Massachusetts both had these contractual exceptions to their usury laws. Noncontractual lending, usually by verbal agreement alone, was a different matter and could be litigated under the usury laws—but of course it was difficult to prove usury without a written contract.

As a result, an unregulated lender could charge whatever the market would bear—that is, whatever his customers would agree to—and did not have to worry much about the consequences. Individuals in need of small loans were not likely to sue because lawyers were expensive and borrowers were typically unable to afford their counsel. But even when a court found in favor of a borrower, the old statutory rates usually entered. When states rolled back or modified their usury laws, they often retained a capture rate of around 6 percent. If a lender were found guilty of charging exorbitant rates, then that rate could be used to settle claims in court between borrower and lender. The net effect of the capture rates was that they appeared to be the same old usury ceilings used since colonial times.

In any case, the patchwork of national and state usury laws was in danger of doing more harm than good. In 1872, the *New York Times* declared that "although [usury] is entirely a dead letter, and is never enforced or regarded, and although it bears heaviest on those whom it is expressly designed to protect—the farmers—yet the prejudice by which it is sustained is too strong to be overcome and it still cumbers the statute book." The British magazine *The Economist* noted that American banks "have to comply with absurd usury laws, which prevent them from charging more than a stated rate for advances [loans]. These laws are of course avoided but still their existence prevents the banks from openly regulating their rates for money in accordance with the conditions of supply and demand."[4] Others were not as certain, however. "We regard the repeal of the usury laws as a capital blunder," the Fitchburg, Massachusetts, *Sentinel* commented in 1878.

Despite the disagreement over the laws and pronouncements about their demise, the fact that they remained on the books provided a warning to lenders. New York's banks and life insurance companies might, for example, comply with the state's usury laws for loans made to in-state borrowers, but the same could not be said for money they lent outside the state. New York City had already assumed the role of the major supplier of credit through its large banks and, while they were wary of charging too much at home, lending to borrowers outside the state was more lucrative. To avoid the 7 percent maximum stipulated by the National Bank Act while still keeping with the spirit of state laws, New York City banks and large insurers lent money to intermediaries in other states that were finance companies and did not fall under the umbrella of many state usury laws because they, technically, were not banks. The rates that finance companies were able to exact from their borrowers proved a strong lure to the banks and brokers that could lend to them on a wholesale basis and thereby avoid the stigma of illegally lending directly to individuals or small businesses. The same was true elsewhere. One loan shark firm in St. Louis was found to be the principal owner of the Edwards securities firm in the same city but lent money for chattel loans under a separate subsidiary to avoid the stigma of being labeled a usurer.

Some Midwestern states that were frequently the targets of high-interest lenders followed the example of Eastern states like Massachusetts, though with less success. Indiana abolished its usury ceiling in the mid-1830s, but reinstated it four years later. Wisconsin ended its ceiling in 1849, but reinstated it after only a few months. In both cases, the public clamored for the protections to be reinstated. "The argument in favor of this policy was that competition in the loan of money, the rate of interest being unrestricted, would produce a great influx of capital to the state. It certainly has produced an influx of money, but not of capital," commented Isaac P. Walker, the Democratic senator from Wisconsin. Walker was referring to money attracted for short-term lending, as opposed to money that would be used for long-term, potentially profitable capital investment. In Indiana, a judge who had presided over many foreclosures observed that "no sooner had the effects of the repeal been developed . . . [when] an irresistible public opinion called for usury laws. Had the legislature not interfered and tied the hands of the spoiler [loan sharks], an immense amount of property would have changed hands in a few years."[5]

Loans to homeowners and the workingman certainly had their appeal. Providers of loans recognized that demand for consumer-related loans was steady. They also recognized that these loans were often the only source of funds for many who were dependent on erratic incomes or low wages. Since the credit markets favored companies and the wealthy, lenders quickly realized they were in the driver's seat when dealing with these customers. As the United States expanded rapidly, the demand for consumer credit would often be satisfied only by unregulated lenders who exacted a high price for their services.

A COMBUSTIBLE MIX

During the latter part of the nineteenth century, many believed the United States was bedeviled by two great social evils: alcohol consumption and loan sharking. The two were considered part of the same overall defect in the human condition and were closely intertwined in the mind of reformers and businessmen alike. "Next to the rum evil, no evil is comparable to the burden laid on a community by the loan shark," declared W. N. Finley, a leader in the war against loan sharks, when the Prohibition amendment was introduced during World War I. The workingman drank too much and put himself, his family, and his employer in difficult straits. He often needed cash to meet everyday expenses and as a result found himself at the mercy of unscrupulous lenders.

The temperance movement, which began organizing in the 1820s, vividly portrayed alcoholism as the country's major social and economic problem. Consumption of beer and spirits caused broken homes, firings at work, and the denigration of women by their husbands. The DuPont chemical company forbade its employees coming to work with alcohol on their breath, and guards were placed at the entrances of its plants to detect the smell of alcohol. Since the consumption of alcohol did not mix well with the sensitive nature of the company's combustible chemical products, the mere suspicion of drinking on the job was cause for immediate dismissal.

Following ratification of the Eighteenth Amendment to the U.S. Constitution in 1919, the production of beer and spirits for personal consumption was outlawed in the United States. The amendment was the first successful attempt at a national sumptuary law, an American version of laws that had been attempted with varying degrees of success since the Roman Republic. Unlike many previous sumptuary laws, Prohibition was aimed at producers and sellers rather than consumers. The idea was that if production was curbed, consumption would necessarily follow.

The same idea was behind the usury laws intended to protect consumers from predatory lenders. To protect society from the evils of indebtedness, laws were aimed at the supply of funds by attempting to control lending rates but, just as bootleggers and smugglers found ways to provide alcoholic beverages to a thirsty public, the suppliers of credit easily found ways around the laws that circumvented the good intentions of their framers. Ironically, the laws gave way to even higher consumer lending rates.

Facilities for saving and managing money were scarce for most individuals before the twentieth century. Banking in the nineteenth century followed a relatively simple model; large urban banks dealt with businesses and wealthy individuals only. Savings and loan associations, or thrifts, were founded after the War of 1812 and made mortgage loans on a local basis to their depositors. In areas where a thrift or a willing local bank did not exist, borrowers were often left adrift for loans, especially for small household loans. More often than not, the would-be borrower did not possess collateral that a small bank would find acceptable. For such individuals, a new source of consumer credit began to appear not long after the Civil War. They were lean operations that could move their offices quickly when necessary. They became known as loan sharks.

The term began to appear in the press in the 1880s. Borrowing from loan sharks often was considered one of the consequences of excessive alcohol consumption, since inebriation made household money management difficult, if not impossible. When the weekly paycheck ran out early, loan sharks provided a vital service, for a high price. Providing credit at high rates as a last resort did not endear them to the public. "The loan shark who lives on blood money is the most nefarious of all the humans," remarked the *Des Moines Daily News* in 1900.

These small lenders certainly counted the poor and ignorant among their clients, but customers came from all walks of life. The business was best described by Clarence Hodson, one of the major figures in the anti-loan shark drive who developed a consumer lending business: "If there are no local licensed money-lenders to supply small loans, the need for loans will nevertheless persist in that community just the same, and loans will be sought and supplied through underground channels, by offering or accepting oppressive terms and usurious rates."[6] It was generally recognized that a borrowing rate of 10 to 20 percent per month was common. Because the loan shark was frequently the only available source of funds, borrowers rarely complained; they could either accept the loan shark's terms or forego the loan.

The standard view of loan sharks today is that they were (and are) an urban phenomenon dominated by organized crime. In the cities before the Great Depression, organized crime did not have an influence in "private lending," as loan sharking was euphemistically known. Crime syndicates that provided consumer loans quickly appeared when other loans were hard to find during the 1930s. In the second half of the nineteenth century, farmers in rural areas also suffered at the hands of high-interest lenders and often dominated the headlines as victims of high-interest lending and foreclosures. Isolated in states with small populations, their choice of lenders was even more limited than that of city dwellers, leaving them vulnerable to a practice that violated state usury laws dating from the colonial period.

High-interest lenders were, nevertheless, easy to find, both in cities and rural areas, although there were fewer in the latter. Newspapers ran ads for loan sharks, sometimes devoting entire pages to them, while many streets had more than one storefront with large signs painted on the windows advertising rates and terms. Loans ran the gamut, from financing farm and home mortgages to purchasing small items costing less than ten dollars. Anti-loan shark societies were founded in the years following the Civil War as the problem of high lending rates began to cause foreclosures of farms and the impoverishment of families. Unfortunately for this movement, many of their arguments focused on the morality of high-interest lending rather than the economics. Their strident tones were more characteristic of a Sunday sermon than of solid economic arguments during this period of rapid industrialization. In language reminiscent of the distant past, the Anti-Usury Society, founded in 1867, resolved that "until our finance is delivered from the morally blinding, insidious and all powerful corrupting power of usury, we cannot reasonably expect that many will maintain their moral integrity or be able to withstand the swelling tide of moral corruption that this wicked system has brought upon us."[7]

In the following decades, Populists seized on the interconnecting themes of government policies, Wall Street bankers, and the overall economic malaise to make their case against loan sharks. This grassroots movement that began in the Midwest and Prairie states during the post–Civil War years focused on the workingman and his troubles and soon became a strong voice in defending the economic rights of workers. Indeed, loan sharks would become a favorite *bête noire* of the Populist movement:

> We want money, land and transportation. We want the abolition of the National Banks, and we want the power to make loans direct from the government. We want the foreclosure system wiped out.... We will stand by our homes and stay by our fireside by force if necessary, and we will not pay our debts to the loan-shark companies until the government pays its debts to us. The people are at bay; let the bloodhounds of money who dogged us beware.

This passionate appeal was spoken by Mary Elizabeth Lease in 1890. Lease was a Kansas Populist who oversimplified the loan shark issue by blaming profligate borrowing for the country's money woes. While "the bloodhounds of money" quotation was perhaps not as memorable as her famous admonition to farmers to "raise less corn and more hell," it certainly made clear the Populists' frustrations with their current conditions.

Given the relative isolation of many farmers and the scarcity of reliable information on events taking place in New York and Washington, D.C., farmers were more likely to be susceptible to conspiracy theories that portrayed the economy as rigged against them. An extremely popular book that circulated throughout the Midwest in the late 1880s was *Seven Financial Conspiracies Which Have Enslaved the American People,* published in 1887 by S. (Sarah) E. V. Emery, a Michigan woman with little experience in politics or in writing until that point.

Emery's book attempted to delineate the several ways in which the average farmer was at the mercy of Wall Street, Congress, the railroads, politicians, and the financial markets. In Emery's account, bankers had used their power to influence government after the Civil War and were now pillaging the country with impunity. The subtitle of Emery's book, *How the Producers Have Been Robbed by the Non-Producers through Evil Legislation*, became a popular refrain of the Populists. Portraying Easterners at the heart of the problem, however, was not entirely without merit.

One passage in Emery's polemic struck close to the heart of many farmers, employing a simple quantity theory of money popular at the time. The Populists' main fear was the contraction in paper money (greenbacks) caused by the resumption of specie (gold and silver backed coin) payments in 1879, after passage of the Specie Payment Resumption Act in 1875. The U.S. Treasury returned to "hard" money to replace the "soft." After the first paper money, or greenbacks, had been created and circulated for several years, specie payments resumed and the amount of paper money in circulation began to fall according to a Treasury schedule, creating a contraction in the supply of paper dollars and depressing farm prices in the process. Farmers relied on inflation to increase their incomes and the contraction of the money supply caused the opposite effect:

> In 1868 there was about $40 per capita of money in circulation; cotton was about 30 cents a pound. The farmer put a 500-pound bale of cotton on his wagon, took it to town and sold it. Then he paid $40 taxes, bought a cooking stove for $30, a suit of clothes for $15, his wife a dress for $5, 100 pounds of meat for $18, 1 barrel of flour for $12, and went home with $30 in his pocket. In 1887, there was about $5 per capita of money in circulation; this same farmer put a 500-pound bale of cotton on his wagon, went to town and sold it, paid $40 taxes, got discouraged, went to the saloon, spent his remaining $2.30 and went home dead broke and drunk.[8]

Emery's case against high-interest moneylenders was more convincing when it used statistics and interest calculations like these. This followed an established tradition often overlooked, since Populism also was known for its fiery rhetoric. In a speech in Kansas in 1886, the activist W. D. Vincent, a Populist activist who became a dominant force in the state's politics several years later, stated that "we as a country are paying out, every eleven years in interest, a sum equal to the assessed value of all our property. In making this calculation the rate was placed at 12 percent simple interest, which no one will deny is much lower than the average rate of interest charged."[9] These simple facts made Vincent's message clear: contracting paper money supply and high interest rates charged to farmers were destroying the workingman.

Another book, *Bond-Holders and Bread-Winners: Portrayal of Some Political Crimes Committed in the Name of Liberty*, by S. S. King, a Kansas City lawyer, also became a popular success after its publication in 1892 and was often advertised in newspapers alongside Emery's book. Readers could purchase them for 10 cents each. King divided the country into two classes: the producers and the wealthy. The producers were the farmers and laborers in the Midwest, Plains, and Southern states, while the wealthy were the owners of financial capital located primarily in the Eastern states of New York and Massachusetts. According to King, the wealthy Easterners owned more assets than all the producers combined and extended credit to farmers through high-interest rate mortgage bonds, which became popular investments. Those sorts of inequalities perpetrated further injustices upon the producers. The rhetorical message was typically Populist and blunt, but the book did cite statistics from the recent 1890 U.S. census in making its case.

Eager to avoid a Populist backlash against high advertised interest rates, loan sharks began attaching fees of all sorts to their loans. Often they failed to mention to borrowers that these fees would substantially drive up the effective rates of lending. Even if the nominal rate of interest on a loan seemed more or less reasonable, the cost to the borrower could be much higher as a result of the fees. Newspaper reports abounded of lenders who demanded up-front fees just to consider a loan. Frequently the fees amounted to more than the loan itself, raising the effective rate of interest to more than 100 percent. Fees were attached to mortgages as well as to smaller consumption loans.

In 1889, farmers recognized the ruse and rose in protest in South Dakota and the furor quickly caught the attention of politicians and the press. The state's official usury ceiling was set at 12 percent, but farmers demonstrated that they routinely were being charged 5 percent or more per month. The protests were heard far beyond Bismarck. The *New York Times* commented that "the money shark is doing more harm and causing more suffering than the drought of 1889. . . . Statehood will enable the people to borrow money directly of Eastern companies, if they desire to do so."[10]

While high interest rates were generally deplored by the newspapers in the East, few substantive comments were to be found concerning the effect of usurious rates on actual farm production. The press kept the focus mostly on the personal hardships of farmers, whose financial needs (both for mortgages and working capital) were understood to be distinct from those of city dwellers. Stories tended to focus on the effects of droughts and winter freezes on farm income and how such losses forced farmers into the clutches of loan sharks. But the effect on state income or the overall economy was rarely, if ever, mentioned.

THE EXCEPTION CLAUSE

One of the Populists' complaints about the economic system being rigged against them appeared remarkably accurate and on target. It centered on the differences between specie (gold and silver coins) and paper money. Clearly, they favored paper money over specie for its ability to inflate prices, which would, in turn, keep incomes from dropping. It was easier for Washington, D.C., to print paper money with no metal backing than it was to produce coins. Technically, coins required metals; paper money required only the desire to produce more currency.

On the back side of greenbacks, the paper currency issued during the Civil War, was the following statement: "This note is legal tender for all debts, public and private, except duties on imports and interest on the public debt." Greenbacks were part of a plan to finance U.S. war needs and were tied to the issuance of Treasury bonds. But technically, the new paper currency was nonconvertible and could not be redeemed for gold. As a result, when an importer needed to pay import duties or when the Treasury was required to pay periodic interest on its obligations, they had to do so in gold itself. Paper money would not be legally accepted because Section 5 of the Greenback Act of 1862 stated that all duties on imports and interest on government bonds be payable in specie only. The language printed on the back of the notes became known among Populists as the "exception clause."

Because specie was made of gold (in whole or in part), many Populists, including Sarah Emery, concluded that bankers had conspired with politicians in Washington, D.C., to get the exception clause inserted into the Greenback Act (Legal Tender Act of 1862). When the paper money was created by Congress to pay for Civil War expenses, it was considered legal tender but was backed only by the "full faith and credit of the United States," a guarantee not yet accepted without reservation. The idea behind the clause was that the effect of paying a foreigner for an import could be offset partially by requiring the buyer to pay the duty in coin, thus reducing the potential outflow of gold. The act also excluded greenbacks from being used as payment of interest on Treasury notes, but there the effect was quite different. Since many Treasury obligations were held by foreigners and represented an export of gold when paid, interest on Treasury notes represented a net outflow of gold (assuming the interest was not reinvested in the United States). The exception clause was, thus, seen as a concession to bankers and their foreign investor clients. Populists naturally seized on both as an example of bankers' collusion with Congress to harm the workingman and the farmer.

The exception clause was not Populist fancy. Addressing an audience in Lancaster, Pennsylvania, in 1863 Republican Congressman Thaddeus Stevens excoriated the clause for its debilitating potential on the workingman, soldiers in need of their pay, and farmers:

When the bill first came from my hand it contained no clause about specie. It provided that the notes should bear the broad name of the United States, and that these notes should be accepted for all things as payment. But when the bill went to the Senate it was so mangled and torn that its main features were altogether changed or modified. There the bill was so altered that the interest was to be made payable in gold and the revenue paid the Government was also made payable in gold.[11]

Stevens remarked that he had "melancholy forebodings that we are about to consummate a cunningly devised scheme which will carry great injury and great loss to all classes of people throughout this Union except one. It makes two classes of money—one for the banks and the other for the people."[12] As far as the Populists were concerned, they definitely got second-class.

Sarah Emery argued that the exception clause elevated the price of gold and depressed the value of greenbacks since it created demand for gold, which, of course, was controlled by bankers. In her *Seven Financial Conspiracies* she repeatedly referred to the New York bankers group as "Shylock," hoarding gold at the expense of the country and forcing it to a premium. As a result, while gold prices rose, commodity prices fell—and the purchasing power of farmers eroded because they used paper currency. The depressed value of greenbacks also helped explain the high interest rates exacted of farmers and those outside the East Coast money centers, where interest rates were lower. For the most part, farmers could only repay their debts with paper money, so lenders charged a premium to offset the depreciation of the paper currency in terms of gold.

Emery also realized that importers were obliged to venture into the New York gold market to purchase the gold they needed to pay import duties. Prices there were high as a result, adding another layer of expense to the import. But when the bankers and brokers became involved, the problem immediately became more complicated. Emery noted that when the importer paid brokers $100 in gold, the broker "immediately invests in government bonds at face value. His next step is to draw interest on his bonds, for the act of February 25, 1862 [the Legal Tender Act] stipulated that his interest should not only be paid in *gold* but in *advance*." Having drawn his gold, she further suggested, "he is prepared on the morrow to sell it to the next importer and with each exchange he clears $185 on every $100 in gold."[13] The exception clause, thus, presented bankers with an immediate arbitrage bonus at the cost of everyone else.

Over 400,000 copies of Emery's book circulated in the Midwest, making it one of the most popular books of the period. It made its point using facts and analysis rather than pure rhetoric (though it was laden with its share of sententious language) and helped highlight financial and economic issues. Her familiarity with recent history and the law made her arguments difficult to dismiss.

Emery's book was roundly condemned by Republicans, who viewed it as a strong rebuke to John Sherman, the senator from Ohio who had been Treasury secretary from 1877 to 1881 under President Rutherford B. Hayes. In his first stint in the Senate (prior to serving in the Hayes administration), Sherman had sponsored the Currency Act of 1870, which kept greenbacks in circulation. Back in the Senate for a second go-round as the political fires of the 1890s were heating up, Emery's indictment of greenback supporters suddenly became a threat to Sherman's incumbency. Others saw it as a rebuke to the memory of President Lincoln himself, although Emery did not criticize him explicitly. Upon first learning of Emery's book, Sherman said he would not respond to it "seriatim," but soon changed his mind. In 1891, he responded to each point in a letter made available to the newspapers. About the exception clause, he wrote:

> This clause had not only the cordial support of [Treasury] Secretary Chase but of President Lincoln and had proved to be the most important financial aid of the government during the war. Goods being imported at coin values, it was but right that the duty to the government should be paid in the same coin. . . . If the interest on our debt had not been paid in coin we could not have borrowed money abroad and the rate of interest instead of diminishing as it did would have been largely increased.[14]

Sherman did not take aim at the technical side of Emery's argument; he instead tried to show that she was incorrect in her conclusions, but only helped to prove them correct. In 1892, despite the popularity of Emery's arguments among his political opponents, Sherman easily won a sixth term in the Senate against his Democratic opponent.

The historic side of the argument was also supported along with the gold trading argument. Greenbacks lost 22 percent of their value against gold in 1862, their first full year in circulation. A low was reached in 1864, when they dipped to 44 cents before rebounding back to 68 cents.[15] Conversely, gold was at a premium and bankers could purchase excess greenbacks with that premium if they so desired. Their increasing revenues led to enormous differences in wealth across the country. Commodity prices in general fell between the Civil War and the turn of the century. Farmers and workingmen slowly were becoming impoverished while Wall Street and Chicago's LaSalle Street prospered. Upon losing his presidential reelection bid to Democrat Grover Cleveland, Benjamin Harrison (who had narrowly defeated Grover Cleveland four years earlier) remarked that "they indicted us first for having too much in the treasury and now they say we have left too little." This was clearly a reference to the Populists.[16] Those who controlled the allocation of credit made sure that money was available for lending, but only at a high price.

The argument had raged for over thirty years with no clear conclusion. Immediately after the Civil War, the *New York Times* reached a conclusion that Populists would have supported even though the movement, let alone the party, had not even been organized. Noting the usefulness of paper money in winning the war, the newspaper concluded, somewhat prematurely, that "they [greenbacks] have served their first and chief purpose so truly and faithfully that the people will never again distrust them—if they ever have done so—will never part with them as a paper currency, save by distribution of a circulation equally national and bearing the same stamp and seal of the Treasury."[17] The newspaper ignored the words printed on the back of the greenbacks because that issue had not yet blossomed into a controversy. The exception clause left a lasting impression that would not recede easily from memory.

Foreign Appeal

Foreign capital was a major factor in America's economic development during the nineteenth century. More than one commentator referred to the source of capital investment as Wall Street *and* London's Threadneedle Street, the heart of Britain's financial district. British investors were the major source of demand for many U.S. railroad bonds and it was well recognized that the railroads and some industrial companies as well as many municipalities, especially before the Civil War, were reliant on British capital. What was less clear was that those investors were becoming more discriminating in their choice of American investments because many had not worked out well in the past.

After a large municipal default by several Southern states on their bonds in the 1840s, the United States was increasingly viewed by foreign investors as a nation of swindlers who failed to honor their obligations. Convincing foreigners to invest was not an easy matter. In one unusual instance before the Civil War, the city of Cincinnati decided to actively court foreign investors after Ohio raised its usury ceiling, as part of the nationwide experiment with higher usury ceilings, to 10 percent. The idea was to attract foreign investors' funds at rates that were still lower than those demanded by Wall Street and local banks. But outside investors would have none of it, deciding that if they did invest, 10 percent would be the minimum rate from which to start. The problem was that a usury law remained on the books. If municipal authorities decided they didn't like the rates they were being forced to pay, they could always invoke the usury laws as protection against the same foreign investors they were trying to attract. As the *New York Times* succinctly stated, "Foreign money lenders might reasonably hesitate to confide in the law of today, authorizing 10 percent interest, which might be broken tomorrow on the first attempt to collect the principal."[18]

As Cincinnati discovered, foreigners viewed direct investment in American companies or private investment in land as preferable to lending money to municipalities. The hope of drawing foreign money to states and territories of the Midwest and Plains was far more realistic for that very reason; raw land was involved. The flow of funds from abroad followed different paths. British money followed the Kansas land boom, and by the late 1880s fourteen British mortgage firms (along with eleven other foreign firms) had funded rural loan agencies to invest in Kansas farm mortgages. These firms represented some of the most visible and sizeable properties in the state.[19] Investing in overseas real estate was a British phenomenon; the country invested about 5 percent of its gross national product in overseas land purchasing and mortgage lending, with North America forming the largest part. British investment extended from Texas north to Manitoba and from Tennessee west to Colorado.[20] The sheer size of the holdings made many Populists suspicious. As a result, several state legislatures reacted by passing laws that restricted the influence of any foreign entity.

Ever since the Homestead Act of 1862, which prohibited non-Americans from acquiring lands from the federal government, an element of xenophobia could be found in the laws that governed the ownership of land and property in the United States. As the extent of British holdings became more widely known, state legislatures began to pass laws that denied legal process to foreign companies, banned nonresident ownership of land (especially farmland), and increased taxes on foreign owners. Most of these laws were passed between 1885 and 1895, when the fervor against high-interest lending was also building. As with states' usury laws, the laws directed at foreign investors were sometimes revoked and sometimes ignored, creating a confusing patchwork for those investors.

The reaction against foreigners holding land was a matter of direct investment. If, however, they owned debentures (bonds) supported by farm mortgages (classified as portfolio, or indirect, investment), there was much less fanfare because many of the would-be critics outside the investment world would never be aware of the phenomenon. Ordinarily, foreign direct investment was viewed with suspicion while indirect (portfolio) investments such as securities drew much less attention. As a result, securities backed by farmland mortgages were developed, appealing to investors who were attracted to the idea of land as collateral. *The Economist*, however, was quick to note that the mortgage companies that peddled these securities had something in common with loan sharks: "It is worthy of note that these mortgage companies are liberal advertisers in magazines and religious weeklies and not in the columns of journals where applications for capital are usually presented to experienced men of business. The inference being that the unsuspecting are their best customers."[21]

During the great land boom of the late 1870s and early 1880s, several foreign investors acquired extensive amounts of acreage despite local laws prohibiting their ownership. The Duke of Sutherland was reputed to have become one of the largest direct owners of American farmland. Many British companies (and later Dutch and German ones) had been formed to buy land directly from the railroads, which was not prohibited by federal law. By 1884, an estimated 21 million acres in the South and West were owned directly by foreign investors. Some investments were for single tracts of more than a million acres. Many of these vast tracts had been acquired before the states began passing land laws to discourage foreign ownership, so the investments were safe. The nationalistic message still was clear all the same. Other kinds of direct investment that had no restrictions on them—mining and oil, for example—became increasingly attractive alternatives, as well. Even so, direct land investments began to be liquidated by World War I because of increasing hostility. British acreage in North America declined by 70 percent from 1885 to 1913 and the foreign menace that many Populists perceived waned.[22]

Money, for a Price

Despite complaints about high-interest lending in the nineteenth century, rates did, in fact, vary greatly from place to place, depending on the type of loan involved. The farther west from the East Coast, the higher rates tended to be for mortgages and business loans. Small lending, which was more commonly provided by loan sharks, tended to feature uniformly high rates regardless of where the loan was made. But in general, time and place were important elements in the price of credit in the decades after the Civil War, with short-term loans more expensive than longer-term ones and remoteness from credit centers only adding to the cost.

In the common law tradition, real estate was not considered movable but a freehold, something fixed that could be owned and passed on in perpetuity. Movable property was referred to as "chattel." A chattel loan referred to a loan on property considered movable; small consumption loans were also referred to as chattel loans. One leading text on law at the time distinguished two types of chattel: personal and real. Personal chattel referred to property literally not tied down, such as furniture, equipment, or slaves (before emancipation). Real chattel referred to real estate (or real property).

One category in particular of real chattel would provide an opportunity for loan sharks. Real chattels also included "chattels less than freehold, which are annexed to or concern real estate."[23] In other words, property attached to the freehold, such as additional acreage added later or outbuildings. This provided many finance companies with a link to the farm itself even if they made chattel loans. If a farmer pledged his outbuildings as collateral for a loan, it clearly was an opening for a loan shark to demand attachment of the farm to satisfy the loan if it went into default.

The borrower was required to provide collateral, usually in the form of furniture, household items, or other personal property. If the borrower fell behind on repayment, the lender would seize the property until payments continued. There was a high cost involved, however. Each time this occurred, the borrower was charged a fee to compensate the lender for his trouble. Fees were a large part of the chattel lending business. Often a lender would not release a loan until the borrower paid the fees in cash up-front. The actual collateral was often not as important (or valuable) as the fee itself. If an unscrupulous lender was forced to move his operation quickly, one step ahead of the sheriff, collateral would do little good. At any rate, lenders were not much interested in the actual value of a borrower's dining table; its real value was in the fees it could generate each time the borrower fell into arrears.

The same was true of mortgage lending. The duration of a mortgage in the nineteenth century was usually just five or ten years, and the payments borrowers made over that time were for interest only. Since amortization of the principal was not included, mortgages required a balloon payment at the end to avoid renegotiation and more fees. In such cases, the value of the collateral—which was the real property—was significant and of paramount importance to the lenders. Despite the fact that their income was highly cyclical and dependent on weather, blights, and other unforeseeable conditions, farmers, especially, were considered prized borrowers by many lenders. In fact, they were generally regarded as better risks than railroad or industrial bonds. On one level, the attraction was obvious. Bonds often dominated the balance sheets of railroads and many industrial companies, where debt-to-equity ratios of 8 to 2 or 7 to 3 were not uncommon. Farmers' mortgages were just the opposite, with farmers holding around 80 percent equity in their farms. The balance was held by private lenders, the largest of whom were insurance companies, based mainly in the East.

Five insurance companies, four located in Connecticut and one in Wisconsin, held 30 percent of the insurance industry's total portfolio of mortgages and had significant holdings in farm mortgages.[24] The attraction of insurance companies to the mortgage market is generally attributed to their need to match assets to long-term liabilities. But the relatively short lives of nineteenth-century mortgages were not the best match, suggesting that the high rates of interest and the rollover nature of the typical mortgage was what really attracted them. When Western Populists ranted about Eastern investors exploiting farmers, their complaints were not unfounded, since the same features of mortgages that attracted insurance companies—which at least superficially appeared to be legitimate investors—also attracted loan sharks.

There were contradictory views of lending rates in the latter decades of the nineteenth century. The first came from Wall Street, the ultimate source of loans. Existing usury laws had little effect on its business because corporate loans were exempt from state usury ceilings and the market view of interest rates prevailed. Henry Clews, a noted Wall Street trader and writer, wrote that the usury laws "are placed on the statute-books in deference to a sentiment . . . that poor people must be protected from the rapacity of money-lenders." In his opinion, nothing could be farther from the truth, as "the alleged principle on which the usury laws are based is illogical." Clews's assessment was based in part on the notion that lending on securities collateral (which was part of his business) was riskier than lending on real property. In other words, those pledging their property against small loans or mortgages were already receiving the best rates available if one assumed that solid collateral meant low borrowing rates.

But the New York money market had its own internal contradiction that showed how confusing the entire issue could be. In the money market, call loans (loans on stock sales) made for a specific term (thirty to ninety days) were subject to New York's usury laws, usually 6 percent per annum. But loans made overnight for more than $5,000 were subject to market rates of interest, which often exceeded 6 percent, reflecting market conditions and attempts by some large banks to manipulate rates. *The Economist* noted that "under the operation of these provisions of the law a borrower of money at call, in excess of the minimum stipulated sum, can be required to pay any rate which may be established by reason of the operation of the unwritten law of supply and demand." As a consequence, "it may be observed that the facilities which are offered for the manipulation of money in the manner indicated result in evil conditions without the least compensating advantage, except for those who are instrumental in their creation."[25]

Thus, the argument that securities lending necessarily reflected high interest rates did not square with the realities of the money market. If a bank or other institutional lender made a loan to a broker or investor, accepting common stock or bonds as collateral, the lending rate should have been higher than that charged on a loan collateralized by property. In reality, it was often lower, and the rates that farmers paid for mortgages collateralized with real property were actually higher. According to the

Wall Street theory, money was nothing more than a commodity and all commodities had their standard prices dictated by the market. But the inversely sloped yield curve that applied to personal lending was evidence of the contrary.

The reality of lending rates was quite different for small borrowers. The rates charged for small loans (under $300) was consistently over 30 percent and often reached 500 percent, depending upon the lender and the borrower's ability to produce reasonable collateral. By contrast, the rates on New York call money for common stocks were even lower than mortgage rates for farms in the Midwest, South, and the Great Plains during the last two decades of the nineteenth century, which typically ranged from 8 percent to 70 percent. Quite often, borrowers in rural areas realized they were paying too much, but there was little they could do to improve their circumstances.

Specifically, many Eastern insurance companies and other large investors invested in farm mortgages through debentures, not directly. Loan agents in the Midwest packaged these loans and put them in a trust that, in turn, backed the debentures. The process was similar to the mortgage-backed securities and collateralized mortgage obligations in use later in the twentieth century. At the time, the model employed was the *pfandbriefen* (mortgage covered bond) issued by institutions in Germany earlier in the nineteenth century. As the *pfandbriefen*, the actual bonds were meant to be stronger than the agents or institution issuing them because of the diversification principle. The issuer promised to cover payments in case payments made to it from the pool of underlying loans failed. But in the case of rural America, packaging mortgage loans was difficult because of the distances involved.

WHAT'S THE MATTER WITH KANSAS?

The major loan agent in Kansas in the 1880s was J. B. Watkins of Lawrence, Kansas. The Watkins firm was one of the more successful of its type and contributed to the farmland boom of the 1880s. Its founder was a lawyer who began working for insurance companies in the Midwest, and when he organized his own company in 1883 he decided to back securities issued against the mortgages with the assets of the company, creating "covered bonds." Watkins was persuaded to issue securities of this type by brokers in the United Kingdom when he first started his firm, assuming that the cover would convince investors that their money was secure.[26] Mortgages were created, bought by the firm, and placed in the hands of a trustee who held them on behalf of investors. Watkins used newspaper advertising extensively to sell his securities and measured his success in terms of the number of securities sold and the number of investors attracted. At the end of September 1893, the firm advertised that it had sold almost $19 million of securities to 4,800 investors. The firm packaged about $6 million in loans between 1883 and 1886 alone, and sold them through agents on the East Coast and in London. Watkins securitized properties all over the state, but those located farthest from his office in Lawrence required more effort to process and required higher fees as a result.[27] The popularity of debentures such as the ones issued by Watkins's firm helped fuel the overall lending boom outside the East Coast. They demonstrated that relatively low mortgage rates, certainly lower than loan sharks were providing, were compatible with good farm credit.

As the number of farms in the country increased, so, too, did the number of banks. The lending situation was greatly aided by the number of state-chartered banks. In 1888 there were over 3,500 state banks; by 1895 there were over 6,100. The number of national banks also increased, though not as dramatically, from 3,100 to over 3,700.[28] Much of this growth was attributable to the land boom. Many ads appeared in newspapers about cheap land available in the Midwest, where people could live in peace and quiet. Railroads commissioned brokers and hucksters to dispose of land they acquired by grants from Congress. The land, some of dubious agricultural worth, was sold cheaply to the unsuspecting (accounting, in part, for the relatively low debt ratios of many farmers). But when crops were threatened, incomes dropped and many farmers had recourse only to loan sharks, who quickly recognized that, in the event of foreclosure, farmers' land was a great deal more valuable than their movable property.

The growth in the number of banks, especially state-chartered banks, followed the growth of the population. The farm population alone rose from 22 million in 1880 to 30 million in 1900 while the number of farms rose from 4,000 to 5,740 from 1888 to 1895.[29] During the same time period, seven new states were admitted to the Union (Idaho, Montana, North Dakota, South Dakota, Utah, Washington, and Wyoming). Clearly, lending was a profitable business. While the exact number of finance companies is not known with any certainty (because so many of them were unlicensed), it would be expected that the presence of so many competing lenders would have forced loan sharks out of business. But in reality, all lenders, legitimate and otherwise, wanted to be in the high-interest lending business. As a result, Midwest and Plains farmers had a choice of potential lenders, but not many offered low-interest rate loans other than firms like Watkins, whose rates were still higher than those available in the East.

By the turn of the twentieth century the Kansas banking commissioner reported that more than 600 banks were operating within the state. During the last quarter of the nineteenth century, farming in general had suffered because of overcapacity, and the incomes of many farmers fell dramatically. In many areas, the cost of planting crops far exceeded the price they fetched upon harvest. Only the high equity levels in their personal finances saved many farmers from foreclosure. The accompanying decline in farm real estate values made many farmers the targets of loan sharks, even when they needed only a small consumption or working capital loan. The proliferation of chattel loans made their real property vulnerable during bad times because lenders would seek to attach the farm as well as the movable property in the case of delinquent payments.

Ownership figures show why Kansas in particular was a favorite with mortgage lenders. The potential for new loans was strong and high interest rates were justified because of the state's size. Kansas had the most mortgage debt of any Midwestern or Plains state but it was also the wealthiest. Among its farmers, 69 percent were owner/operators, while 31 percent were tenant farmers. While roughly 55 percent of the farm owners were mortgage-free, the other 45 percent had mortgages of some sort. Most important, 36 percent of the value of owner/operator farms ($74 million) had liens against them. The average interest rate for a mortgage in Kansas in 1880s was 8.83 percent for real estate with dwellings and 8.71 percent for acreage alone. Wisconsin had lower rates, with the average mortgage at about 7 percent. In neighboring Minnesota, rates were about one to one-and-a-half percentage points higher. In contrast, the rates in New York were 5.53 percent for property with dwellings and 5.80 percent for acreage. New Jersey, Connecticut, and Massachusetts showed similar or even wider spreads when compared with South Dakota, North Dakota, Montana, and Wyoming.[30] In other words, the farther the state or territory from the East Coast money centers the higher the mortgage rate attached.

Kansas was especially hard hit by loan sharking. The state attracted a wide variety of lenders, and when crop failures came, high-interest payments could not be met and foreclosures hit the state's economy hard. The economic effects were felt by loan sharks, as well. As one Kansas farmer remarked:

> All alike, loaner and borrower, banker and farmer, were overwhelmed in a common ruin. The three hundred exploded loan agencies in operation in Kansas, together with their bankrupt head centers, situated in Kansas City, which went down burdened with millions, and the general hegira of the people from the region affected all attest the terrible effects to those immediately concerned as well as to the reputation of the state at large.[31]

The loan sharking problem helped create an exodus from the state only a few decades after the lure of cheap land initially caused an influx of settlers.

Not all the damage of high-interest lending was inflicted on farms. The *Western Kansas World* noted that "mortgage companies say that foreclosures on city properties are as frequent as on farms. This clearly shows that farmers are not the only class suffering from the depression."[32] Kansas's farm depression attracted a wide array of hucksters, storefront preachers, and "demagogues" (as one newspaper referred to them) who offered relief for farmers—for a price. For the preachers, that meant a donation; for the demagogues, it was usually a vote in an upcoming election. Nevertheless, as the mortgage crisis was unfolding in Kansas, there were efforts by some who, in order to reverse the exodus of farmers and lenders, claimed there was no crisis at all. One reader wrote to a newspaper asking about a comment he had read in a rival, business-friendly newspaper that there had only been six foreclosures in all of Kansas in 1890. The same article also claimed that the cost of planting corn was only 10 cents per bushel which would, when harvested, fetch many millions for farmers who would be even better off than before. The reader's response was simple: "It is a direct insult to the intelligence of every loans agent and farmer in the state."[33]

The mortgage and lending crisis was reported by the Populists in a formal document that was much more analytical and less emotional in tenor than the remarks of some of their leaders in the 1890s. They produced a handbook of facts and figures to refute the claims of those who said that the financial situation in the state was normal. The handbook estimated that approximately $391 million of mortgages was outstanding in Kansas. Even after making allowances for overestimates, the figure would not be lower than $260 million, far higher than the official $236 million reported in the 1890 federal census. The same document also reported the interest rates of Kansas mortgages in the range of 10 to 70 percent. The Populist estimate used a constant 8 percent throughout the state, despite the fact that it was considered low.[34]

Farmers continued to suffer from the fragmented nature of banking before the establishment of reform efforts in agrarian finances later in 1916. Commodities prices slumped after the Civil War as slackening demand depressed the price of foodstuffs. Lenders and investors crossed state lines seeking borrowers but did so indirectly. A national banking system did not exist despite the fact that the National Bank Act of 1864 created "national banks," a designation that the larger banks received by agreeing to submit to the regulation of the Comptroller of the Currency, also created by the act. States' prerogatives concerning bank regulation and usury ceilings still prevailed although many bankers recognized that the United States was desperately in need of a central bank that would be able to allocate credit more uniformly on a national basis.

In the Pits

Among the many problems affecting farmers' ability to earn a livelihood, the commodities futures markets in Chicago were at the top of the list. They were blamed, along with Wall Street, for the erratic changes in the availability of money and the wild swings in commodity prices. Eastern bankers held credit in their hands, while traders on Chicago's LaSalle Street manipulated agricultural prices for their own benefit. Farmers were intimately familiar with the latter. From its inception before the Civil War, the Chicago Board of Trade (CBOT) handled virtually all the U.S. trade in agricultural commodities futures contracts. Yet few traders ever called for the actual delivery of the commodity being traded. This was antithetical to the founding objective of the exchange, which was to serve as a place where forward deliveries could be negotiated to ensure farmers could sell their crops at a certain price in the future.

Speculation in the Chicago commodity pits occasionally had a severe impact on prices. In the decades after the Civil War, the most widely traded commodity in the futures pits was wheat, the major agricultural product of the American Midwest. From the early days of the CBOT, wheat trading became known as "wind wheat." This meant that farmers and traders suspected that wheat was never meant for actual delivery and that the wind could affect its price as much as any other factor. Within a few years, that term was given additional significance by cornering operations mounted by infamous pit traders.

In a corner, a trader would attempt to dominate (corner) the available or visible supply of a commodity, temporarily forcing up futures prices. In the early decades of the CBOT, cornering operations had been dominated by two pit traders, Benjamin Hutchinson and P. D. Armour, both of whom became legends in Chicago but were often vilified on the farms for their deleterious effect on prices.

The largest cornering operation of its type was mounted in 1897 by Joseph Leiter, the son of a Chicago businessman who, after graduating from Harvard, was entrusted with $1 million of his father's fortune. Leiter's plan was to corner the supply of wheat by emulating previous cornering operations by Hutchinson. One trader remarked that "it can't be done again. The market is too big, too immense." But Leiter proceeded nevertheless, and after several false starts began to mount his corner. The syndicate he formed to pursue the operation cornered nearly 16 million bushels of wheat at a time when world reserves of the grain were running low. In addition, Leiter planned to corner wheat for delivery in December, when the supply was naturally short because of winter weather. Just as it appeared that Leiter had successfully completed his corner, the plot thickened.[35]

While Leiter's syndicate was buying all the futures contracts available, P. D. Armour and his agents had begun selling. Suddenly, other traders were not sure that the market had been cornered after all, especially since Armour was taking the opposite trading position. In a classic confrontation on the floor of the CBOT, Leiter told Armour he would force him to settle (buy back his short sales) contracts at a great loss. Armour became so infuriated that he devised a method to break the corner rather than capitulate. He ordered his agents to send all visible wheat through Duluth, to be forwarded to Chicago. He then hired adventurous seamen who were willing to sail the Great Lakes in the dead of winter to deliver the wheat. He even hired tugboats to break the ice on the lakes so the boats would arrive before the delivery date of his contracts. To the surprise of the CBOT, Armour delivered his wheat on time, adding to the visible supply, depressing prices, and, in the process, breaking Leiter's corner. Armour's actions turned Leiter's $7 million profit from the corner into a $9 million loss.

Initially, Leiter's attempt to corner the market was popular with farmers, who were elated over the increase in the price of wheat. Criticism of the speculators who drove up the price was nowhere to be found. But when the forces of supply and demand again set the market price, the abundant wheat harvest meant a return to depressed prices.

At the same time, the Progressive movement was gaining strength and would prove to be a more significant adversary than the Populists. The rumors that speculators and rapacious Easterners dominated the futures markets would continue, but calls for regulation and trading ethics also began to be heard. Their comedic value was also on display. In 1895, the play *Other People's Money* began a brief run in New York. The comedic actor Hennessy Leroyle starred in the role as king of the Chicago wheat pit; he just happened to bear a striking resemblance to Joseph Leiter. One memorable line from the play: "There is nothing so good as money, and no money so good as other people's."

"AUNTIES AND UNCLES"

As the spread of high-interest lenders demonstrated, lending became big business after 1880. The farm lending problem would be tackled by Congress in 1916 when the Farm Loan Act was passed, but in the intervening years lending became something of a national pastime. Farm mortgages were only a part of the overall problem of high-interest lending in the post–Civil War decades as lenders developed other ways to provide credit than chattel and mortgage loans. With the United States industrializing at a rapid rate, money lending became a favorite pastime of just about anyone who had excess cash and was in search of a safe, high-yielding investment. Loans were advertised in newspapers from a wide variety of sources. Merchants, lawyers, banks, finance companies, and pawnbrokers all offered their money to consumers.

Between 1890 and 1900, call money rates in the New York market ranged from 3.5 to 6 percent. At the same time, mutual savings banks offered customers a deposit rate of just 4 percent. As a result, those with cash to lend were drawn to chattel and mortgage lending, as rates were much higher. Investing in a securitized debenture, the safest method of lending to farm mortgagees, could yield around 6 percent, while direct chattel lending could fetch much higher returns.

Everyone joined the game, and from all walks of life. In 1894, Chicago was experiencing financial difficulties, and money to pay for essential public services was in short supply. To meet its payroll obligations, the municipal government paid many employees with vouchers, which employees then sold to lenders at a discount to obtain cash. That the city would ever redeem the value of the vouchers the lenders bought up was doubtful; but the lenders, as creditors to the city, would be in a strong position to demand future concessions. Brokers also eagerly bought up judgments against the city that it could not afford to pay; for example, when a municipal worker was injured and the city was found negligent. As one newspaper reported, "the judgment draws interest and there are lots of people willing to buy it from the lucky litigant and hold it for the interest—indefinitely it would seem."[36] Or at least until the city could afford to settle the account. To free market advocates, these ploys simply added liquidity to a system that was desperately short of it; to detractors, they were nothing more than extortion at high interest rates.

In their frequent ads in daily newspapers, loan sharks would advertise lending rates that appeared to abide by official usury ceilings. What they failed to mention were the fees that could push the effective rate of borrowing much higher than advertised. But not all lenders advertised publicly—or needed to. Many employers lent money to their employees at extortionate rates, keeping the process from public view. In 1911, a scandal was exposed at the Bureau of Engraving and Printing, the agency of the federal government that printed the country's currency and stamps, when it was discovered that senior employees were lending money at usurious rates to lower-level employees. The practice was not confined to men ("uncles") but included women ("aunties"). The head of the department remarked, "I understand that my bureau is not the only one in which this practice is going on . . . I do not think it necessary that they resort to Shylock methods to make a living."[37]

Similar problems were reported in other major cities. In some cases, municipal authorities actively intervened to protect their own workers and residents from outside lenders and punishment for falling behind on payments. The governor of Missouri and the two highest ranking officials in the St. Louis police department traveled to New York City to intervene at Western Union's headquarters on behalf of employees in St. Louis whose jobs were in jeopardy after dealing with loan sharks. When the workers fell behind on their payments, the loan sharks had their salaries garnished, and that meant immediate dismissal from the company. As a result of the meeting, Western Union agreed to pursue dismissals only in the most egregious cases in the future. The trip had an additional consequence. One of the police officials was also a well-known attorney in St. Louis, and he offered to take up the case of anyone in similar circumstances in the future, pro bono. Reports had circulated widely of borrowers who could not afford to repay loan sharks committing suicide, and it was hoped that simple legal recourse, unaffordable to many in debt, would help avert such dire outcomes. The *New York Times* optimistically remarked that "the outcome of the fight is looked for with interest, as its results may be far reaching."

Police in some large cities were also involved in high-rate lending. Louis Dalrymple's famous cover for *Puck* in October 1894 listed it as one of many grievances against police in New York. New York City police also were investigated for acting in concert with pawnbrokers to warehouse stolen goods. In Chicago, municipal authorities enacted a short-lived sumptuary law prohibiting women from frequenting certain saloons in the theater district after numerous complaints of rowdiness and illicit behavior. After money changed hands between the establishments and the police, women were allowed to return, on the provision that they could be served only soft drinks. Chicago police officials were also implicated in acting in concert with a firm of loan sharks, presumably to direct their lower-paid subordinates to them for business. One local newspaperman commented that "these blots on the city's life have been permitted to exist without their paying someone for the privilege is too much for sophisticated belief."

Taxing Issues

For most of the years after the Civil War, loan sharks lent out their money, collected their interest, and enjoyed their profits without having to pay a dime to the federal government in taxes. Suspended in 1872, no income tax was levied by Washington, D.C., for the next twenty-one years. But a new tax came into existence in 1894 that imposed a tax of 2 percent on incomes over $4,000. At a time when the average annual income was barely $1,000, the tax would affect only 85,000 earners in a population of 65 million, according to one congressman. Because the tax was comprehensive and included earnings from investment sources as well as earned income from employment or business, those affected by the tax included lenders and investors, as well as those who earned interest on real estate. The tax met with fierce opposition in the East, where incomes were higher and where many lenders resided, but was supported by people in the rural South and Midwest. Opponents of the tax claimed that the country's top income earners would move abroad rather than pay the tax. The lines were drawn along social and income lines, as the tax was clearly a class tax aimed at high earners.[38]

The tax was almost immediately challenged in federal court by parties who were opposed to the tax on passive income. The following year, the Supreme Court, in *Pollock v. Farmers Loan & Trust*, found the law to be unconstitutional.[39] Congress would not institute a new tax on personal income until 1913, with passage of the Sixteenth Amendment. The lack of an income tax for nearly four decades was crucial for lending in the United States for two reasons. First, it had an impact on the structure of mortgages, since many loans were structured as interest only; lenders were only interested in the interest income produced, and borrowers were faced with repaying principal as a lump sum at the end of the term. Second, the treatment of interest derived from real estate as income suggested that if an income tax were passed in the future, it was reasonable to assume that interest income would be included, as it eventually was. The combination of the two, along with the general neglect of the state usury laws, opened the way for continued high-interest lending after 1895.

Stories of suicides, broken families, and destitution continued to be heard as before. But in some cases, the press was not always helpful. A Buffalo newspaper ran an incredible story on its front page about a property owner who had purportedly approached a loan shark to obtain a loan of $3.50 to pay his servants. The man told the shark that he owned $10,000 worth of property, meaning he could collateralize the loan many times over. The loan shark was unimpressed and told the man he would need to pay a fee of $2.00 just to be considered for loan. After the man handed over the fee, he was told he would then have to wait a year for his loan. When he returned the next year, he was told he would need to pay another fee of $1.50. The story clearly strained the imagination, with fees equaling the amount the man wanted to borrow in the first place. The larger point, however, is that reporting on loan sharking was inconsistent at best. The story was not unique. Papers around the country routinely reported similar incidents.

A story reported in New York City demonstrated that some judges were becoming tired of the antics of loan sharks. A complainant sued a loan shark for kicking in his door in his absence and repossessing the furniture he had used as collateral for a small loan. His eight-year-old daughter was home alone at the time and bewildered by the incident. After hearing the complaint, the judge bound the loan shark over for trial and recommended criminal charges against him as well, claiming he had no respect for privacy or personal property. Similar events occurred in rural areas but the stories traveled slowly and by the time they reached their intended audience their shock value had diminished substantially. Urban states had no better protections against loan sharks than rural areas, but in the latter high interest rates simply were considered the costs of doing business given intangibles such as weather, insect infestations, and remoteness.

Panic and Conspiracy

In the decades following the Civil War, the United States experienced several panics in the markets. The most notable, the Panic of 1873, was triggered in no small part by the infamous gold corner by Jay Gould in 1869, which, in turn, caused a run on several well-known banks, notably Jay Cooke and Company, several years later. The link between gold, greenbacks, farm prices, and the cost of money became well established. The United States experienced another banking crisis in 1893. Although it would be the last of the century, it proved to be one of the most serious. The term panic, defined at the time as a massive loss of confidence in the markets, was entirely appropriate. The fragmented nature of banking, the tenuous position of gold, and the country's reliance on foreign capital were all on full display. According to the Populists, all were self-induced because of faulty legislation and bankers' greed. The Gilded Age, created in part by an increasing reliance on finance at the cost of farming, was also in full bloom by the 1890s.

The panic began after silver entered the gold discussion. The United States was a debtor nation, owing more to foreigners than it earned from them. By the beginning of the 1890s, this dependence became very clear when foreign investors began to panic over the gold–silver debates that had been waged in the United States, especially since the Specie Payment Resumption Act of 1875. In 1890, President Benjamin Harrison signed the Sherman Silver Purchase Act, which required the Treasury to buy a specific amount of silver each month to maintain its price. Politically, this was a bow to the Western mining states in Congress. But the policy also suggested a move toward bimetallism, with two metals (gold and silver) backing the currency rather than just one (gold). The clear preference was for gold but politics intervened on behalf of silver. Seeing the resurgence of silver as an example of American equivocation regarding the dollar, foreign investors began to sell American securities. They had read of the fiery speeches in favor of silver by William Jennings Bryan, the firebrand lawyer and opponent of gold and the rhetoric of Populism added to their uncertainty. British investors had already begun to liquidate many of their landholdings and took this new opportunity to unwind other investments. This caused an outflow of gold from the country and precipitated the Panic of 1893. It began to appear that Populist fears about the reliance on British investors were well founded.

The gold reserve of the United States had fallen to low levels in part because of revenue losses created by protective tariffs. What was considered an adequate reserve level of $100 million was breached in January 1893 and investors began to sell securities. In February, the New York Stock Exchange had a record trading day, with over $6 million worth of bonds traded. As a result, President Grover Cleveland, who defeated Harrison in the 1892 election, asked Congress to repeal the Silver Purchase Act in an attempt to bolster the Treasury's gold reserves and restore order in the financial system. A special session of Congress was convened in October and, after a heated debated, both houses voted for repeal. In the interim months, however, the reserve situation had become even more acute. Reserves dropped to around $80 million and numerous business failures followed. Over 500 banks and 15,000 businesses failed nationwide. By the end of 1893, an estimated 30 percent of all American railroads had filed for bankruptcy.

Investors' faith in American investments was also shaken in August 1894, when the federal government announced its first budget deficit, a $60 million shortfall, since the Civil War. The Cleveland administration proposed the first of two bond issues, of $50 million each, to shore up the Treasury's finances. Both were heavily subscribed by New York banks, which paid for their subscriptions in gold. This temporarily solved the Treasury's immediate problems. However, since the Treasury was using the proceeds of the two sales to pay back debt that was currently maturing, within a year the Treasury was back in the same position. The Treasury needed, somehow, to regain some of the gold it had lost when foreign investors sold their securities. In a desperate attempt to reverse the outflow, President Cleveland struck a deal that would allow the Treasury to sell bonds to foreigners, who would pay for their purchases in gold coin.

To pull this off, Cleveland enlisted the help of major Wall Street banks, including J. P. Morgan & Company and August Belmont & Company. Both institutions had enviable reputations at the heart of U.S. financial markets but were, as noted earlier, derided as "Shylock" by Sarah Emery and other Populists. Conspiracy theorists held that Shylock—the vast cabal of New York bankers—had seized control of the gold supply after the Civil War and used it to keep prices low, to the everlasting detriment of farmers ever since. Morgan and his banker allies sold $50 million worth of 4 percent bonds to a syndicate that paid a premium for them. They were then sold to foreign investors for a higher price. With the purchases boosting its reserves, the Treasury was spared the indignity of a default by the United States on its obligations although the rate of interest on the Treasury bonds was considered high. An official Treasury document justified the transaction by stating that "it must be conceded that the risk which the purchasers ran of failing in their attempt to supply the Treasury with gold was so great that they were justified in making hard terms.[40] But silver advocates and Populists were highly critical of the deal. The syndicate of bankers had netted about $6 million on their trading of the deal, which seemed to confirm the belief that Shylock controlled the financial system for his own gain.

Despite these measures, saving the Treasury came at a price to the bankers. The wave of criticism sparked by the affair was directed against bankers in general and Jews in particular. (Belmont was the U.S. representative of the Rothschilds, the Jewish family that had amassed the largest private fortune in the world). One critic characterized President Cleveland as a tool of "Jewish bankers and British gold." Cleveland had defeated Benjamin Harrison in the recent presidential election in 1892 in part because the public believed that Harrison was part of the tariff problem that had caused the contraction in the availability of money. The writer Henry Adams pointed out the dangers of having so much

American debt in foreign hands when he claimed the "Jews of Lombard Street" (by which he meant the Rothschilds in London) "threaten to withdraw their capital if there was even a danger of free coinage of silver." In the eyes of Adams and many others, foreign investors not only controlled the flow of American capital, they also apparently helped decide the silver question in favor of gold.

The liquidation of securities and land investments during the early and mid-1890s created an untenable situation for many leveraged investors and businesses that relied heavily upon borrowing. The panic took its toll on the mortgage industry when the Equitable Mortgage Company of Missouri, which had offices in New York and London, was unable to meet interest payments on mortgage-related debentures and became one of the most notable casualties of the panic. The company had been founded in 1884, expressly to make loans to farmers in Missouri and surrounding states. According to the company itself, Equitable had been able to meet its obligations, including paying an annual dividend of 10 percent, without fail until the financial crisis of 1893 (although nine years was not a particularly long history). The panic laid bare Equitable's precarious financial situation, however. When it was organized, Equitable had capital of $2.1 million. By 1894, it claimed assets of only $600,000, with $940,000 in interest payments due on its bonds and debentures at the end of the year. Equitable's unpaid liabilities to British investors alone totaled £1 million.[41] The firm's failure not only left its investors in the lurch but helped cast a darkening shadow over the new securitized market for mortgages.

Doubts about the market for mortgage debentures began to develop well before the panic unfolded. In fact, Equitable was just one of dozens of hastily founded lending companies whose financial situation deteriorated as the agricultural economy worsened and more and more farmers defaulted on their mortgages. Another company that failed was Kansas City's Jarvis-Conklin Mortgage Company, which—like Equitable—maintained offices in New York and London. A correspondent of the *Financial Times* asked company officials as early as 1891 about the mortgages it held and was told that they were "judiciously chosen and safe."[42]

Three years later the company was in receivership and faced claims of nonpayment from its bond investors after many of the mortgages it underwrote had failed. Since the company's dealings had beguiled more than just a handful of investors, the collapse of Jarvis-Conklin received widespread attention. The firm had used a subsidiary to buy up foreclosed mortgages and then leveraged the purchase when it bought them from the subsidiary at a higher, inflated price. When the new mortgages defaulted, the losses were unsustainable and the pools failed. An English investment journal remarked that "these mortgages have been hawked up and down the country [UK] as good advances against properties worth two and a half times their face value. The whole thing was a screaming farce in which all who had a hand must have laughed at the innocent faith of the British investor."[43] Jarvis-Conklin was sold to another, larger firm in 1895 and, despite the negative press, continued in business with the same management.

J. B. Watkins's firm in Lawrence, Kansas, also failed. It filed for bankruptcy and was placed in receivership in April 1894. The firm had become aggressive in land deals in the late 1880s and early 1890s at a time when the farm depression was worsening. At the time of its bankruptcy, J. B. Watkins & Company listed assets of $7.77 million and bills payable of $80 million. But the firm had cash on hand of only $18,229, and interest due from borrowers totaled $124,000.[44] Clearly, the inability of farm mortgage holders to meet their mortgage payments strained the firm, which did not have the resources to pay its bills.

Debenture holders were not the only investors damaged by the mortgage crisis during the panic. Many of the mortgage companies that had been organized in the farming states held few assets other than the property they bought. Creditors who lodged complaints against them often found that there were few, if any, assets to be liquidated to satisfy their claims. In some cases, an Eastern state's attorney general (often the attorneys general of Connecticut or Massachusetts, where many debenture investors resided) would request that his Midwestern counterpart (often the Kansas attorney general) require stockholders in an insolvent company to add additional capital to the firms' balance sheets to satisfy the claims.

When the attorney general of Massachusetts wrote to his Kansas counterpart about the matter, he received the following reply: "Our statute is in substance that . . . such execution may be issued against any of the stockholders to an extent equal in amount to the amount of stock owned by him, together with any amount unpaid them. This execution against the stockholder however cannot be issued except upon motion and notice to the stockholder."[45] This practice, common for investors in bank stocks in the nineteenth century, extended shareholder liability beyond paid-in capital and exposed them to more liability, usually double the amount paid in. The mortgage companies were included because they were often owners of one or more banks in their home region that did the original lending. Kansas was one of many states where the concept was written into its constitution. The notion of extended liability, as opposed to the contemporary limited liability, was imported from Britain in the colonial period and was adopted by many American states.[46] This problem developed three years before the crisis occurred, when the mortgage companies and their securities first showed signs of weakness. It was another contributing factor to the liquidation of many British investments in the United States because British investors did not want to incur financial double jeopardy by having to pay in additional amounts equal to their original stock investment. British investors were already in the process of liquidating many of their land holdings and took the opportunity as another sign to exit.

Within a year, however, the severe depression began to abate. The silver debate would continue, but gold remained as the standard for the dollar. The United States was still feeling the effects of unequal credit allocation and an inelastic (inflexible) currency. There was no central authority over the supply of money, such as a central bank, that could turn on the tap when necessary to provide the economy with more cash. That function was still filled by the major New York banks. Seizing upon this, Populists established another link in their attempt to connect domestic ills to foreign and banker cabals. Nevertheless, the influence of the Populists began to wane after the election of 1896. Five years earlier, the movement had organized into an official political party (the People's

Party) and, in 1986, supported William Jennings Bryan as their candidate for president.

Unfortunately, Bryan was also the candidate of the Democrats. On July 9, Bryan sealed the nomination with a fiery speech to the national convention in which he again advocated for silver as an alternative standard. "You shall not crucify mankind on a cross of gold," he thundered to the assembled delegates. Bryan lost the election to the Republican candidate, William McKinley, by more than 100 electoral votes by splitting the electorate, which had become increasingly urban and whose workers were more likely to work in factories than on farms. Factory workers feared the inflation that adding silver to the mix would create. Silver was their enemy but remained the farmers' friend, helping to raise farm prices and their incomes.

From this point on, the Populists' influence on regulating usury and loan sharking would be limited at best. Many of the states in which they appeared strong and vociferous never passed meaningful legislation to control the problem. In the early decades of the twentieth century, Populism would be supplanted by another movement that would have a greater voice in shaping solutions to social problems. The Progressives and their ideas appealed to all political parties, and the movement would include them all in its ranks. Unlike the Populists, many Progressives were based in urban areas in the Northeast, well educated, and better able to organize into a substantive political force.

CHAPTER TWO

A VENERABLE PRACTICE

AS THE POPULIST MOVEMENT BEGAN TO FADE AFTER THE elections of the 1890s, Progressives stepped into the breach by adopting many of the agrarian reformers' goals. But their methods differed. Many Progressives held high public office and were committed to creating change by using their insider knowledge of politics and government to attack many of the problems the Populists had only ranted about. Rapid social change was affecting many parts of American life. Loan sharking was at the top of the Progressives' wish list as a problem to be eliminated.

Loan sharking did not command the attention of the most powerful Progressives, however. The broad Progressive movement for social reform included three successive presidents in its ranks: Republicans Theodore Roosevelt and William Howard Taft, and Democrat Woodrow Wilson.

They were the direct opposite of the Populists, displaying Progressive ideas and policies alongside more traditional positions characteristic of their parties. The strong-willed Roosevelt, who took office in 1901, was an environmentalist and supporter of antitrust policies while, at the same time, being a firm believer in a strong military. Taft, who had served as solicitor general for the Benjamin Harrison administration and then as a federal judge, openly admitted that he had always wanted to be a justice on the Supreme Court, an appointment he would receive from Warren Harding in 1921 after he lost his bid for a second term to Woodrow Wilson in 1912. He initiated dozens of antitrust lawsuits and supported the founding of the Interstate Commerce Commission to regulate railroads. Wilson, the first president to have earned a Ph.D., had served as governor of New Jersey after eight years as the president of Princeton University, and was a strong advocate of international peacekeeping efforts by championing the League of Nations. Despite their political differences, all three could claim membership in the fraternity of progressivism for at least some of their policies. The social and economic legislation passed during the two decades of their presidencies, from 1901 to 1921, was the some of the most momentous since the Civil War. But the matter of loan sharking and usury was not among them.

The competition for legislative priority was intense during that time. Prohibition, the income tax, universal suffrage, and direct election of senators were some of the Constitutional issues on the agenda. Even the Progressives' two great pieces of financial reform legislation—the Federal Reserve Act of 1913 and the Federal Farm Loan Act of 1916—did not address usury and loan sharks directly (though it was assumed they would be subdued by other aspects of those laws). Financial issues had a reputation for being slippery and fast, like a loan shark absconding across the Hudson River to New Jersey to avoid New York authorities. Direct remedies for loan sharking would eventually proceed at state and local levels rather than in Congress, as would the first attempts at regulating securities markets.

High interest rates for small borrowers created a double-edged problem. Existing debt at usurious rates caused foreclosures, especially in the

Midwest and Plains states, and cast long shadows over the back-to-the-farm movement that had begun with the land rush after the Civil War. It cast equally long shadows over American manufacturing. Throughout the late nineteenth and early twentieth centuries, manufacturers continued to bring new consumer products to market. Yet, to consumers who were buried in debt already or lacked the means of obtaining credit, these innovations might as well not have existed. It was hard to sell to customers saddled with debt. High interest rates were creating a permanent state of indebtedness among lower-income Americans (farmers in particular) who could never pay off their debts, especially those interest-only mortgages that required a lump-sum payoff of the principal. In the absence of a central bank that could allocate credit nationwide, merchants and manufacturers were left to tackle the problem for themselves with the aid of their bankers.

The role of the Federal Reserve, established by Congress in 1913, in farm credit creation was viewed skeptically during the early years of World War I. In its early days, the Fed would be involved predominantly with credit market conditions affecting banks and Wall Street and less with agriculture (although there were some provisions for dealing with short-term farm debt). The Fed purposely had limited influence in agriculture. "Whether the Federal Reserve Act will suitably facilitate short-term credits or seasonal credits for agricultural purposes remains to be demonstrated," commented one senior agriculture banker.[1] A few years later, as an indication that more help was needed, Congress created the Federal Farm Loan Act to extend smoother credit to the agricultural sector. As it turned out, the Federal Farm Loan Act became the central bank for farmers and was all that stood between them and their traditional loan shark lenders.

Despite the fact that the farmers' plight had been recognized and well publicized, there was little political action or sympathy for farmers outside the agricultural centers. The Farm Belt was a long physical and emotional distance from Wall Street and the gap never got narrower. Two Americas had emerged by the late nineteenth century: one of farmers and the other of city dwellers. Senator Henrik Shipstead, a Farmer-Laborite

Republican from Minnesota, remarked that "my idea of New York, and by that I mean the controlling interest there, is that they sit back and look upon the rest of the country much as Great Britain looks upon India." The East was viewed by many as a colonial power intent on imposing its will on the rest of the country, especially when it came to the allocation of credit. The mortgage bond fiasco and the monetary claims of nineteenth-century Populists had not been forgotten.

The war against loan sharks would not be won by new credit institutions, however. A vigorous campaign in the press, supported by avid anti-loan shark forces, was waged to protect borrowers from exploitation and predatory lending. That so many loan sharks were so active nationwide became an embarrassment, with potentially damaging effects on the economy. Despite representing opposite sides of the economy, both farming and working for an urban municipality were losing their attraction as ways of making a living because so many workers from each sector were heavily indebted with no real process of extricating themselves.

Salary Buying

The first program loan sharks devised that became commonplace for many urban workers was called salary buying. Today the practice is known as payday lending. The phenomenon, which began in the late 1890s and became a booming business within ten years, was especially pervasive in urban areas because of the concentration of factories, offices, and municipal governments—places with lots of workers who were often short on cash. Salary buying was a simple scheme in which a finance company paid a worker an advance on his weekly pay. When the worker was paid, the lender would deduct his fee, leaving the worker with less than the full value of his pay. The percentage charged usually amounted to more than 20 percent per pay (240 percent on an annualized basis) and was even higher in some cases. The benefit to the worker was that the worker received proceeds a couple of days before he was actually paid, so the transaction appeared to be a third-party advance on his next pay. The lender claimed it was not a loan but only a discounted advance and, hence, usury laws did not apply. The high rates of interest suggested otherwise.

Salary buying was far more attractive to loan sharks than chattel lending (loans for small purchases). It was contractual and involved less record-keeping and fewer worries about the actual collateral. It was also much more profitable. One New York City loan office reported a net gain of $541 on loans of $1,899 in just one month, a return of 28 percent for the month and 342 percent annualized. The annual net income from an operation with $10,000 to lend at that rate of return would be over $34,000.[2] With returns exceeding almost anything else in the markets, many established loan sharks were soon looking for new investors with fresh cash to help expand their businesses.

One of the major expenses of running a loan office was newspaper advertising, which often amounted to as much as 30 percent of operating expenses. In New York, salary buyers advertised mainly in the *New York World*, spending twice as much on ads in that newspaper as in any other. The expense was usually well worth it. One man entered the business in New York with $25,000. Three years later he was offered $60,000 for the business, after having made $110,000 on his original investment.[3] Returns of this nature lured many newcomers to the salary lending business as well as those involved in chattel and mortgage lending. The more successful loan sharks were able to grow their businesses from local concerns to national firms. More than one operated in several cities and some even established branches abroad. New York's D. H. Tolman, the most successful (and the most notorious) salary buyer of the early twentieth century, had more than sixty offices in the United States and Canada by World War I. His success led to prosecution within ten years.

Borrowing against salary was anathema to most employers and was a cause for dismissal if detected. Ironically, this often made the potential borrower who worked for an employer with a strict dismissal policy a good credit risk in the eyes of the salary buyer. The implied blackmail in the situation was obvious. The agreement between salary buyer and employee was confidential, but if the borrower could not meet his obligation, the lender would consider it a breach of contract and notify the employer, resulting in the firing of the employee. Loan sharks also employed women who would suddenly appear at the places of work of borrowers (mostly men) who fell behind on their repayments and shout at them to pay back their loans. This was referred to as a "bawling out." Often, if the borrower did not work for a particularly strict employer, the lender would require additional co-signers to the contract, all of whom could be held liable for the debt and possibly risk losing their own jobs if their employers were informed. Clearly, borrowers who needed the occasional salary advance walked a fine line with financial catastrophe.

While salary buying is assumed to have been big business in the early twentieth century, estimates of the actual size of the market are rare. One estimate claimed that there were about thirty different loan offices operating in New York City alone, whose $300,000 of invested capital grossed about $1.2 million a year. Considering that the average loan was for $20, this suggested that about 15,000 employees used the services of salary buyers. Many employers were proud that their no-tolerance policies greatly reduced the number of employees who had to be dismissed, but on further examination the situation was more complicated. At least one manager of a no-tolerance firm actually acted as an agent for loan sharks, helping them procure customers among his own employees in exchange for a 6 percent commission.[4]

There was a widespread assumption that a vast majority of the workforce in the cities was underpaid and had trouble making ends meet from week to week. In 1911 the *New York Times* reported that "recent investigations have shown fairly conclusively that in every city of more than 30,000 population there is one usurer to every 5,000 to 10,000 people; in cities where manufactories employing large numbers of workmen have congregated these figures are greatly increased."[5] Some office workers in New York believed that their entire company's workforce was indebted to salary buyers and could not exist without them. While their suspicions may have overestimated the mark, the reaction among some employers, church groups, and small-town bankers indicated that there was more truth to the belief than officially admitted. As a result, the movement against loan sharks began with humble origins but gained considerable momentum very quickly.

PAWNBROKING

Arguably the oldest form of lending, pawnbroking was not always viewed with the same disdain as other forms of high-interest lending. Part of the reason had to do with its historical origins in the Middle Ages, when the Catholic Church sanctioned the establishment of public offices called *montes di pieta* (mounts of pity) to lend money to the poor at low rates of interest. This was at a time when the Church otherwise forbade the charging of interest entirely. The *montes* took their lending model from pawnshops, which had been in existence for more than a thousand years. The lending process required the borrower to leave a personal item as collateral for the loan, similar to the pawnbrokers' methods established centuries before. If the item was not bought back, it was sold with no further consequence.

Prior to the 1890s, there were ambivalent feelings about pawnbroking in the United States. The majority of observers were on the negative side when it was discussed in policy circles. Pawnbrokers were accused of fostering alcoholism by providing ready cash, encouraging theft by purchasing stolen items, and encouraging slothfulness among the population.[6] Pawnshops appeared to have been more popular among the general public, at least compared to mutual societies (savings institutions owned by their depositors) in their early years. But this was probably because the overwhelming majority of mutual society customers had no prior experience of any sort with banks and did not understand the processes by which bank loans were made. For example, pawnbrokers gave cash on the spot and did not require credit checks or other borrower paperwork.

Despite being an ancient institution, not all pawnbrokers were the same. In the United States and Great Britain in the late nineteenth and early twentieth centuries, pawnbrokers were privately operated. On the continent, most pawnbrokers were municipal institutions whose activities were closely supervised by the local government where they operated. Their rates were closely controlled; they were required to hold pawned items for a specified amount of time and to dispose of unclaimed items at public auction. The differences evolved from the notion in continental Europe that pawnbrokers, indeed, were usurers and, therefore, required close regulation. In the United States and Great Britain, pawnbrokers claimed to provide a vital service to those in need of fast cash and were accepted on that basis.

Although often criticized as just another form of loan sharking, pawnbroking occasionally drew praise as a necessary economic function. Pawnbroking was chattel lending, and in New York the law was very specific about the type of property that could be pawned. Personal clothing was included with the other forms of tangible property. On May 10, 1896, an article titled "Pawnbroking Not Piracy," appeared in the *New York Times*."[7] In it, supporters of pawnbroking equated pawnbroking with the activities of remedial loan societies to help reduce the indebtedness that had sprung up in some cities as a way to provide much-needed liquidity to the poor. Much of their defense centered on the rates that New York allowed pawnbrokers to charge. Pawnbrokers could charge as much as 30 percent per year on loans up to $100 and 18 percent on loans over that amount; the same rates allowed for consumption loans generally, but amounts exceeded by loan sharks who, technically, were still limited by New York law to 6 percent per annum. Most pawnbrokers operated within those rates because they were licensed and could not legally exceed them.

Pawnbrokers, thus, occupied a middle ground between low-interest lenders such as mutual societies (when they could be found), which charged only the maximum under usury laws and the high-interest loan sharks. How high those interest charges were depended in part on how long the item was pawned. With the repurchase price increasing each month the item was kept in hock, at a certain point it became impractical for the customer to buy it back. The mark-up price reflected the rate of interest charged although, technically, the pawnbroker could argue that he was not charging interest at all. In any case, the rate of interest was calculated over a short period of around six months, after which it was safe to assume the customer was not returning to repurchase the item.

As a result, arguments raged over proposals in the New York state legislature to reduce the legal rates; the public protested that pawnbrokers were simply loan sharks preying on the poor and destitute. The argument in favor of maintaining the present interest rates centered on pawnbroker activities. Supporters asserted that when pawnbrokers advanced cash to those wanting to pawn personal clothing, such as a winter coat, it demonstrated their willingness to lend despite the apparent risk of questionable collateral. Yet many customers would pawn a coat in spring, hoping to redeem it before winter began, indicating poor financial health. While the economic argument was sound, the issue underlined the desperate financial straits of many of the working poor because of high interest rates. The pawnbroker was the workingman's lender of last resort, however, and high rates were justified to compensate for this sort of high-risk lending. When compared with the practical side, the economic argument usually won the day.

THE REMEDIAL REACTION

The first defensive shot in the war against loan sharks began in the 1880s and was fired by employers, small bankers, and churchmen who founded what became known as remedial lending societies. These groups took several forms, including mutual savings banks, employer-organized lending groups (which eventually evolved into credit unions), and church loan bureaus. They were known as remedial societies because they helped borrowers disentangle themselves from onerous debts. These organizations would allow the average worker, who had been all but ignored by existing banks for decades, to establish legitimate banking relationships that would enable him to borrow for a home or other purchase at less than extortionate rates of interest.

Remedial lenders were commercial enterprises but strove to charge reasonable rates of interest. Mutual societies were usually limited-purpose banks that took deposits from and made loans to their members. They were among the oldest financial institutions in the United States. The Philadelphia Savings Fund Society and Boston's Provident Institution for Savings both dated their origins to 1816. Since they were mutual organizations—that is, they were owned by their depositors—there was a strong incentive for borrowers to repay on time. They were also local in nature, which meant that members of the association tended to know one another. The main objective of the mutual societies was to provide consumption loans and loans for purchasing a home. Unlike traditional banks and commercial lenders, they did not provide loans for capital investment or working capital to business. They required that the borrower have a savings account before a loan would be considered. They were dedicated to doing business with the workingman and would take deposits as little as a nickel or a dime. Many of them, in fact, made this clear in their very names, such as the Dime Savings Bank of New York.

Credit unions also trace their origins to the remedial, anti-loan shark movement. They operated in much the same fashion as mutual savings societies, although membership was limited to employees of a specific organization or industry, or some other group dedicated to protecting its members. Credit unions frequently were organized by employers who realized it was good business to help their employees avoid loan sharks. Some were organized along ethnic lines or catered to immigrants of a specific country or their descendants. In the early days, credit unions were concentrated within two distinct groups: employees of private organizations and government workers.[8] Massachusetts passed the nation's first credit union law in 1909, and the first credit union opened the following year. The law was strongly supported by Edward Filene, the president of the Boston department store that bore his name. Filene became a vigorous advocate for credit unions after taking a world trip in 1908 where he observed first-hand the success of small consumer banking institutions in Europe. With the aid of a Canadian who was well-versed with similar institutions in Canada, Filene helped draft the Massachusetts law that became the model for many other states. The majority of credit unions established in the years before World War I were based in Massachusetts, New York, and Rhode Island; ironically, the idea was slower to spread to the Midwest and Plains states, where sources of cheaper credit were more sorely needed.

These groups proved popular and profitable. Between 1896 and 1900, the amount of mortgages reported by mutual savings banks increased significantly—by 25 percent.[9] Their rate of growth demonstrated that demand existed for loans at reasonable rates of interest, provided they were supported by a corresponding compensating balance (money held on deposit at the bank as collateral). During the last years of the nineteenth century, mutual savings banks paid 3.5 to 4 percent interest on deposits, while charging 6 to 7 percent interest on personal loans and mortgages. The spread between the two was more than adequate to ensure a profit for the lender, as long as loans were extended prudently.

The establishment of remedial lenders followed quickly after the passage of legislation in several states designed to distinguish between chattel, salary, and mortgage loans and to establish rates for them that fell within existing usury laws. In some states that had effectively abolished their usury laws, such as Massachusetts, the rates followed those in neighboring states so that loan sharks would not be tempted to migrate there from places with more onerous restrictions on lending. In 1894, the Provident Loan Society of New York was chartered to provide small loans to customers who might otherwise fall prey to loan sharks. To avoid the temptation of overcharging, Provident's charter mandated that officers of the society were not to be compensated for their service and that the company could charge its customers nothing other than interest. The interest charged was a maximum of 3 percent per month for the first two months and 2 percent thereafter, with a one-time filing fee of three dollars. The maximum loan that could be borrowed was

$200. The model was soon copied by new lending societies in other states. The Workingmen's Loan Society, established in Rhode Island in 1895, made loans of up to $1,000 at an interest rate of 1 percent per month. In New York City, the Hebrew Free Loan Society charged no interest at all to qualified borrowers.

Churches also joined the movement. In one of the better-known experiments, St. Bartholomew's Church in New York City opened a remedial lending society in 1895 with $25,000 capital, about twice that of the average loan shark office in the city. Its mission was to extend chattel loans to those in need of no more than $50 at an interest rate of 6 percent. In its first year, it made loans of $30,000, about half of which was repaid within the first six months. Even though demand far exceeded the lending capital available, the success of the experiment induced church officials to make the program permanent. "It is in no sense a charity but strictly a business enterprise," commented the rector of the church. Borrowers were expected to make their payments on time, though the plan would exercise leniency when circumstances warranted.[10] The society provided small loans at rates that were almost 1 percentage point lower than New York's official usury ceiling at the time and a full 30 percentage points lower than the lowest loan shark rate. The church proved that the usurious level of interest was a genuine moral problem and that the economic argument that what mattered was the availability of funds, was false. Providing loans at high compensatory rates for the lender was, indeed, usury, and its parishioners proved that correct. The old statutory usury rate was a holdover from the past but even the average worker had it in the back of his mind as fair and just and jumped at the opportunity to borrow. Although obvious, it proved that the demand for borrowed money depended on the interest rate charged and that individual borrowers were, indeed, aware of the rates they were offered. This simple experiment by St. Bartholomew's provided some proof that there, indeed, were many working people in dire economic straits who did know the difference between 6 percent and 240 percent or more. The fact that many borrowed at loan shark rates was an unofficial indicator

that society had a serious problem that lenders had no particular interest in solving.

DISCOVERING CONSUMER CREDIT

While the farmers had their credit problems, they also became a focal
point of a retailing phenomenon that began on a massive scale in the
decades after the Civil War. The retail department store got its start in
East Coast cities and for decades remained primarily an urban institution. Retailing on a large scale is generally attributed to John Wanamaker, who opened his first store, a men's clothing store, in Philadelphia
in 1861. The store opened just as the ready-to-wear clothing industry
began to grow larger. Wanamaker expanded into dry goods in 1875, and
two years after that he created the forerunner of the modern department store by opening a number of specialty shops around his flagship
store.

Because of the distances involved and the difficulty of making payments to merchants, farmers in the Midwest and Plains states were typically considered to be beyond the reach of the market that stores such as
Wanamaker's could serve, but, in the 1870s, Wanamaker and other retailers began to close this distance. Wanamaker constantly strived for
innovation in his retailing business. He was among the first retailers to
spend considerable sums on advertising in newspapers. After raising a
significant amount of money for Benjamin Harrison's successful presidential campaign in 1888, Wanamaker was named Postmaster General
by Harrison, a post in which he served from 1889 to 1893. It was his
tenure as head of the post office that opened the door even further for
the mail-order catalog business.

The first mail-order business had been started several years before,
in Chicago, by Aaron Montgomery Ward. While working in St. Louis,
Ward recognized the problems faced by farmers who, because of their
isolation, could not shop for consumer goods. In 1872, Ward opened a
retail mail-order house that bought dry goods directly from manufacturers

and offered them for sale by catalog, thus eliminating the need for local showrooms and suppliers. Ward's business proved popular very quickly, not just among farmers but the urban public as well. His first catalog was printed on one page; by 1895, the Montgomery Ward catalog ran to 500 pages (and weighed four pounds) and was a staple in both rural and urban homes. Part of Ward's appeal was a liberal returns policy, which minimized the risk of purchasing goods that the consumer could not first pick up and try out or that were damaged in shipment.

By 1888, Montgomery Ward's annual sales exceeded $1 million. Another major retailer and catalog company was Sears, Roebuck, which was founded by Richard W. Sears and Alvah Roebuck in 1886 as the R. W. Sears Watch Company. The company changed its name to Sears, Roebuck & Company in 1893 and expanded into mail-order sales of household items and clothing. Like Montgomery Ward, its focus was on rural areas where retail stores were in short supply. Coinciding with the rise of the Grange movement, which advocated for a variety of social and economic policies to improve conditions for farmers, the catalog companies could plausibly claim they were making a tangible difference in the lives of rural Americans.

The mail-order business was aided by the introduction of rural free delivery (RFD) by the postmaster general in 1895, an innovation that had originally been proposed by John Wanamaker during his tenure. In 1891, Wanamaker had written about the benefits of RFD in social as well as practical terms: "A great deal is said about the desertion of the farm. . . . The regular arrival of the paper or magazine, the easier ways to correspond, the general process of sending and receiving things by mail will not only keep the girls and boys at home and make them contented there but will add to their ambition and determination to make the old farm pay."[11] Wanamaker also opposed the use of the mail by state lotteries to sell tickets nationwide. The Louisiana Lottery had been very successful in selling tickets out of state but had been widely criticized for mismanagement and fraud. Cleaning up the use of the mail was in keeping with what was seen as its potential social benefits—that Rural Free Delivery would somehow add to the intellectual development of those isolated in rural areas. The lottery, on the other hand, simply sapped people of hard earned savings. Ideas of that nature were reiterated many times in the years leading to World War I by those wishing to stem the migration from rural areas to the cities.

Buying from a mail-order catalog required the customer to pay by some sort of money order or bank draft. Retail checking accounts were still uncommon for most people, due to the lack of banking facilities, so mail-order goods were usually purchased with stamps or money orders. Before long, merchants realized they needed to extend credit to their customers, and to do so successfully, they would need a viable system of credit that provided financing for their wares at rates that substantially undercut loan shark rates. Many stores already offered credit on an individual basis as a convenience, but in general the rates they charged were very high. In fact, the lending charges were often more profitable to the merchant than the markup on the items sold, and these customers soon came to realize that the convenience of credit came at a high price. Merchants also allowed customers to put away money on a regular basis to make their purchases at a future time. This was typically called the "layaway" plan—the customer laid aside money for the item. Layaways were marketed under a variety of names, including the "Christmas Club." A customer would begin setting aside cash with a merchant in January, and by the following Christmas, she would be able to take that item home. The merchant set the goods aside for the customer but would not release them until payment had been received in full.

While layaways would remain popular for several more decades, they would lose ground to the new installment credit plans introduced during World War I. The concept was simple, but at the time somewhat radical. Consumers were required to make a down payment on a purchase and then pay the balance in equal installments. Automobiles were the first big-ticket items to be sold in this manner, with the Maxwell Motor Car Company being the first manufacturer to offer its cars "on time" in 1916. A purchase required a down payment of 50 percent, with the balance to be paid off in eight equal installments. Most other car companies eventually followed suit, but the costs to the consumer were not low. New cars bought on installment plans incurred annual finance charges of 11 to 23 percent, while used cars ranged from 16 to 43 percent.[12] Many other big-ticket consumer items, such as refrigerators and farm equipment, were offered on installment, and eventually the practice spread to all sorts of consumer goods. The only qualification was that the item purchased had some relatively long-lasting value so that its collateral value provided the creditor with protection should the borrower fall behind on payments. The chattel loan was alive and well, only now it was being used to fund new purchases.

The PANIC OF 1907

The fortunes of the stock market were closely related to the credit markets before World War I, although the direct link was not often clear. Banking and securities were integrally related and securities speculation usually had banking consequences or vice versa, making panics unusually severe and sometimes long-lasting because of the lack of a national securities regulator. As a result, banks and securities firms usually attempted to resolve market problems on their own, as they had during the nineteenth century. The stock market and the denizens of Wall Street were viewed with suspicion, and events just after the turn of the century only strengthened the feelings of mistrust.

By the start of 1906, the stock market was approaching bubble-like proportions. The market had risen sharply since J. P. Morgan merged three giant steel companies to form the United States Steel Corporation in 1901. Over the first half of 1906, however, the market's rise was interrupted by a sharp sell-off amid widespread bearish speculation. The sell-off angered the New York press and brought denunciations raining down on the heads of the New York banks. In the plunge, the price of U.S. Steel dropped from the mid-fifties to less than $10 a share. Over the next few months, the market recovered and prices began to rise again, but the absence of a regulatory entity that could calm the market, a central bank, was increasingly worrisome, even to some on Wall Street, since the markets were becoming larger and more complex, along with the economy. If the market fell again, many of the banks that were heavily involved in speculating—including big trust banks, which managed money invested on behalf of estates and companies—would likely go under. Many trust banks had made margin loans to market speculators while accepting securities as collateral. If stocks fell, the trusts and their investors would be badly hurt. Without a central bank, there was no one to provide them with liquidity in the event of a depositors' run or if they needed cash to prop up their positions.

Because of their substantial stake in the trust business, the heads of many Wall Street banks wanted to assemble a pool of money to be used should a crisis develop. A few years earlier, several New York banks had collected money to found their own trust institution, the Bankers Trust Company. The market reaction the bankers had feared came in March 1907, with stocks losing almost 10 percent of their value over a fifteen-day period. Many politicians, including President Theodore Roosevelt, blamed the dismal economic climate on the concentrated power of of the country's banks which alone decided if credit was needed in the markets. The next six months saw the market steadily erode.

Then, on October 21, a run developed on the Knickerbocker Trust Company of New York. Depositors lined up in front of the bank's headquarters to demand their funds. Many of them were unsuccessful in collecting. The bank closed the next day after an auditor found that its funds were depleted beyond hope. A few weeks later, the bank's president, Charles T. Barney, shot himself.

After Knickerbocker's failure, Wall Street banks, led by J. P. Morgan & Company, banded together to ensure that the banking system remained intact. They met in New York with President Roosevelt's secretary of the Treasury, George Cortelyou, who provided them with $25 million from the Treasury to keep the system from collapsing. The money was deposited in the national banks in New York for the purpose of adding funds to a system sorely in need of more liquidity. It was the job of the large New York banks to apply the funds as they saw fit to prevent further panic and runs by depositors. In many ways, this infusion of Treasury funds was an extraordinary gesture. Roosevelt's reliance on Morgan underscored the tremendous vacuum in the United States's financial system; the Treasury of the largest emerging economy in the world had to transfer funds to private bankers to prevent a financial collapse.

Despite the gesture, the stock exchange began to sag under the weight of margin selling. Ransom Thomas, the president of the New York Stock Exchange, pleaded with Morgan for more funds to support it, fearing it would not be able to weather the day without aid. Morgan and other bank presidents responded by pledging money, and the New York Stock Exchange was able to remain open. When Morgan's support was announced in the exchange, pandemonium broke out and the uproar echoed down Wall Street. When Morgan asked what the noise was, he was told that the traders on the exchange had given him a roaring ovation.

More than one detractor claimed that the bankers had orchestrated the panic to make speculative profits by using their inside knowledge of banking to make money in the stock market. When the Knickerbocker Trust Company, a retail bank with many depositors, failed and bankers refused to prop it up, the view was bankers would not support other banks that did business with the public that they did not control. A pledge to do so came only after the Knickerbocker failure, triggering a stock market rally. Morgan's reputation was enhanced. After bailing out both the banking system and the New York Stock Exchange, Morgan was literally deified in the press as "our savior."

Senator Robert La Follette, a Progressive Republican from Wisconsin, was one of the most ardent proponents of the conspiracy theory that this panic was engineered by and for the benefit of Wall Street. La Follette represented a generation of Americans who favored competition rather than the concentration of industry into large trusts (or monopolies). La Follette was not convinced by the media accounts. "Morgan gave out, as reported in Wall Street, that the Knickerbocker would be supported [by the other banks] if it met the demands of the depositors who had started a run on it. There was nothing in subsequent events to indicate that there was any sincerity in that promise. . . . Support was not given, it was withheld," La Follette stated later in 1907.[13]

Nevertheless, Morgan's reputation as a savior was further enhanced again just a few days after his rescue of the stock exchange when he saved the city of New York from insolvency, in a manner reminiscent of his bailout of the U.S. Treasury over a decade before. Mayor George McClellan made a personal appeal to Morgan, who agreed to underwrite the sale of $30 million of city bonds. The bond issue was successful, and after several difficult months this panic began to abate. Morgan was now seen as the savior of the banking system, the stock exchange, and New York City all at the same time. But the lessons of the past had not been forgotten. If La Follette's views were any indication, many in Congress would soon be clamoring for financial reform.

MOVES TOWARD REFORM

The outcry for reform rising from Progressives forced bankers to consider the increasing tide of opinion against them. Around the turn of the twentieth century, the idea of a European-style central bank was discussed as a remedy for the country's credit market conditions, but most bankers were not wholeheartedly in favor of the idea. Those who did favor it came from those Wall Street banking houses that better understood central banking and whose founders were German Jews who had immigrated to the United States in the nineteenth century.

Worried about another liquidity crisis, Congress, in 1908, passed the Aldrich–Vreeland Act. Its sponsors included traditional Republicans in addition to Democrats who had close ties to the banking community. The act created an emergency plan to issue currency in times of monetary crisis and formed the National Monetary Commission, which was charged with examining the currency situation and studying ways to make the credit markets more stable.

Shortly thereafter, in 1910, a group of Wall Street bankers met clandestinely on Jekyll Island in Georgia. The meeting was intended as a forum to frame a Republican alternative to the banking reforms making their way through Congress, which was under Democratic control for the first time in twenty years. The group drafted what became known as the Aldrich Plan, named for the head of the National Monetary Commission, Republican Senator Nelson Aldrich of Rhode Island; the plan would become the blueprint for the Federal Reserve system. Ushered through Congress by Carter Glass, a Republican congressman from Virginia, the plan passed in almost its original form; it was the model on which compromise between Wall Street and reformers would later be centered when the Federal Reserve was introduced. An elastic currency that could be controlled by a central bank-type institution was one of its stated objectives.

One of the senior bankers present at the Jekyll Island meeting was Paul Warburg of the Wall Street investment bank Kuhn, Loeb & Co. Warburg, who had left his native Germany to settle in New York in 1902, was in favor of a central banking-style institution and made his opinions known to his colleagues. He was later confronted in his office one day by James Stillman, chairman of the National City Bank of New York, who wanted to know why Warburg supported such a radical change in American banking. "Warburg," Stillman asked, "don't you think the City Bank has done pretty well? . . . Why not leave things alone?" Warburg's answer came without hesitation: "Your bank is so big and so powerful, Mr. Stillman, that when the next panic comes, you will wish your responsibilities were smaller."[14] Some, if not many, Wall Street bankers realized that another panic should be avoided at all costs. The Fed was about to be created.

THE BIRTH OF THE FED

In the months leading to the passage of the Aldrich bill, drafted after the meetings and many discussions in Congress, its success was anything but assured. President William Howard Taft decided to send the members of the National Monetary Commission to Europe to study central banking methods. It was an unusual move by usually insular American politicians. The banking system was being prepared for broad changes in the way business was conducted. Speaking at the Economic Club of New York in 1909, Senator Aldrich had announced, "I have a plan which was suggested by the Ambassador to France . . . to make the United States the financial center of the world, a position she is entitled to by virtue of her resources, her vast accumulations of capital, and her surplus capital." Aldrich did not reveal the plan at the time but told the assemblage that he hoped they would support it. Considering the vast changes the plan would entail, it was unrealistic to expect immediate acceptance; personal diplomacy would be needed to pave the way.

Aldrich already had the support of President Taft, who was determined to correct the problems in the banking system. "Mr. Aldrich states that there are two indispensable requirements in any plan to be adopted involving a central bank of issue," Taft remarked in September 1909. "The one is that the monetary system shall be kept free of Wall Street influences and the other that it should not be manipulated for political purposes." Taft understood that it was important to appeal to those critics of the financial system who favored even more radical change than Aldrich would propose. Noting that Aldrich was viewed with deep suspicion by people from Western states, Taft added, "If, with his clear-cut ideas and simple but effective style of speaking, he makes apparent to the Western people what I believe to be his earnest desire to aid the people and to crown his political career . . . it would be a long step toward removing the political obstacles to a proper solution of this question."[15]

The Aldrich bill did not pass Congress on the first effort. As the American correspondent of *The Economist* noted in April 1912, "It is admitted by everybody that no measure of banking reform can be passed at the current session of Congress. . . . There seems to be no chance of getting any relief from the present disturbed conditions in our banking system until a new President is inaugurated."[16] The correspondent attributed the delay not to bankers but to radical elements among the Democrats, notably factions favoring William Jennings

Bryan, who caused the more conservative members of Congress in both parties to act slowly rather than insert measures in a bill they thought to be unwise.

The Economist's reporter proved correct. After Woodrow Wilson was elected president, and after years of discussion, the Federal Reserve Act finally passed both houses of Congress in December 1913. The new central bank would be called a "reserve" rather than a central bank, partly to assuage the reservations of some bankers. The powers of the new central bank were contentious, but in the end were fairly well received in the banking community.

The major point of contention in the formative stages was the composition of the Fed itself, which gave the large New York banks a significant role but denied them seats on the system board. Many on Wall Street wanted bankers to be represented on the Federal Reserve's Board of Governors, but President Wilson was firmly opposed to the idea from the very beginning. In a meeting at the White House with key lawmakers framing the legislation, Wilson responded to their arguments: "Will one of you gentlemen tell me in what civilized country of the earth there are important government boards of control on which private interests are represented?" Senator Carter Glass, a major architect of the legislation who was present at the meeting, recalled the silence that followed as the longest single moment he ever experienced. Wilson pressed on. "Which of you gentlemen thinks the railroads should select members of the Interstate Commerce Commission?" he asked.[17]

The issue was not raised again and bankers were excluded from the Fed's board. Bankers would, however, be represented on the boards of the twelve district Federal Reserve banks. The district banks were spread throughout the country, each with its own management board.[18] Local bankers from the districts were allowed a limited number of seats. The Board of Governors in Washington, D.C., which was composed of five paid directors, made policy for the entire system. The new regulatory body was charged with maintaining watch over credit conditions in the country, requiring reserves of those banks over which it had authority, and was given powers to intervene in the money market if necessary. But the most contentious issue of all was the Fed's ability to issue notes.

The elastic currency was the most prominent economic issue facing Congress when it passed the legislation. The dollar had been tied to Treasury securities since the nineteenth century and had to be freed from them it if it was to become responsive to changing credit conditions. The new law allowed the Fed to issue Federal Reserve notes backed not directly by Treasury securities but by the full faith and credit of the U.S. government, a concept that had become more acceptable since the Civil War. If the economy slowed down and needed a stimulant, the Fed could provide it without asking the Treasury to issue more bonds. Commercial banks also needed the ability to convert bank deposits into cash if required. Gold still was the standard for the dollar, but war was about to break out in Europe, obscuring the issue.

The New York Federal Reserve Bank would be central to the entire system, reigning supreme over the other eleven district banks. It was clear that the locus of financial power was still in New York rather than in Washington, D.C., where non-Eastern interests would have preferred it to reside (although the practicality of that was questionable). When the blueprint for the Fed was drawn, open-market operations (the buying and selling of money market securities by the Fed) were granted to each of the twelve district banks individually rather than centralized into a system operation (as it would be in the 1930s). This meant operations performed by the New York Fed would be seen as most important, and New York remained the center of the financial universe.

The Fed's primary focus was the commercial banks; other sorts of banking institutions were outside its ambit. Unless the commercial banks started serving retail customers and farmers in a meaningful way, credit conditions would not improve for large segments of the public. The Fed recognized the plight of farmers almost from the beginning. Farmers had a difficult time every year during the period of "crop movements," the time when farmers sent their crops to market. Any fluctuations in money market rates during this period could be very disruptive to the prices farmers received when their crops were sold. As a result, in 1915, the Fed sent letters to its twelve district banks urging them to ensure that their day-to-day operations went smoothly so that inefficiencies would not hurt their impact in the credit market. The *Boston Daily Globe* remarked that the new emphasis "represents a radical change from the program previously followed and means a great deal to the business interests of the United States."

Farmers no longer would be reliant upon local banks that got their money from New York correspondent banks. Banks could now rediscount agriculture paper they held directly with the Fed banks. "All this means cheaper money for the farmer-borrower," the paper continued, "and in the end cheaper money for everyone who has high grade collateral to pledge."[19] Many Wall Street bankers soon recognized this as one of the consequences of the new central bank—a flow of funds out of New York to local and regional banks around the country. But Farm Belt fears still were not assuaged.

Concentrated Power?

Before the Fed was created to regulate the banks, self-regulatory function and control of credit was provided by what became known as the "money trust," the Gilded Age term referring to the concentrated powers of the large, urban banks. The term was coined by Minnesota Congressman Charles A. Lindbergh. The actual power in this group was held by the large New York banks, which dictated their needs and objectives to others around the country. Like Robert La Follette, Lindbergh was a Progressive Republican who had become disenchanted with Wall Street, and in early 1912 he launched an investigation into the practices of the putative money trust. The hearings would be convened by a subcommittee of the House Committee on Banking and Currency, which came to be known as the Pujo Committee, named after its chairman, Democratic Congressman Arsène Pujo of Louisiana.

In Lindbergh's view, the Federal Reserve was nothing more than another large, unaccountable trust. Its founding was a product of self-serving bankers and their political allies in Congress. This was a state of affairs that suggested the public was not being served by them but merely stood as pawns in their larger game of financial dominance. The Aldrich–Vreeland emergency law was viewed skeptically. Lindbergh remarked, "Its ostensible purpose was to provide an emergency currency, but the real purpose was to get a monetary commission which would ultimately frame a proposition for amendments to our currency and banking laws which would suit the money trust."[20] Lindbergh owed many of his views to the Populists of previous decades. While his opinions on the money trust centered mostly on commercial banks and their influence on money, credit creation, and the stock market, they owed a distinct debt to the agrarian movement and its interpretation of monetary affairs since the Civil War. His views on the exception clause (the requirement that tariffs and interest on Treasury bonds be paid in gold, not greenbacks) closely followed those of the Populist writer Sarah Emery.

In his 1913 book *Banking and Currency and the Money Trust*, Lindbergh quoted from a letter written by the secretary of the Associated Bankers of New York, Philadelphia, and Boston in 1877 to the group's members concerning the resumption of specie payments in 1875: "To repeal the Act creating bank notes, or to restore to circulation the Government issue of money, will be to provide the people with money, and will therefore seriously affect our individual profits as bankers and lenders. See your Congressman at once and engage him to support our interests, that we may control legislation."[21] The forty-year-old controversy briefly came to the forefront again. This comment supported the old Populist notion that greenbacks were worth less than gold in terms of purchasing power. By extension, an institution such as the Federal Reserve that supported the bankers' special interest group only furthered its aims at the expense of everyone else.

The Pujo Committee's hearings made the fears of Lindbergh and La Follette abundantly clear. Samuel Untermyer was the committee's chief counsel. Never a friend of bankers, Untermyer enjoyed the distinction of being their first congressionally appointed inquisitor. His method of interrogating the bankers called to testify was probing and direct.

Untermyer summoned most of Wall Street's senior bankers to testify before the committee, including J. P. Morgan himself, a man not accustomed to being asked to explain himself in public. Untermyer's investigations uncovered labyrinthine connections between the banks and the nation's largest companies. Partners of J. P. Morgan & Company were revealed to directly or indirectly hold over 340 directorships in 118 corporations, representing over $22 billion in market capitalization. J. P. Morgan & Company also held directorships in five major insurance companies. And this paled in comparison to the combined influence of the other banks. Senior partners of the fourteen banks mentioned by the Pujo Committee held 103 board seats in sixty insurance companies, many of which overlapped.[22] Even more damning, the committee demonstrated that the overlap existed even among the banks themselves because of interlocking directorships (each bank holding at least one directorship on the board of the other). Those institutional relationships became the focus of the Clayton Antitrust Act of 1914, which attempted to control the concentration of financial power by banning interlocking directorships.

After the Pujo Committee hearings concluded in 1913, J. P. Morgan & Company sent an open letter to the committee to argue that there was, in fact, no such thing as a concentration of financial power among the New York banks. If there appeared to be such a thing, it was only because all the major banks were located there; there was nothing sinister about it. Blaming the country's ills on an acknowledged antiquated banking system, Morgan's letter strongly suggested that the committee had overstepped its bounds in its investigation. Conspiracies among bankers did not exist, it claimed, in an effort to debunk Progressive notions that banks manipulated the economy for their benefit. The letter also dismissed the idea that bankers had created the Panic of 1907 for their own enrichment: "In order to sustain the theory that the panic of 1907 had been 'engineered' one must attribute to the 'engineers' not only the power but some motive for their assumed achievements."[23] Morgan claimed that the stock market debacle and credit market crisis in 1907 had hurt bankers as badly as everyone else and that they did not profit from it.

Despite the fanfare, the hearings did not produce hard evidence of a money trust. Most of Wall Street and the press thought they only helped shed a favorable light on the bankers. The bankers may have felt that the politicians did not know what they were talking about technically, but they conducted themselves politely. The *New York Sun* sarcastically commented that the Pujo Committee "is indebted to Mr. Samuel Untermyer for exhibiting to it . . . that type of financial ability and integrity which is highly desirable that the legislative mind should study and comprehend."[24] Many observers began to believe that Congressman Lindbergh's characterization of the banks had no merit. Nevertheless, the hearings came at a sensitive time for the banks and financial markets and contributed to the controversy surrounding the Fed.

KING OF THE LOAN SHARKS

While the banking system occupied center stage in discussions about credit after the Panic of 1907, criticism of loan sharks continued but did not draw the same sort of headlines. That began to change in the years leading up to World War I as the public clamor against loan sharks, as well as attacks against them in the press, became more pronounced. When action was finally taken, it was surprisingly easy to put some loan sharks out of business. Ironically, the first successful battles against them were won in the cities rather than the rural areas where the cause had been championed by Populists for so long.

In the twenty-odd years since salary buying had become popular, many loan sharks were able to scale up their operations and establish offices across the country. The ability of individual lenders to maintain a network of far-flung offices was additional proof that unlicensed lenders did good business. Often, an office in one state would make a loan using the facilities of one in another state rather than its own. By doing so, the originating office could add another fee for the transaction, increasing the effective cost to the unsuspecting borrower. When officials in one city discovered that their local lender was actually a branch office of a company headquartered in another, discontent quickly rose to the surface. Loan sharking had always carried the connotation of carpetbagging outside the Eastern money centers, and large lending operations, making small loans became ready targets of those opposed to high-interest lending.

The best known of the high-interest lenders was Daniel H. Tolman, a New Yorker who had more than sixty offices across the United States and in Canada. Tolman's operations were the same as the original salary buyers of the late nineteenth century. Most of his customers were small borrowers in need of loans of $50 or less. The offices usually bore Tolman's name and were staffed mostly by women well trained to deal with male customers. They were instructed to respond to customers who complained about Tolman's terms by explaining that they were "only women" and did not make business decisions. It was assumed that men would not complain too strenuously since they did want to be unkind to women publicly.

Despite trying to soften its image, loan sharking could not shed its predatory reputation. When some of the newspapers and local politicians searched for a target for investigation, Tolman's name was on the top of most lists because his name was the most visible of the private lenders.

Tolman's lending practices came under attack in the early 1910s from the press in different cities at the same time and for similar reasons. An effective anti-loan shark campaign closed his office in Cincinnati after its manager was arrested by local authorities for violating usury laws. In Washington, D.C., newspapers were vocal in their opposition to him. In 1912, D.C. police arrested and charged the manager of the Tolman office, the manager's son, and the manager of another lender, the Household Loan Company, with violations of the local usury law. The son was released on $50 bond.

The arrests were based in part on complaints raised by a local woman who claimed she had fallen into the clutches of loan sharks. Her husband had borrowed $15 from Household, agreeing to pay it back in eight monthly installments of $3 each. When the husband died suddenly, his widow was left destitute and she sought another loan from Tolman to pay back the first from Household. Though she had no prospect of repaying the original high-interest loan, Household insisted that the original terms be honored first. Complaints of a similar nature had already prompted the police to raid most of the city's loan offices for failing to comply with an act of Congress (which made laws for the federal district) that made it illegal for an unlicensed lender to charge more than 6 percent per annum for loans. Licensed lenders were permitted 12 percent, following a 1910 law. Household and the local Tolman office, both unlicensed, were clearly in violation of local law because their rates were far in excess of the legal rate.

On the West Coast, Tolman fared no better. The city government of Tacoma, Washington, prohibited loan sharks from dealing with municipal employees or having anything to do with city hall. In late 1912, the *Tacoma Times* encouraged one of its readers, a municipal worker, to challenge the local Tolman office on an outstanding loan. The lender quickly recognized trouble and packed up his office, sold the fixtures, pulled his ads from the newspapers, and moved out of town. The newspaper claimed full credit for the affair: "Tolman operates offices in more than 60 cities of the country and so far as is known this is the first time he has been successfully squelched and driven from any city although his system has been the butt of warfare on many occasions."[25] The entire affair ended quickly; only fifteen days elapsed between the customer's complaint and Tolman's departure.

Tolman's surrender in Tacoma was a prelude to a much nastier battle closer to home. Following the success of other states in pressing usury charges, New York brought Tolman up on usury charges and convicted him in October 1913. Tolman was also convicted on similar charges in New Jersey around this time, though the New York conviction would prove much more serious. The New York complaint was filed by a clerk who had borrowed $10 from Tolman's company in New York and claimed he was charged interest and fees of 200 percent. Tolman was sentenced to six months in prison. At his sentencing, the judge declared,

"You are one of the most contemptible usurers in your unspeakable business. The poor people must be protected from such sharks as you. . . . Men of your type are a curse to the community and the money they gain is blood money."[26]

Tolman's son offered to tear up $500,000 of outstanding small loans in exchange for a pardon from New York Governor Martin Glynn. The governor refused. When the moneylender himself heard of the offer, "he declared he would rather serve out his sentence than 'thus forgo my manhood.' "[27] While incarcerated in Hart's Island Prison, Tolman served on the grave digging detail assigned to burials in the potter's field, a job reserved for the least popular inmates. He was released after serving his term and retired to his home.

On his death in 1918, his estate was believed to be worth about $7 million, proof that the salary buying business, indeed, had been lucrative. But he remained despised to the end. After his death, a popular business magazine remarked in Shakespearean tones that "Tolman chose great riches coined from the tears and the blood of his fellow creatures. He died rich, very rich, but his name was one accursed."[28]

A COORDINATED ATTACK

The travails of Tolman and other loan sharks demonstrated that curtailing loan sharks was difficult at the local level. Despite the establishment of the Federal Reserve in 1913, regulation of the financial sector of the economy did not always operate at the national level let alone on the local or state level where it would be enforced, if possible. In the years preceding World War I, high-interest lending existed side-by-side with another phenomenon designed to empty customers' pockets: speculation in the stock market. The same federal versus state and local regulations, if they existed, could be found there as well.

A rash of speculative securities offerings, buoyed by a strong stock market following the recession of 1907–08 and strong earnings for farmers, was promoted by hucksters, both in person and through the mail, to unsuspecting customers. Savings banks and other retail depository institutions offered low rates on deposits at the time, and the lure of high returns induced many novice investors to subscribe to these offerings instead. They often lost substantial amounts of money in short periods of time. One newspaper editorial compared the hucksters to the notoriously corrupt officials of the Louisiana Lottery Corporation, which had attempted to distribute its lottery tickets nationwide through the U.S. mail in the late nineteenth century. The editorial concluded that "probably the Louisiana Lottery was a conservative business enterprise when compared with many of the schemes now appealing to the gullible under the guise of investments."[29]

The soliciting and selling of securities of a dubious nature prompted many states to pass "blue sky laws," the first attempts at meaningful securities legislation in the country. Kansas passed the first blue sky law in 1911, and Indiana, Michigan, Arizona, Vermont, Ohio, and others followed (as did the Canadian province of Manitoba). The Kansas law required securities sellers to register their offerings with the state and to provide financial information about the companies whose securities were being offered as well as the brokers selling them. On its own, the blue sky law was innovative but it was hampered by the public's apparent appetite for high returns. Nor was the law helped by the Kansas banking department's announcement that state bank deposit rates would be limited to 3 percent, a change designed to protect the banks from ruinous competition.[30] Usually this meant competition from out-of-state banks, notably national banks.

Another example of state action was directed against the insurance industry in New York. In 1905, the Armstrong Committee (named after State Senator William W. Armstrong) began delving into the affairs of the Equitable Life Assurance Society and the activities of bankers and their relations with insurers. After a four-month investigation, Wall Street banks emerged looking particularly ravenous. The Equitable alone was sitting on a horde of $500 million in cash and liquid assets, and its link with Wall Street banks, especially J. P. Morgan & Company, looked particularly suspect. Politicians in the state capital at Albany had also been enjoying the insurers' largesse. The insurers reportedly kept a slush fund to bribe state leaders and maintained a house of ill repute in which to entertain them. The most damning revelations, however, centered on the matter of insurance companies' purchases of securities from bankers. One of the committee's favorite witnesses, George W. Perkins, a partner at Morgan and at the same time an executive at New York Life, described how his company regularly bought securities from Morgan and was given special treatment when selling shares or subscribing to new issues.

The publicity from the Armstrong hearings caused many states to consider measures to regulate the insurance companies within their own borders. State action became even more imperative after legislation was introduced in Congress seeking a federal law to regulate the insurance industry, a measure many states opposed. As far as they were concerned, insurance remained a local matter that should be controlled at the state level. Accordingly, over 100 governors, attorneys general, and insurance commissioners met in Chicago in 1906 to discuss a uniform insurance law they could all agree upon. It was doubtful whether insurance regulation could be constitutionally justified in Congress, so many of the states then adopted their own insurance laws, including New York in 1906.

But a change in public opinion was being fueled by the revelations of investigations such as the Armstrong Committee. It was also being compelled by writers such as Frank Norris, who wrote about the corruption and greed endemic among commodities traders and business leaders; the muckraker Ida Tarbell, who exposed the machinations of John D. Rockefeller and the Standard Oil trust; Upton Sinclair, who wrote about abuses in Chicago's meat packing industry in his novel *The Jungle*; and the journalist Gustavus Myers, who documented and made public the dubious practices the wealthy used to accumulate their vast fortunes. As a result, public opinion in the 1910s was veering strongly toward the position that all big business was corrupt. The firming of public opinion against the moneyed class would soon be put to use against loan sharks. As with the regulation of the insurance industry, most meaningful action would come at the state and local levels.

Battle lines against loan sharking were drawn in New York City by two young men in their late twenties: Raymond Fosdick and Arthur Ham. Fosdick was a young Princeton graduate and law student at Columbia who was working for the city in 1910 as commissioner of accounts. From this vantage point, Fosdick examined efficiency in the city government and was able to help implement several measures that saved the city hundreds of thousands of dollars. One of the studies he undertook was of loan sharking and its effects on city employees. The results were disheartening and prompted the city to declare war on high-interest moneylenders.

As commissioner, Fosdick worked directly for Mayor William J. Gaynor, who assigned him jobs that would not endear him to the subjects of his investigations. He investigated police corruption and the efficiency of public works departments, taxicabs, and city-run ferries. Many local politicians thought that, because of his age, Fosdick would not produce reports of much value, but he constantly produced results that yielded wide publicity and impact. His loan sharking report was critical of the city's many unlicensed lenders, and he described their techniques in detail. Since the report had been commissioned by the city, its primary focus was on salary buying and its effects on city employees. Later, in 1915, it was revealed by the city paymaster that 2,700 city employees were having their wages garnished by salary buyers or other small lenders. The borrowers ranged from day laborers to municipal court judges.

Fosdick's report revealed that many of New York City's unlicensed lending offices were actually owned by individuals from outside the city. "Seventy-five percent of the capital invested in these loan agencies in New York apparently comes from the West. We can't push off so far as I can find the shame of this business on other races," the report stated.[31] By "West," Fosdick meant Americans of European origin; by "other races," he meant the usual implication that loan sharking was often in the hands of Jews. As an example of someone from the West, Fosdick cited a loan sharking company in the city that was owned by the deacon of a Congregational church upstate. When city investigators went to interview him, they were kept waiting outside the church because the deacon and his family were in prayer inside. Other owners, Fosdick found, came from Connecticut and Pennsylvania. One of the more extensive loan sharking operations in the city was Edwards and Company, which was owned by a woman whose name had already surfaced as a loan shark in St. Louis more than a decade before.

Fosdick's report also documented several instances of official corruption. In one case, several loan sharks offered a bribe of $250 to a state assemblyman to help kill a loan shark bill that was about to be introduced in the assembly. The bribe fell through when the legislator demanded no less than $300 and the loan sharks would not pay. The bill introduced new lending rates, breaking the old 6 percent ceiling and allowed qualified lending to approach pawnbroker rates. The bill was given impetus by familiar stories of loan sharking that ran from the tragic to the inept. In one case, a city fireman reportedly fell into the clutches of loan sharks following the death of five of his children over a matter of months. Hard pressed to pay for the funeral arrangements, he borrowed from unlicensed lenders, who charged him more than 200 percent interest. At the end of the loan period, the fireman was indebted to the loan sharks for more than he had originally borrowed. In a case with a completely different kind of outcome, an unnamed young man who had decided to investigate loan sharks on his own purposely borrowed from a Tolman office with no intention of paying back the money. The young man ignored the requests for repayment of the loan and was somewhat surprised to discover that the Tolman company did not pursue him and let the matter drop.

The Fosdick report did not have an immediate effect on enforcement in New York City, but it did add to the momentum already building against loan sharking. Fosdick left his job as commissioner a year later, after two and a half years in the post, and the mayor was not unhappy to see him go because of the unwanted publicity brought by his investigations. While Fosdick viewed loan sharking as an injustice that led to great inefficiency in local government and the larger community, other New York institutions had their own problems with the practice and seized upon the investigation to pursue their own ends.

One of these institutions was the Russell Sage Foundation, which had been founded in 1907 from the estate of the late Wall Street financier to study and propose solutions for problems facing the poor. Ordinarily, investigations of salary lending to employees of the city government were the province of state or local officials. The Russell Sage Foundation felt justified in launching its own investigation on the grounds that the people most affected were New York City employees who were signed up for salary buying programs and that the economic impact was too great to ignore. Arthur Ham, one of the foundation's investigators, commented that "one only has to take into consideration the fact that no lien is so good to a loan shark as a lien on a city employee's pay envelope."[32] The foundation's investigation provided economic analysis for the war against loan sharking in New York City. In 1909, the foundation proposed that the fifteen remedial loan societies that existed in fourteen of the largest cities in the United States combine to form the National Federation of Remedial Loan Associations. The foundation also established a Division of Remedial Loans under the direction of Ham, who was then in his late twenties. He was charged with studying the existing loan associations and advising those who wanted to form new societies. For a year, Ham worked in the offices of the Provident Loan Society, which by that time had been in the remedial loan business independently for fifteen years. Ham produced several in-depth research reports that proved instrumental in attacking the existing usury laws on an economic basis.

Ham reiterated previous critics' suspicions that the average American worker could not make ends meet and, thus, often sought the assistance of loan sharks. "The average annual wage of the American workingman is not more than $500. This falls far short of the minimum expenditure upon which it is estimated that a normal standard of living can be maintained," Ham wrote in 1911.[33] He reported that, of all loan companies doing business in New York in the early nineteenth century, only three were doing a legal business, including St. Bartholomew's, the remedial society that had started as an experiment by the church in 1895. All the others routinely violated the 6 percent usury law. And the reason for that was simple, in his opinion. Small loans could not be made profitably within the legal limit. "A profitable business at 6 percent is impossible," Ham concluded, citing the costs of doing business as a lender. "The interest on a $50 loan at 6 percent per annum for six months would be $1.50. . . . Apart from direct evidence bearing on the point, it is clear that 6 per cent would not cover expenses."[34] This assessment was directed at the small loan business only. By the time interest was charged and fees collected, the effective rate of lending could treble. Even at double the legal rate, legitimate lenders would find it difficult to make small loans due to the administrative costs and work involved. The void left by the absence of legitimate lenders was filled by loan sharks, with their hidden fees and misleading rates.

As a result, the Russell Sage Foundation concluded that the best way to attack loan sharks was to raise the legal lending rates rather than attempt to enforce unrealistically low rates. Interestingly, this conclusion was at odds with a fifteen-minute silent film the foundation funded in 1912. In *The Usurer's Grip*, a family man falls into the clutches of a loan shark but is by chance redeemed by a friendly businessman who directs him to a nearby credit union for a loan on better terms. The credit union's 6 percent loan enables the man to get back on his feet. It was an uplifting story, but flew in the face of Ham's analysis that suggested such low rates were unworkable. For those already in the clutches of loan sharks, the Russell Sage Foundation urged borrowers to simply refuse to pay usurious rates. It teamed with the Legal Aid Society to provide legal relief for borrowers threatened with legal action.

But these were stopgap measures; a blueprint for the future was the foundation's avowed goal. Using the pawnbrokers' rates as a guide, the idea was to allow interest rates of around 3 percent per month (36 percent per year) on short-term loans. At these higher rates, lenders would be induced to make loans to lower income customers (in theory, at least) while being compensated for the risk involved. But the higher rates would still be much lower than the rates charged by loan sharks.

This compromise between unrealistically low and exorbitantly high interest rates became the cornerstone of the long legislative battle that followed. In early 1914, New York Governor Martin Glynn acceded to requests by the Russell Sage Foundation not to appoint a state supervisor of finance companies as required by recent legislation passed in Albany. The foundation discovered the same law would allow rates on small consumer loans to rise to 8 to 10 percent per month, violating the state's current (and most of its past) usury ceilings in the process. It would also eliminate the imprisonment penalty for convicted usurers and eliminate the notice that was required before informing employers of their employees' indebtedness to a loan shark.[35] These provisions had passed through the legislature without much scrutiny.

While the anti-loan shark forces marshaled their resources, lenders proved equally adept at keeping one step ahead. New York loan sharks frequently loaned money to the unsuspecting by offering loans using securities as collateral, a trick that confused borrowers by adding another layer of complexity to the process. Several New York City assistant district attorneys were kept busy tracking down borrowers who told stories of approaching a loan shark for a loan only to be told that the loan shark only lent money on securities, such as stocks. The borrower was then referred to another party who sold the securities to him at an inflated price. The money for the purchase was loaned to him. When they were presented to the lender as collateral, they were discounted and he was given a loan for a diminished value. In some cases, the borrower would end up paying an effective interest rate of over 200 percent for the borrowed sum. One of these lenders specializing in the demand for securities as collateral was the much-reviled Tolman, who at the time was still facing usury charges in New York after being found guilty in New Jersey. Tolman was quoted as saying, "I am a banker. I accept nothing but commercial paper—notes with two names to them."[36] The reference was to the simpler type of salary loan he made, ignoring the more complicated securities collateral type.

A report circulated several years later suggesting that this method of discounting collateral had not actually violated the usury laws in New York. Franklin Ryan of the Harvard Business School published a major study on consumer lending in 1924 that described methods of avoiding usury laws and outlined this technique in some detail:

> It is legal for a note broker to sell commercial paper at seven or eight percent or any higher rate, and it is legal for a bank to buy this paper, provided the title to the paper is definitely fixed as the note broker's . . . in the transfer of such paper the ownership passes from the seller to the buyer at a fixed price and the undisputed owner of the paper has a right to fix any price for his own property that he can get.[37]

Ryan was referring to short-term corporate debt (commercial paper) while Tolman and other sharks simply used the name to disguise salary buying and other types of packaged consumer loans. Ryan also noted that requiring a potential borrower to use the money lent to purchase securities first (to be used as collateral) and then discounting them heavily was another way the usury laws could be circumvented legitimately and much higher interest charged.

Newspapers joined with the Russell Sage Foundation in deciding not to rely upon the intentions of city and state officials to investigate loan sharking and took it upon themselves to support the underpaid municipal workers. The *New York Globe* was in the forefront of reporting on loan shark excesses. Newspapers began to refuse to run advertisements from unlicensed lenders, with the *New York Times* announcing in 1911 that it would not accept ads from salary buyers or chattel lenders. The paper had already unofficially been pursuing a policy of that type for a couple of years. In 1910, it remarked that loan sharks "should be advertised for what they are, not for what they intend to be in the lying announcements which they cannot at any price get into any column of this paper."[38] At the same time the newspaper offered a reward for information that it was being used to plant false reports on companies to influence the price of their stocks by traders.

LOAN SHARKING IN CHICAGO

Shortly after the revelations of the Fosdick report and the policy recommendations made by the Russell Sage Foundation, the anti-loan shark movement migrated west from New York City to Chicago. As in New York, salary buying was a widespread practice among city employees and other workers. The Illinois legislature had passed a law in 1905 to regulate the practice, but it was subsequently overturned by the state supreme court. The local Legal Aid Society estimated that the city had approximately 125 loan shark offices, more than any other large city, making loans of $50 on average to over 70,000 customers per year. The average effective interest they charged ranged from 10 to 20 percent per month. According to one commentary, Illinois laws facilitated such high rates by making it "very difficult to foreclose on household goods." As a result, sharks charged even higher rates for loans without collateral. The Legal Aid Society's recommendation was to place a monthly limit on consumption loans of 4 percent.

In 1911, the *Chicago Tribune* also launched its own anti–loan shark campaign and banned high-interest lenders from advertising in its pages. Other Chicago papers followed the *Tribune's* lead, and soon only three papers were still accepting ads from loan sharks. Loan sharks responded by increasing the volume of their advertising in the three holdouts. The *Day Book,* one of the papers that refused loan shark ads, recounted the story of a loan shark who took his business to one of the three instead: "One loan shark admitted the other day that he paid *The News* $180 in one week and got 20 customers. And he said suckers were cheap [even] at $20 per head." Any lead that panned out would return that $20 charge quickly and probably would provide a long-standing customer in the process.

In 1916, Chicago was ready to build on anti-loan sharking campaigns that had had some success in other major cities. Earle Edward Eubank was hired by the Chicago municipal government to produce a report on loan sharking in the city. Just thirty years old, Eubank had grown up in a family of Christian missionaries and had written a thesis at the University of Chicago in which he discussed the economic factors that led to the disintegration of families in urban America. Eubank's report for the city was published under the auspices of the Chicago Department of Welfare. In New York, the Fosdick investigation focused mainly on efficiency in municipal government; Eubank, instead, focused on the effects on the family and the social fabric generally. Ham's and Fosdick's findings figured prominently in the Eubank report, however, and they all dovetailed with the aims of the Russell Sage Foundation.

City campaigns of this sort were very effective against loan sharking. Arthur Ham wrote to Fosdick before the official Chicago campaign began: "Perhaps the most notable campaigns, because of the success which accompanied them, were those of New York in 1910–1911 etc., San Francisco in 1911, Buffalo in 1912, Portland, Oregon in 1913, Dayton in 1915, Omaha in 1915–1916. Each of these resulted in the passage of much needed legislation and the organization of a remedial loan society."[39] Chicago was fertile ground for loan sharks, because Illinois's 7 percent state usury ceiling prohibitions were too low to encourage legitimate lenders and too porous to be enforced in any event: "no punishment can be meted out to the extortioner as the law stands at present, for any exaction in excess of seven percent," Eubank wrote.[40] As a result, the number of lenders in Chicago exceeded most other cities: the study found 229 firms in the lending business at one time or other, 139 of which were active in the fall of 1916. That resulted in a loan shark business of almost $12 million per year, since each firm did about $85,000 profit on average. As the report stated, "A genuine dyed-in-the-wool loan shark apparently considers his business to be losing out unless he is able to double the amount he loans every year."[41] And Eubank pointed out that many of the firms operating within Chicago were funded with cash from the East Coast. Similar to Fosdick's reports in New York, there was always a suspicion that loan sharking originated outside the affected areas.

Loan sharks were much more organized than they appeared to the casual observer. While many operated from offices with no names on the door, others proudly advertised their services in newspapers and the mail. But they had one common denominator completely unknown to the public. In Chicago, they operated a joint clearinghouse, much in the same way banks and brokers used a clearinghouse to settle transactions. The clearinghouse operated on a no-name basis; members were charged an annual fee but remained completely anonymous. When an applicant for a loan applied at a member firm, his name was checked with the clearinghouse so it could determine whether he was creditworthy enough to borrow. That decision was based upon previous history with other members, in a manner similar to the legitimate credit agencies that were developing at the same time. Someone who had a poor history with one loan shark found it difficult to borrow from another. Contrary to popular opinion, loan sharks did not want to make loans only to find borrowers defaulting. The clearinghouse was a good method of protecting their investments.

The Russell Sage Foundation cited the progress that had been made in finding alternatives to the loan sharks. Benevolent societies, credit unions, and remedial loan associations all had made great strides in providing nonpredatory loans, but their presence had not extirpated the loan shark threat by any means. Ignorance of the effective rates of interest charged, embarrassment at using the loan shark's services, or fear of one's employer were all cited as reasons customers continued to do business with them despite the newspaper and municipal campaigns. All the signs pointed to a population either living above its means or one that was underpaid and not able to cope with daily expenses. Arthur Ham claimed that none of the unlicensed lenders in existence when his campaign began were still in business three years later. The remark was possibly correct, but it only applied to the visible loan shark offices, not to those who discreetly remained behind the scenes.

New Banks for the Retail Customer

The same wave of anti-loan shark activity that swept through New York, Chicago, and other major cities in the 1910s also prompted entrepreneurs to create a new breed of bank that would make low-rate loans to individuals (as benevolent societies did) but would still manage to turn a profit. The founders of these new institutions were not necessarily motivated by an altruistic desire to help consumers steer clear of loan sharks (though many definitely were); it was, instead, to stimulate demand for their goods.

One early proposal for a retail-oriented bank came from Julius Rosenwald of Sears, Roebuck. Rosenwald had been a long-time supplier of men's clothing to Sears, Roebuck when, in 1895, he purchased a portion of Alvah Roebuck's ownership stake. As vice president of the firm, he helped Richard Sears organize the company's enormously successful initial public stock offering in 1906, underwritten by Rosenwald's Wall Street contacts at Lehman Brothers and Goldman Sachs. In 1911, Rosenwald, now president of the company following Sears's retirement, established Sears, Roebuck's consumer credit operation; they were one of the first major retailers to do so. In his proposal for what became known as an industrial bank, Rosenwald planned to offer low interest, 5 percent loans to customers in a manner similar to the benevolent societies. "These banks, it is hoped, will in large measure eliminate the loan shark evil flourishing all over this country," Rosenwald stated. "We aim to kill this system which encourages the small man to borrow beyond his means."[42] Presented as a philanthropic venture, Rosenwald's bank reputedly had Andrew Carnegie and Vincent Astor as coinvestors although their actual involvement was not clear.

The first industrial banks were referred to as Morris Plan Banks, named after Arthur J. Morris, a lawyer who, in 1910, founded the Fidelity Savings and Trust Company in Norfolk, Virginia, to make affordable small loans to people of modest means. Another industrial bank in St. Louis, the Industrial Loan Company, opened in 1913 and claimed great success both in its operations and its effect on local loan sharks. The bank's cashier claimed that nineteen loan sharking companies had been put out of business, saving people $17,000 in interest payments in the process. These banks, like the one Rosenwald began, also offered savings plans that encouraged workers to put aside money for a rainy day, protection from shortages of cash that might otherwise lead them straight to the loan shark. In addition to serving the working class, Morris Plan lenders also offered their services to small businesses that often could not obtain credit from traditional banks.

The avowed purpose of this model was not to provide low-interest loans, however. Even though the nominal lending rates were low, by the time the discounting of notes, fees, and other charges were factored in, the rates were higher than the maximum permitted by the usury laws in many states.[43] Still, they were lower than loan shark rates. The industrial banks, thus, carved out a niche between commercial banks, benevolent societies, and loan sharks. In time, the potential profitability of the industrial banks began to draw the attention of large commercial banks.

While Morris Plan institutions were touted as banks for the people, they did not enjoy great success. In a speech in 1916, Arthur Ham described the virtues of "people's banks," but never once mentioned industrial banks. Instead, Ham chose to emphasize credit unions. Noting the success of credit unions in Europe, where they had originated a half-century before, Ham described the basic formula that made credit unions successful, albeit on a small scale. "In a joint stock bank the shareholders and constituents are mostly different people—a condition which keeps distinct the interest of the buyers and sellers of credit. In a credit union, the interests of borrowers and lenders are identical." When the borrowers and the lenders are from the same community—when they are, in fact, the same people—the nature of making loans changes. A violation of the obligation to the credit association, as Ham put it, "invites self-ostracism."[44] The industrial bank model fell outside this community concept.

Despite their appeal to reformers like Ham, the number of credit unions grew slowly. Ham noted that there were only fifteen credit unions in New York City at the beginning of World War I. Among them were organizations formed by employees of John Wanamaker, the Equitable Life Assurance Society, and the American Can Company. A great many existed on a less formal basis, however. Other similar lenders were private and were called *axias*. They operated much like credit unions, although they were unlicensed and, therefore, unregulated. New York City alone had hundreds of such institutions, many of which were organized along ethnic or religious lines. But they were not low-interest lenders, and because they were private, fraud and embezzlement often existed within them. In some office buildings, dozens of them were listed on the building directories but many others operated less formally, meeting once per week in a social hall where deposits were taken and loans made. Most of them were not permanent institutions and dissolved at the end of a financial year, making a payout to shareholders (depositors) of around 10 to 12 percent.[45]

At the same time, retail lending by a commercial bank began in California at a bank founded by A. P. Giannini in San Francisco. Giannini's novel lending practices did not attract much attention at first. The son of Italian immigrants, he had founded the Bank of Italy in 1904 with $150,000 in borrowed money, to serve San Francisco's immigrant community. Giannini's reputation spread when the bank managed to stay open during the great 1906 earthquake; Giannini had rescued the bank's cash from the fire and looters by loading it onto a horse-drawn vegetable cart and taking it home with him. When other bankers refused to open their institutions after the earthquake, Giannini insisted on opening, often extending credit to customers who were, trying rebuild homes or businesses. He did this business based only on a handshake or a signature on a scrap piece of paper. The gesture was well-received and made Giannini something of a folk hero.

The bank remained a California institution for twenty years. In 1919, he changed the name of the institution to BancItaly Corporation and, in 1928, put it under the umbrella of the holding company called Transamerica Corporation so it could expand nationally. He then bought the older Bank of America in New York and adopted its name. When Giannini's bank moved east in the 1920s, it soon attracted the attention of other New York banks. After studying Bank of America's model, these institutions decided that the market Giannini had tapped was too big to ignore, though it would take them several more years to offer their first small loans.

In 1928, the National City Bank of New York became the first to announce its small loan program. Its president, Charles Mitchell, declared that the bank recognized that working-class customers, previously ignored by large banks, needed and would receive assistance from his bank. "Our contacts with people of this class have given us a confidence in the integrity and character of the average individual," Mitchell declared. "While it is not our purpose to encourage anyone to borrow except under the stress of circumstances, we have faith that loans so made can and will be paid when the spirit of thrift can be kept alive."[46] National City's announcement was met with great enthusiasm by the public. The *Boston Globe* remarked that "by charging only 6 percent interest, [the bank] is doing something to spoil the business of the loan sharks." On the first day it opened its doors for retail lending, National City received 500 new applications for loans. Within several years, the bank had made 67,000 loans totaling $23 million (at an average of $342) and was generally accepted as the leader in small loans among the larger lenders. Over this time, National City recorded a loan loss rate of less than a quarter of 1 percent while approving 88 percent of customers' loan applications. In fact, most of the larger banks that entered the retail lending business recorded similar results.[47]

Similar comments came from the New York Trust Company in a survey it conducted in 1928. It stated that "in the past twenty years, loan sharks found ample opportunities for exercise of their unsocial activities. With banks reluctant until recently to assume any portion of the service . . . the need was met in large measure by loan sharks at unconscionable cost to the borrower." The bank also noted that the small loan laws gave rise to the need for more capital on the part of lenders, creating an opening for the large banks to fill the needs of small borrowers because they possessed capital smaller lenders could not raise.[48] As a result, the large banks were drawn to the business by both demand and resources that smaller lenders could not muster.

THE FEDERAL FARM LOAN ACT

Despite the new Federal Reserve, the problem of farm credit remained. The new central bank was intended to coordinate credit for commercial banks and many farm credit institutions were not commercial banks. A system of credit was needed that would address the farm credit problems that had caused such uproar in the past. The closest thing to a system that had existed in the past was the poorly assembled mortgage debentures that had broken down when foreign investors could no longer be convinced to provide capital. In 1912, the Taft administration dispatched a delegation to Europe to study how the Germans and the French supplied their farmers with credit, just as it had dispatched a delegation to study European central banking systems in 1909.

The delegation spent two months in Europe studying agricultural finance. The difference between European and American financing was embarrassingly simple: the Europeans had institutions dedicated to providing it and the Americans did not. In Europe, the institutions that provided farm financing fell into two distinct types: cooperative societies that were responsible for short-term loans and land credit banks that were responsible for mortgages. The cooperatives did not make loans to farmers for consumption purposes or to pay off previously incurred debt. The loans were usually intended as working capital advances. But what impressed the delegation most was the European model for providing long-term credit. In the United States, farm mortgages were typically only three to five years in duration and required interest-only payments, meaning the entire principal had to be paid off or refinanced at the end of the mortgage. The length of European mortgages, on the other hand, extended up to seventy-five years and included amortization payments. The American delegation estimated that the average life of these mortgages was fifty-six years. Furthermore, bonds issued to finance farm mortgages were covered by the same association that sold them to investors, unlike some old American debentures where the cover did not extend back to the bond issuer, usually a mortgage company located in New York. To avoid excess leverage, associations never made a loan to a farmer for more than two-thirds the value of the land involved.[49]

One avid supporter of adopting the European's model for financing farmers was Myron Herrick, a former governor of Ohio and ambassador to France under President Taft. The productivity of American farmers had lagged behind French and German farmers, and sagging incomes had slowed the back-to-the-farm movement of the post–Civil War era considerably, especially since the 1890s. Without reforming farm finance, the migration to the cities would only continue. Herrick's views on the matter were blunt: "The overcrowding in our cities is producing a large class of people whose low moral and intellectual standards make them unfit for citizenship. It is the existence of this class in increasing numbers that makes it more difficult for us to assimilate the foreigners that immigrate to this country."[50] How improvements in agricultural efficiency and finance would help eliminate the urban underclass was not clear, but the general idea was to clear them out of the cities. Others expressed the idea in more structured terms. The idea behind rural credits, the term used to describe farm credit at the time, was to entice city dwellers, especially recent immigrants, to the farm, thereby reducing the problems of the city—crime, overcrowding, and unemployment—in the process. Herrick hoped that reforming farm finance would have a similarly positive impact on rural life that Rural Free Delivery supposedly had twenty years before.

Herrick had few expectations for the Federal Reserve in agricultural finance. Based on his reading of the National Monetary Commission's report that originally proposed the Federal Reserve, Herrick surmised that the central bank would have little effect on the market for farm-backed debt. Unlike other securities held by commercial banks that could be discounted by the proposed Fed for cash, farm credit would continue to languish without central bank support, with the result that farm mortgages would remain prohibitively expensive. "In some parts of the country farmers have to pay as high as 10 percent for their loans and in other localities similar loans can be made for 6 percent. There are in this country no organizations by which loans on land—the safest of all security—can be mobilized and access obtained to the wide, stable investment market," Herrick commented.[51] The model that most appealed to Herrick for supplying the much-needed credit was Germany's *Landschaft* system of cooperative mortgage societies. These groups sold individual mortgages to investors, backed by all members of the society. A similar function was performed in France by the Credit Foncier, a state-sponsored bank that made agricultural loans and marketed bonds with its own guarantee. The guarantees in either case made the bonds highly marketable and appealing to investors.

The United States lacked any sort of analogous institutions dedicated to agricultural finance, as Professor E. W. Kemmerer of Princeton University was surprised to discover after writing to the U.S. Department of Agriculture in 1912 to request information on agricultural credit. The department responded succinctly: "The only really agricultural cooperative credit societies of this country are maintained by the Jewish colonies [communities] which were planted by the Jewish Agricultural and Industrial Aid Society." Even the department seemed surprised at the lack of cooperative credit institutions in the country, noting that "whole counties have been populated in the Northwest [of New York State] by European agriculturists who came from neighborhoods where they were familiar with agricultural cooperative credit and yet not a society of cooperative credit for these immigrants has been established from the beginning to the present time."[52] As in other areas of the country, the absence of legitimate credit facilities opened doors for loan sharks in the agricultural areas of upstate New York.

The Jewish Aid Society had been founded just two years before, in 1910, with the express purpose of providing agricultural credit to Jewish farmers. It did so only on a long-term basis, by providing farmers with second mortgages on their properties. By lowering the rates charged on them it was able to indirectly provide short-term funds for farmers by saving them money that could be used for other productive purposes. Most of the society's offices were located in New York. After just two years in operation, the Jewish Aid Society showed a net profit of 12.5 percent and a high repayment rate. But its greatest success was in marginalizing the two great enemies of New York's farmers: the loan sharks who now had low-interest rate competition, and the shopkeepers, whose store-provided credit often kept farmers on a very short leash. "The pernicious activity of the local usurer has been largely curtailed. The overbearance of the local storekeeper is in evidence no longer and the farmer is now treated as a respected customer," enthused Leonard Robinson, the society's general manager, in December 1912.[53] Despite its success in New York, however, the Jewish Aid Society attracted very little attention when Congress began considering farm legislation in 1914. It received scant attention even in influential policy circles; Arthur Ham on occasion mentioned the various agricultural cooperatives operating under its umbrella in the same vein as credit unions, but not in the context of agricultural credit.

The matter of rural credits was widely seen as vital to the Democrats' political fortunes. In early 1916 over 100 rural credits bills were proposed in Congress, and it was widely understood that one had to be successful if the Democrats wanted to retain the White House after Woodrow Wilson's first term. The war also played a major factor. As the secretary of the American Rural Credits Association visiting New York commented to the *New York Times*, "The support of the farmers, which would be engaged by rural credit legislation, is necessary to the Democratic Party in the Middle West to offset the pro-German vote which will be solidly Republican. You cannot imagine the sentiment against Wilson among those or pro-German sympathies in the West. It is much more intense than in this city."[54]

The Federal Farm Loan Act passed Congress in 1916, two-and-a-half years after the creation of the Federal Reserve. As with the Fed, the act divided the country into twelve districts, each with a Federal Land Bank at the center of operations, overseen by a five-member Federal Farm Loan Board in Washington, D.C. Many cities lobbied Congress to host the land banks, and numerous hearings were held to determine the winners.[55] At the behest of Secretary of the Treasury William McAdoo, who also served as chairman of the Farm Loan Board, "no such districts shall contain a fractional part of any state." This was a clear reference to Federal Reserve districts, which were apportioned differently and divided some states between districts.[56]

The law stipulated that no mortgage supported by the new farm system was to exceed 6 percent. The bonds sold by the land banks were pegged at 5 percent interest, about 100 basis points below the loans charged to farmers. The difference was used to cover the expenses of issuing the bonds. The mortgages supported by the system ranged from five to forty years to maturity for amounts up to $10,000. The act was accompanied by instructions demonstrating how amortization actually worked, since the idea was new to American mortgage financing in general. The bonds created by the new farm loan system would differ substantially from the older debentures that had caused so much controversy in the nineteenth century. "The greatest undermining influence, however, in connection with the operations of these early debenture companies was the practice of substituting inferior mortgages for collateral securities withdrawn," later remarked A. C. Wiprud, the vice president of the Federal Land Bank of St. Paul.[57] Until the Trust Indenture Act was passed almost twenty-five years later, the safety of collateral remained a crucial element in investing, especially when mortgage-backed securities were involved.

A tax exemption given to both the land banks and bond investors proved equally important for the success of the new system. The land banks were exempt from federal tax on their holdings, and investors in the system's bonds also enjoyed tax-exempt status on the interest they received. This was done to achieve equitable treatment on both sides of the financing equation. However, many local jurisdictions objected to the exemption for investors on the grounds that they wanted to be sure that local loan sharks, who were suspected of investing in the new bonds, were taxed on their earnings. This was, in part, a reaction to the fact that for most of the years following the Civil War loan sharks had not been required to pay any federal taxes on their earnings. Passage of the Revenue Act of 1913 reimposed a federal tax on income, including income from real estate. A clever way for loan sharks to get around the tax would be to invest in tax-free bonds, such as the new farm bonds. The only drawback was that the loan sharks would have to accept the lower interest rates on the new bonds. Looking back in 1921, A. C. Wiprud brushed aside the critics who had wanted to see the loophole closed for the "Shylocks." "Whatever merit or lack of merit that argument had, it is entirely out of place in the new system. . . . Under this system, the rate to borrowers will be correspondingly reduced."[58] The new system, according to Wiprud, was not intended to be retaliatory; its benefits were to be found in the low interest rates farmers paid for credit.

Many in the farm states favored the new law, especially its limit on interest rates. This was particularly important because the new Federal Reserve was able to control bank reserves and discount money market paper but did not have the power to declare an interest rate ceiling other than to declare its discount rate, certainly not subject to state usury laws or the 7 percent national bank usury ceiling. Still, this did not mollify dissenters such as the socialist *Northwest Worker,* which dubbed the new rural credits law a "fake." The newspaper described the farm act as nothing more than an extension of banker power into agriculture. The *Northwest Worker* urged Congress to vote against the bill, arguing that Wall Street and Eastern money interests supported it only because of the favorable tax treatment it accorded to farm credit bonds. The paper urged its readers to write their congressmen to "kill it now to pave the way for a real, fair, and popular rural credits system."[59] Like so many popular appeals, however, the *Northwest Worker* was more adept at formulating polemics against the bill than proposing a better system of providing lower-cost credit to farmers.

One area the 1916 act did not address was the need for short-term credit facilities. Congress would attempt to address this shortcoming in the Agricultural Credits Act of 1923. This law created twelve Federal

Intermediate Credit Banks (one in each of the twelve districts established by the Federal Farm Loan Act), which served as banks of discount
to agricultural cooperatives, commercial banks, and other lenders. They
did not lend directly to individuals. Commercial banks displayed no enthusiasm for the program, and the intermediate credit banks did not improve the flow of short-term credit to farmers. This strained the system
and still left the door open for high-interest lenders.

In July 1916, when President Woodrow Wilson signed the Federal
Farm Loan Act into law, most of the government's attention was con-
sumed by World War I. After the U.S. entry into the war against Germany and the Central Powers in April 1917, many critics viewed the
farm bill as a diversion of critical war resources for the benefit of just a
few farmers. Nor did the German origins of the new law sit well with
everyone. One prominent critic was William Marshall Bullitt, who
had been Solicitor General of the United States in the Taft administration and was now a prominent attorney in his native Kentucky. Bullitt
invoked the country's fervent anti-German sentiment to cast suspicion
on the new law. "The Farm Loan Act was chiefly written by a man born
in Germany, and was modeled upon the Austrian scheme," he remarked to a meeting of the Farm Mortgage Bankers Association in
September 1918. Bullitt was referring to one of the members of the
team President Taft had sent to study European agricultural credit institutions. Bullitt also questioned the constitutionality of the act, suggesting that amortizing farm mortgages over periods as long as forty
years meant that most mortgages would outlive their borrowers and
the usefulness of the land that collateralized them. Turning four
decades of farm turmoil on its head, he declared the Farm Loan Act
"essentially a scheme to assist the borrower at the expense of the
lender."[60] This view considered farmers a special interest group that
was not entitled to the lower mortgage rates the new agency was designed to produce. Following this logic, farmers would exploit the new financing arrangements by renegotiating their existing mortgages rather
than contracting new mortgages. The criticism was a reaction to the

new system of farm credits that favored the older, nineteenth-century laissez-faire model. Also evident was that a new financing agency based on European cooperative ideas was not widely embraced outside the Farm Belt.

An ESTABLISHED PRACTICE

Within a year of the Federal Reserve being created, one of its board members—John Skelton Williams, who was Comptroller of the Currency in the Wilson administration—shocked Wall Street and financial reformers alike when he published the results of a survey of national banks around the country and found that 1,200 of them, 40 percent of all national banks, were charging interest rates above (often well above) the legal maximum of 7 percent. Williams himself preferred a maximum rate of 6 percent, the same as the discount rate established by the new Federal Reserve. Williams's decision to publish the survey was met with protests from the banks themselves, as well as the American Bankers Association, which claimed the survey was an intrusion into the way they conducted business. Williams found that the national banks that charged the highest rates were located in rural, agricultural states; Texas and Oklahoma were home to the most (287 and 168, respectively), followed by Tennessee (113) and Kentucky (89). Banks in these states claimed they were being charged 6 percent by the money-center banks in the large cities for interbank loans and had no choice but to charge higher rates to their customers as they passed the charges on to compensate.

Williams's initial response was to ask the banks to reduce their rates to reasonable levels and to recognize the Fed's discount rate as the maximum allowable rate, not tack on additional percentage points. Those that refused received stern letters from the comptroller in which he suggested that bank directors who allowed their institutions to charge usurious rates would leave themselves open to legal liability. He also suggested that his office could sue the banks to obtain relief for borrowers.

In most cases, these threats were enough to compel banks to reduce their rates, at least temporarily.

As a former president of the American Bankers Association, Williams realized that his report, by divulging the confidential practices of the banks, had the potential to cause great embarrassment. Although he did not identify banks by name, Williams did report on some of their replies to his requests for information. Perhaps the most revealing came from an unnamed bank president who told the comptroller that it would be unreasonable to require his bank to reduce its lending rates all at once because, as Williams recalled, "as national banks in many sections of the country have been charging usurious interest for fifty years or more, it was harsh or quixotic to attempt to reduce these rates at one time or to insist that the banks should cease suddenly a practice so venerable however great the hardships that might have been inflicted unlawfully in thousands of instances."[61] The response was not as disingenuous as it sounded. Most banks, including national banks, were unaccustomed to inquiries about their businesses and saw little wrong with charging high rates.

Williams's report contained a number of controversial legislative remedies to the widespread problem of usury at the national banks. He proposed an amendment to the National Bank Act of 1864—which in addition to creating the system of national banks also created the Office of Comptroller of the Currency—that would allow the Department of Justice or the Comptroller of the Currency to bring suit against usurers to compel them to lower rates. He also proposed a cap on savings deposits at national banks of 4 percent. The lower cost of funds would presumably translate into a lower cost of borrowing. This idea gained widespread support in some states, while banks in other states sued. In some cases, banks merely challenged Williams's authority as comptroller to propose statutory changes, while others challenged the legitimacy of the comptroller's office itself. National banks were not accustomed to dealing with an activist comptroller like Williams. When he successfully pursued the directors of Riggs National Bank in Washington, D.C., for irregularities in the bank's reserves, Riggs, in turn, sued the comptroller in retaliation.

It was at Williams's reconfirmation hearings in 1919 that the banks retaliated against him in force. They accused Williams of corruption and levied charges that he had abused the powers of his office by making unlawful attacks on bankers. The charges were not proved. In their testimony to the committee, the bankers made it clear that the only action they were accustomed to when there was a problem was a letter from the comptroller asking them to correct it. Beyond that they were free to correct the problem however they saw fit, without further investigation by officials in Washington, D.C. They did not understand or appreciate the activities of a regulator who might have thought them to be in violation of the law, as in the case of usury charges, or other imprudent banking practices. Although a final committee vote was never taken on Williams's confirmation, he continued in the post until 1921, when Republican Warren G. Harding moved into White House.

Usury laws as well as sumptuary laws persisted throughout the Progressive Era even as they were undergoing a slow period of redefinition. The laws had become ingrained in the American psyche and were destined to persist for many more years despite the best efforts of reformers, not to mention bankers, to rescind them. Delivering a Supreme Court decision about financial contracts in California, Oliver Wendell Holmes wrote, "No court would declare a usury law unconstitutional, even if every member of it believed that Jeremy Bentham had said the last word on that subject, and had shown for all time that such laws did more harm than good. The Sunday laws [also], no doubt, would be sustained by a bench of judges even if every one of them thought it superstitious to make any day holy."[62] The presence of usury laws and the day of rest had become so entrenched that everyone presumed them inviolate, but they were having a difficult time justifying why they should still be acknowledged since, like Prohibition, they were being violated with impunity.

The debate over loan sharking and usury began and gained serious momentum in the early twentieth century and would be prominent throughout the 1920s. The boom years leading to 1929 would prove that embedded high interest rates also had become a way of life for manufacturers and builders as well as banks and loan sharks. And the reality that loan sharking was not confined only to unlicensed lenders but was becoming rapidly institutionalized began to set in.

CHAPTER THREE
THE STATES ATTACK

MARK TWAIN ONCE QUIPPED THAT IF A MAN OWES A BANK a dollar and cannot pay, he has a problem. If he owes it a million and cannot pay, the bank has a problem.

That remark more than adequately described the situation that characterized borrowers and lenders as the 1920s began. Small borrowers continued to suffer while large borrowers with problems severely affected many banks. American society had become driven by consumers, and the economic problems characteristic of the decade were set to collide with substantial force.

After the Federal Reserve and the Farm Credit System were created, reformers claimed a major victory over the unequal allocation of credit. But the average citizen in need of a small consumption loan disagreed, since those loans remained largely in the hands of unlicensed lenders. The situation was improving rapidly, but credit for individuals still required attention since loan sharking remained a thorny problem. Usury had receded from the political argument over mortgages to an extent, but extortionate private lending remained.

At the same time, banking problems remained endemic. The rapid spread of banks in the nineteenth and early twentieth centuries was followed by a dramatic series of failures in the 1920s. During the mortgage securities crisis of the 1880s and 1890s, many banks were formed to issue debentures on behalf of mortgage companies; the same took place again when banks were created to funnel money during the short-lived property boom in the 1920s. They were so closely linked to the industry that when the boom ended so did their ability to pay their liabilities. These problems were directly related because many banks were seeking higher rates of return and avoided both consumer lending and the usury ceilings that sometimes constrained it.

Even the Russell Sage Foundation admitted the problems in dealing with loan sharks. Recognizing the efforts before 1910 as unsystematic and doomed to failure, the foundation later noted that "social ills were thus often increased rather than cured. Money lending at high rates being outlawed, the lender would charge even higher rates to compensate for the stigma attached to his business." The newspaper campaigns that often triggered legislative action tended to force loan sharks to raise their rates even further to compensate for their increased risk of prosecution. Only the state of New York had an official charged with monitoring small lenders; without someone responsible for this kind of supervision, no state could effectively enforce any usury laws on their books. The remark made by a federal judge in a loan sharking case adequately summed up the conundrum when he reflected on a case before him. He stated that loan sharking practices had "brought on conditions which were yearly reducing hundreds of laborers and other small wage earners to a condition of serfdom in all but name."[1]

The economy was growing but the usury debate had not abated. Loan sharks charged excessive interest on loans but, as unlicensed lenders, the remedies against them were limited to customer complaints or lawsuits, both unlikely in most cases. Banks and finance companies that did make small loans to individuals and small businesses were limited by legal ceilings but often evaded them by charging stiff fees because the legal limits were uneconomical for lenders. This created a vacuum in which loan sharks continued to flourish. Swedish economist Gustav Cassel described usury as "that surplus price which the lender is able to exact because of the defective organization of the market, or where the circumstances, particularly the risks, are of such an extraordinary character that no market could possibly exist."[2] That comment, originally written at the turn of the century, still succinctly characterized retail credit before and after World War I. Business credit was more than adequate, except for small businesses, which often found themselves in the same position as consumers.

Cassel's description had been framed in the nineteenth century, several years before the Russell Sage Foundation began its small loan crusade. It laid the foundations for future discussions of usury by using economic argument rather than emotional language. Banks and other lenders constantly used technical terms when arguing their positions on high-interest lending, though their detractors often fell short of forceful arguments when morality was invoked rather than economics. If usury was indicative of surplus capital available for lending under defective market conditions, then new credit market reforms were long overdue since loan sharking was so widespread. The question was whether the new Federal Reserve and the Farm Credit System were the cure or only palliatives for the imperfect marketplace. Would reforms and new credit facilities for institutions find their way down the chain to the consumer?

Aware of constitutional questions about state versus federal power raised by the passing of the Rural Credits Act, the Russell Sage Foundation added its support when it made it clear that state intervention against predatory lenders was part of a government's police power. According to its interpretation, the state could intervene in business affairs to protect the natural rights of the poor or needy against lenders who, in the name of profit, would impinge on those rights by exacting ruinous rates of interest. Using an argument reminiscent of John Locke and the founding fathers, Russell Sage argued that "the right to acquire property and the right to contract with reference to it are natural rights which men in the rudest state of nature exercise at will; but when they enter into a social compact these rights are to a very great extent placed under control of the government thus formed."[3] The police power found in government jurisdiction extended to stipulated rates of interest found in state statutes. This is what was known in the eighteenth and nineteenth centuries as "statutory usury," the original 6 or 7 percent ceilings found in most states. To strengthen its argument, the foundation cited several dozen state and federal court cases. No one disputed the states' right to set interest rate ceilings; the only real problem was the centuries-old attempt to determine what that ceiling was to be.

The years immediately after World War I provided an answer of sorts. Lending for consumption underwent a transformation as initiatives by the Russell Sage Foundation and the states were instituted. Many usury ceilings were raised, but they were not abolished. At the same time, the installment loan became the norm for consumer purchases of big-ticket items such as automobiles and large household appliances. Farm mortgages became longer in maturity and rates were subject to the intervention provided by the land banks. Residential mortgages were still short in maturity but were augmented by second mortgages that were granted to many borrowers and used to effectively stretch payments. Market rates and commercial loans were unaffected since usury ceilings did not apply to them.

After John Skelton Williams's remarks about banks charging usurious rates in his report during World War I, it was evident that the meaning of the term usury was still unclear in the minds of many. Franklin Ryan of the Harvard Business School remarked that "the amazing thing about the speech was, not that banks were breaking the usury laws, but that Mr. Williams thought that usury laws ought to be obeyed." A consensus concluded that the higher interest rates on consumption loans tolerated by the Uniform Small Loan Law (USLL) had made the idea of usury laws obsolete. Williams angered many again when he charged the banks with usury in 1920, declaring that they were still charging too much interest on call loans (loans on stock market transactions), a questionable remark since ordinary call money did not fall under any existing usury guidelines. Franklin Ryan commented on the second accusation, saying that "the New York call-loan rate is a resultant of economic forces and is followed by all bankers in making their call loans."[4]

After the war, what seemed to be only a technical stock market development occurred that would have profound implications for the economy later in the 1920s. The New York Stock Exchange established a call money desk on its floor to help brokers fund their trading positions. This brought credit directly to traders. The call money, or broker loan, market, indeed, was mostly free of usury laws but not entirely. Brokers also extended "term" call loans to customers, many of whom were investors borrowing $5,000 or less, in addition to overnight loans tied directly to daily trading positions. In New York, where most of the loans were found, this did fall under usury laws, since the amounts were not considered "corporate." Investors of all types used these loans to pay for new issues of securities. If a new issue of stock in syndication required payment in seven days to settle, investors would borrow the amount from the term loan market. Often the rates exceeded the legal limit of 6 percent for noncorporate loans in New York. If they did, that technically meant they were usurious. Later in the decade that would expose the bank lenders to potential charges of usury. Additionally, the corporate loan exemption did not extend to partnerships, and most brokers were organized as partnerships at the time. This suggested that either small customers or brokers could sue the bank lenders for usury, although there is no record of any having done so.

In the earlier part of the 1920s this problem went mostly unnoticed as the stock market gained momentum, but within six years the usury problem would begin to affect the supply of broker, or "street," loans made available. As the New York movement against loan sharks gained strength, lenders became especially uncomfortable about supplying funds to the market at higher rates and often withdrew them at short notice since the loans were still technically callable. The stock market suffered badly at those times, and the small investor suffered especially. The white elephant of usury remained prominently in the background of the strong bull market that was developing after the early 1920s.

OLD FEARS AND NEW HOPE

The aftermath of World War I reignited the usury debate despite the strides made in controlling loan interest. Farmers now had mortgages that were longer in years and priced lower than those in the past. The intermediation created by the Farm Loan Act (or Rural Credits Act) lowered mortgage rates on agricultural land by 150 to 200 basis points. This provided much-needed relief, but in the eyes of farmers it was not enough.

Despite the new Farm Credit System, the fears of farmers were realized when commodity prices declined, forcing their incomes down from levels achieved during the war. One of the farmers' suspicions was that the Fed would continue to manipulate the supply of credit to them, just as they suspected the bankers' coterie had done for decades. During World War I, farmers enjoyed high prices for their crops; inflation had always been preferred to price stability or declines. When the war was over, they harbored a suspicion that the Fed would deflate prices for a while to compensate for the rise in wartime inflation. Representatives of the Fed met with the American Farm Bureau Federation in 1921 to address the farmers' fear that "they have no financial system designed to meet their needs." Old suspicions died hard; farmers believed that "money is borrowed from Federal Reserve banks to be re-loaned on Wall Street." They also expressed concern about any attempts at deflation, even though New York Fed governor Benjamin Strong told them deflation was inevitable after the previous inflation.[5]

As their revenues declined, farmers again were susceptible to loan sharks. Between 1920 and 1927, the average farm mortgage foreclosure rate increased 450 percent. Foreclosures in the Plains states were as much as ten to twelve times the number experienced in New York or Massachusetts.[6] The divide between the East and Midwest grew wider as farm prices flattened out or declined while the manufacturing and services economies grew.

Introducing a national loan law was nearly impossible, so a drive began at the state level to reform usury ceilings despite the obvious pitfalls. Similar to the Prohibition amendment, the idea began to wind its way through state legislatures as a state law beginning in 1917. Several states already had small loan laws on the books, often having adopted the language of a Russell Sage Foundation draft that had come to be known as the Uniform Small Loan Law (USLL). New Jersey passed the first comprehensive law in 1914, better known as the Egan Act, which was vigorously supported by Arthur Ham, who spent considerable time lobbying for it in Trenton. At the time, it was touted as "the most significant piece of financial legislation ever enacted in New Jersey."[7]

In 1917, Illinois, Indiana, and Maine passed legislation and others began to follow. Most allowed interest to be charged at 2.5 to 3.5 percent per month, with a lower rate to be adopted after six months if the loan was not repaid. Lenders were required to be licensed in their states and had a number of regulations placed on them regarding fees and business methods. In the newly liberalized environment the new definition of usury suggested that only criminal usury, with rates above the state limits, was now defined as loan sharking; high-interest lending up to 40 percent (on an annualized basis) per year was deemed appropriate and legal because of the risk factors associated with small consumer loans.

But that general 40 percent level still was higher than any official rate ever charged for credit in the country by legitimate lenders. The assumption was that unlicensed lenders would lend money to anyone foolish enough to sign an agreement with them, but once borrowers were aware of licensed lenders who would charge the new, stipulated rates, then unlicensed demand would diminish, eventually driving the loan sharks out of business. The clearinghouse procedures established by groups of unlicensed lenders some years before were only set up to ensure that borrowers were not indebted to other loan sharks; it was not understood as, nor could it claim to be, a form of consumer protection. At rates often exceeding 400 percent per year, the greatest risk to a loan shark was that his borrower might also be indebted to other sharks, making repayment impossible.

Franklin Ryan of the Harvard Business School contributed to the drive to abolish usury laws by publishing one of the few studies of usury outside of the widely regarded Russell Sage Foundation. In 1924 he concluded that usury ceilings in the states should be abolished: "Such a statutory maximum is powerless to control the market rate of pure interest, is mischievous and detrimental in its effects upon business relations, and does not recognize the fact that the loan charge may vary with the duration, amount, and security of the loan." His conclusions were based upon market theory at the time, especially in light of the actions of the Federal Reserve. He found that the Fed's discount rate did not conflict with state usury laws because the Fed banks could rediscount at any rate they wished and were not subject to state usury ceilings. He also concluded that the provisions of the USLL were in accord with economic theory and could not be attacked on those grounds. He gave his support to the new Farm Credit System by remarking that farmers never could obtain low-cost loans under existing usury laws. That problem was "on its way to a solution by the new federal agricultural credits systems and their excellent devices for lowering risks on loans."[8]

In 1922, the American Industrial Lenders Association, representing the industrial banks, announced another drive against loan sharks. The group strongly favored the USLL and urged that it be passed as quickly as possible by all the states. As the USLL wound its way through state legislatures, many believed the usury debate had ended. The drive to license small lenders apparently was succeeding. Nine states had passed the USLL by 1923 and most of the others followed suit by 1930. The new regulations proceeded slowly, however. In contrast, by 1920 over two-thirds of the states had passed their own versions of blue sky laws covering securities sales. No federal legislation had yet been passed for the securities markets.[9]

The remedial loan was offered by many lenders, following guidelines set by the Russell Sage Foundation, that carefully monitored the fees and repayment terms attached to them. These were small loans for less than $300, used primarily for consumption, usually to tide the borrower over a rough patch when salary would not cover an unexpected expense. The allegedly low interest rates attached meant that the borrower could actually pay back the debt in reasonable fashion without becoming permanently indebted to a loan shark. Commercial lenders were attracted because the new set of rates was considered "scientific," a term used by loan shark foe Clarence Hodson.

Descended from an old colonial family, Hodson already had extensive banking and business experience when he began to cooperate, through his own organization, the Legal Reform Bureau to Eliminate the Loan Shark Evil, with the Russell Sage Foundation in its loan shark war. Using the USLL as a guide, he opened the first office of his Beneficial Loan Society in Elizabeth, New Jersey, in 1913, the year before the state passed its first small loan law. Within a decade, Beneficial was the largest nonbank lender of small loans in the country. Remedial loans were very successful and widely heralded as the death knell of loan sharks, a conclusion that was reached too quickly.

Acceptance of the new usury ceilings was not always easy or automatic. Wisconsin finally passed its version in 1927, allowing an initial 3.5 percent interest per month for loans $300 and lower. The bill had been vetoed twice by Governor John J. Blaine, a Progressive Republican and ally of Robert M. La Follette, who claimed that a 1923 version was nothing more than legalized usury. "The bill legalizes usury to the extent of four times and more of the legal rate of interest," he said when vetoing it for the second time.[10] The Russell Sage Foundation took exception, pointing out again that legitimate lenders could operate profitably at the new rates despite the fact that the loans were for small amounts, and the law eventually passed.

Between 1915 and 1929, the USLL generated $819 million in small loans in those states in which it was adopted. The growth rate in loans generated was 20 percent per annum. The general framework of the law appeared good for business. Most of the growth was recorded in urban areas rather than rural. This represented about 2 million borrowers with licensed lenders, with an average loan of about $100 each by 1930. The average loan was considered remedial and short-term, requiring repayment within a year.[11] By 1930, thirty-six states had passed a version of the law. Among the twelve that did not were those where the rhetoric had been pitched strongest against loan sharks and high interest rates in general in the period leading to World War I. These were also some of the states with the highest rate of small bank failures; notably Kansas, North Dakota, South Dakota, Oklahoma, and Montana.

CLAIMS OF VICTORY

The two great social evils plaguing the United States were thought to be waning in the early 1920s, and expected to be joined by a third. Prohibition was in force, the USLL was underway, and securities protection laws had been passed by a number of states. Legislative action against social problems thus appeared successful, and many thought the battles were almost over. But these social ills were dynamic. They would emerge in new forms, appearing as benefits rather than evils. In the case of usury and loan sharking, they would take refuge in institutional structures.

The continued prevalence of loan sharking in 1921 prompted the Harvard Law School to create a group of thirty-six students to do *pro bono* work on behalf of the poor. Defense against loan sharks was one of their major tasks. This contrasted with claims of just the opposite in other parts of the country. In 1924, St. Bartholomew's Church in New York City announced that it was discontinuing its loan program and benevolent society. The church had 3,700 members and its pastor decided they no longer needed the inexpensive loans that had been offered for thirty years. The pastor declared that "the loan sharks have been driven out of business; new laws have been passed to curb the rapacity of money lenders; other agencies have arisen to relieve temporary poverty. And above all, the closing of the saloons and the increase in wages have so swollen the deposits in the savings banks that those who formerly were relieved by the Loan Association are now independent."[12] The link between alcoholism and borrowing from loan sharks appeared to have been severed.

The announcement followed closely on the heels of other developments that also seemed to suggest a victory over loan sharks. As early as 1917, Frank Marshall White, a reporter and editorial writer, also pronounced loan sharking all but dead, in part because many former loan sharks had become licensed lenders under the guidelines of the Russell Sage Foundation. "The small loan business, as formerly conducted throughout the United States," he wrote, "was consummate knavery."[13] White estimated that 20,000 former unlicensed lenders had gone legitimate out of an estimated 50,000 in existence before the anti-loan shark campaign. Arthur Ham made similar comments, leading other commentators to join in the victory remarks. Editorials in city newspapers expressing comparable views reinforced the sentiment.

Loan sharks receded from view. Many became licensed lenders rather than fear the wrath of state legislators and the press. Clarence Hodson wrote that "experience shows that when a state enacts reform loan legislation, that about one half of the former loan sharks in that field remain in business and conduct it thereafter upon a lawful basis in wholesome competition with the new loan agencies."[14] But the trick of lending at high rates of interest had been ingrained in the financial services industry generally and would be difficult to remove. Salary buying remained a problem, along with other questionable practices. But the stand-alone loan sharks operating from rented offices appeared to be in full retreat. Many of the tricks they had used in the past were becoming institutionalized, associated with the productive process and the new American mantra of economic growth.

Despite the early obituaries for loan sharks, the credit landscape in the 1920s was similar to that which preceded it except that there were more sources of credit for individuals. Credit unions offered the lowest interest rates, ranging from 6 to 18 percent. Industrial banks charged from 17 to 35 percent, remedial loan societies from 12 to 36 percent, and axias from 18 to 30 percent. Loan sharks, where they existed, still charged the most, from an astonishing 240 to 480 percent.[15] But older distinctions became blurred because of the boom. Were those individuals borrowing from loan sharks using the money to purchase consumer goods or to cover shortages of cash? The distinction was not clear, but based on the activities of loan sharks it appeared that many were still comfortably ensconced in the salary buying business.

The mayor of New York agreed. In 1918 John Hylan asked for an inquiry into the activities of loan sharks who had been plying their trade with members of the armed forces on active duty. He noted the unpatriotic nature of the lending but acknowledged that loan sharks had been drawn to soldiers and sailors because the city had suspended buying tax liens during the war, forcing the servicemen to look for other sources of revenue. Loan sharks were in the habit of buying the loans at deeps discounts and then holding them until the city, as Chicago had done with similar sorts of paper, redeemed them at par at a later date. The rates that the lenders obtained through the discount were quite high. Without them, loans sharks reverted to their traditional prey, individuals with urban jobs. Failing that sort of revenue, military personnel were a safe bet.

The matter of discounting interest became central to the usury debate. Charging interest above the legal limit was relatively easy to prove for small loans but more difficult to demonstrate when discounting was involved. When tax liens were discounted by lenders, a sharp rate of discount could be detected, but when the amount was closer to the legal rate, conflicts ensued. In 1920, the Supreme Court decided a usury case in which a nationally chartered bank discounted a loan by 8 percent in Georgia, where the usury ceiling was 7 percent (*Evans v. National Bank of Savannah*).[16] The plaintiff claimed the rate was usurious because it was discounted—the discount was greater than 7 percent and certainly exceeded the usury ceiling—and because it deprived the borrower of the nominal value of the loan.

The court ruled on behalf of the bank. In its decision, it noted that state usury ceilings applied only to fixed interest and bound a national bank operating within the state. But discounting fell under federal law, and that meant that the discount could be at a higher rate than state law. This occurred because discounting had not been envisioned in the early colonial and state laws on usury; only fixed (or stated rates of) interest was addressed at the time. The *Wall Street Journal* summed up the case succinctly by noting that "from this it may be deduced that the national banks have the right to discount notes at the highest rate of interest permitted in the state where the transaction takes place and reserve the charge in advance."[17]

THE CONSUMER CREDIT BOOM

In the early 1920s the United States emerged as a creditor nation for the first time in its history. The amount of domestic savings and investment available for domestic purposes and capital export to foreign borrowers meant that the country was no longer dependent on British and other foreign investment to finance its industry and infrastructure. The pendulum had swung in the Americans' favor. The war temporarily curtailed foreign investment in the United States and, with it, the fears that foreigners exercised an invisible control over the country.

The capital exports in particular rivaled those by Britain before the war. Between 1923 and 1927, $2.6 billion worth of foreign bonds were issued in the U.S. bond market and half of those paid more than 7 percent interest. The *Chicago Daily Tribune* noted that some Americans were "ashamed" of the yields as usurious but the newspaper noted that "the high yields of most of the foreign issues floated in this country are neither an indication of risk in the investment nor of avarice on part of the lenders."[18] Unfortunately, the comment proved incorrect on both counts.

Following World War I, an enormous amount of liquidity was released into the hands of consumers that resulted in booms in purchases of consumer durables, nondurables, and property. The result was impressive. During the 1920s, the population grew by 15 percent. With it, demand for consumer goods was strong. In 1922, 60,000 households owned a radio; by 1929 over 10 million did. In 1922, 24 percent of the national income was held by 5 percent of the population. By 1929, it was held by some 26 percent, indicating a narrowing in income inequality And within the same time period, the average hourly wage rose from 48 cents per hour to 56 cents per hour, an increase of 16 percent. The growth in wages was not strong given the robust nature of the economy, but modest wage growth was aided by very slow inflation; consumer and wholesale prices remained fairly stable throughout the decade.

On the other side of the coin, farmers did not participate in the general euphoria. Commodity prices declined after 1920. Mortgage foreclosures increased dramatically, especially since farmers increased their mortgage borrowing significantly in the latter years of the war when commodity prices were high. But the truly sharp rise recorded during the 1920s was in financial asset prices and, to a slightly lesser extent, in property.

The stock market recorded significant gains until 1926, when a correction set in, after which it continued its upward momentum until October 1929. Combined, the stock and consumer booms ushered in the new era of consumer dominance of the economy. During the 1920s, consumption accounted for about two-thirds of gross domestic product, a level that would maintain for decades. Credit played a significant role in this phenomenon, but savings originally triggered the boom. The source of this vast amount of cash was the savings bonds sold during the war. Between 1917 and 1919 the Treasury sold $21.5 billion worth of Liberty loans, the nickname for war bonds. They had the advantage of being free of federal tax and, by the early 1920s, they were maturing.

While the average outlay by the retail investor was only $100, on aggregate the potential market was enormous. As the ubiquitous Charles Mitchell, president of the National City Bank of New York put it, "the development of a large, new army of investors in this country who have never heretofore known what it means to own a coupon bond and who may in the future be developed into savers and bond buyers" was the ultimate reward of the Liberty loan program. Both the stock market and the bond market would benefit in the 1920s. Manufacturers of consumer goods also experienced their greatest profits, attracting much of this cash flow into their products.

The boom in the production of consumer durables and nondurables in the 1920s was facilitated by a boom in credit facilities for the average consumer. Newly licensed lenders—many of whom were former loan sharks, industrial banks, mutual savings associations, and credit companies—all began extending consumer loans to the consumer, the newly discovered driver of the industrial economy. The consumer responded willingly, and the greatest economic boom in American history was underway. The strong market for residential housing also helped immeasurably. All of the newly built homes and apartments required furnishings and a myriad of other newly introduced consumer durables and nondurables.

After World War I, two axioms concerning credit were heard. The first was that farmers were solid credit risks for mortgage investors, echoing similar comments made in the nineteenth century. Second, the average consumer proved to be a much better credit risk than previously thought. A study by the Twentieth Century Fund (one of the first think tanks) proclaimed that "the common, average American workingman seems to be as good a credit risk as the man of property." Noting that finance companies and other lenders experienced no greater losses lending to the workingman than to others with substantially more assets, it concluded that "almost all agencies of mass credit show losses of less than one percent of their volume of loans."[19] The term "agencies" was not meant in a governmental sense; it referred to finance companies, remedial loan associations, and banks of all sorts involved in creating consumer credit.

The darker side of that statistic was that about 40 percent of lower-cost consumer loans were used to pay off higher-interest rate loans, a legacy of loan shark loans made previously. The ostensibly-receding loan shark was replaced by credit companies attached to manufacturers that charged higher rates than the USLL allowed in most states. The consumer boom of the 1920s was proving that other forms of hidden charges were built into prices.

Many manufacturers' credit companies built interest charges into installment plans that went unmentioned and undetected. Offering a loan on a new car helped the manufacturers and made borrowing simple for the customer, but the interest rates attached were steep. Only two studies appeared before the 1929 crash that examined installment selling and its costs to the consumer. Both bore witness to the fact that usury was not a dead issue.[20] Ninety percent of automobile purchases, especially for lower-price models, was done on installment plans. Characteristic of all installment plans, the rates charged were unregulated.

Immediately after the war, manufacturers recognized the need for extending credit to customers. In 1919, General Motors created the General Motors Acceptance Corporation (GMAC) to lend money to its dealers and customers, following in the footsteps of the Maxwell Motor Car Corporation, which had begun offering credit during the war. Within three years, the operation was a success, lending over $225 million. GMAC became the largest installment credit company in the country. The concept proved so popular that Citroen of France soon began using it to provide credit to buyers of its cars. Ford established its credit subsidiary in 1928 with the stated purpose of helping everyone own a Ford. It stated that it was not establishing the company to make a profit but only to provide finance for buyers. Within two years, it had provided $425 million in financing to 800,000 installment buyers. At the time, the least expensive car cost slightly less than one year's salary for the average workingman (wages rose from about $1,100 to $1,500 a year over the decade).

Installment credit had become so popular by 1926 that many of the leading lenders formed a wholesale company that would serve as a backup by purchasing their notes at a discount to provide liquidity. The American Rediscount Corporation was formed with capital of $31 million to provide a market for some of the paper created by installment credit companies. There was a general fear that abuses by some companies could lead to problems in the credit market if they sold their notes to private individuals like loan sharks. Within just ten years after Maxwell began offering installment payments to customers, the business had become so large that the company was formed. It was touted as a Federal Reserve for installment companies.

High rates continued for installment buying, often exceeding 40 percent. The rates indicated that the USLL was having some effect on lending to consumers but they were at the upper limits tolerated by the new state laws. While those interest charges were high, not much criticism was raised. The Federal Trade Commission reported to the Senate in 1922 its study of the retail furniture business, showing that the business had a net profit margin of 28 percent, including installment charges. It was estimated that the mark-up in the business, after installment charges were added and costs to dealers had been included, was around 200 percent over production costs.[21]

Mild criticism of this sort of usury was not considered serious. The main concern surrounding installment buying was excess. The average worker was being marketed a range of household appliances and automobiles that he could not afford. The result was reminiscent of earlier fears that insufficient credit facilities would put a damper on industry eager to bring new products to market. Franklin Ryan noted that "the worker's standard of living will not improve rapidly while he carries such a multitude of burdens. . . . When installment buying reaches its peak . . . where is business going to be found?"[22]

While the concern was valid, the matter of high interest charges had been overlooked. Critics like Roger Babson warned about the potential pitfalls of offering installment credit to those of limited means but the arguments fell mostly on deaf ears. When consumer credit was included in the cost of a good, it seemed to be more palatable than when a financial service company or bank charged a high rate of interest to a customer.

The countercharge to these allegations was simple. Installment lending was more similar to small loan lending than it was to commercial lending, and the installment seller had to be expected to raise interest rates because the counterparty risk was greater.

Once high interest rates became embedded in the sale price of an item, charges of usury faded since it was assumed that the real cost of interest, difficult to calculate, aided economic growth. One common, but invisible, method of concealing high interest charges was the practice of including interest on the sale price of a car when the manufacturer and its credit unit required a down payment of one-third. The customer paid interest on the entire amount rather than the two-thirds, but the charge was never revealed. Another was to charge interest on an unpaid balance; although exactly the amount or the method of calculation was not clear, it certainly favored the seller at the expense of the buyer.[23] Once high interest rates became institutionalized, they receded from view unless they were charged by a highly visible consumer lender or a loan shark. Installment companies, especially those representing major manufacturers, were accepted as above reproach because they put consumer durables within the reach of many who did not have enough cash on hand to purchase them outright.

THE LAND BOOM

The consumer boom of the 1920s was accompanied by a boom in land prices. The best known and most publicized was the Florida real estate spiral that began after World War I. At its height it displayed every dubious marketing trick in the book to entice investors to buy worthless land that had been advertised as suitable for recreational or retirement living. In a period during which loan sharking was being pursued with renewed vigor despite the perception that they had been conquered, high-interest lenders found new methods of disguising the cost of a high-interest loan. The eventual property bust caused many of these practices to surface.

Land prices in Florida increased when developers began offering lots advertised as suitable for home building. The publicity and ads in New York and Midwest newspapers helped prices rise. Newspapers were replete with stories that Palm Beach was being developed into a high-end resort area with $30 million from a well-known investor. Small investors thought they saw opportunity and followed suit. Between 1921 and early 1926, the number of building permits, property transfers, and all other statistical measures related to the boom increased ten times.[24] Many buyers purchased land sight unseen, based only on the advertisements. Often, a parcel of land was flipped several times in a day until a maximum price had been reached. The entire state was billed as a great real estate development.

Many of the properties were touted in extensive advertising campaigns as being near cities such as Miami, Orlando, and Jacksonville when, in fact, they were located far outside a city's limits. One, called Manhattan Estates, was listed as being near the city of Nettie. In this case no such city existed. Many developments were nothing more than small, scrub pine lots supported by poor, if any, infrastructure. Subsequently, it was discovered that developers, including a man named Charles Ponzi, offered lots for as much as ten times their original cost. Using a technique he had employed in the postal reply coupon fraud some years before, Ponzi sold investment certificates in the real estate project, promising investors a large dividend of 200 percent within a few months. He then used the funds raised to buy property for resale to the public. The proceeds of the new sales were then used to pay the dividend. If no money was available to pay it, investors would be offered land instead. As one commentator later remarked, "he apparently solved the problem of embarking on real estate operations without capital." The scheme worked for five years, before he was found guilty by a Florida jury of violating state statutes regarding trusts.[25]

The bubble burst when charges of fraud were leveled at property developers. Having little incentive to pay for the greatly inflated properties, many buyers abandoned them, leaving lenders holding worthless mortgages. Ironically, many of these mortgages were for amounts that were actually less than the ceiling for small loans ($300).

The failures began in late 1925. Land was worth just a fraction of its previous value and the quick wealth it had created disappeared. A sharp stock market reaction followed in March 1926 as shares related to Florida property dropped precipitously. Within several months, the banks felt the effect and a large number around the state closed their doors although, for the most part, they were relatively small operations originally chartered during the land boom.

The social problems caused by the collapse were dramatic. Thousands of migrants from the north, notably New York, began leaving Florida in full retreat from the bust. The newspapers referred to them as "driftwood." Neighboring states began to complain that property boom refugees from Florida were putting a strain on their economies. Spartanburg, South Carolina, had to provide a soup kitchen to feed them so they would not beg on its streets. North Carolina police warned the drifters that they were not welcome on their roads. They called them hobos sleeping in automobiles rather than boxcars. The Florida economy did not recover quickly. By the late 1920s, it was in a severe depression and there was open talk of revolution if the populace in general did not find enough to eat. The affair was an eerie precursor of the Great Depression, both in social and economic terms. The property bust proved that declining prices had ramifications for banks, stock market investors, and the allocation of consumer credit.

A DECADE OF BANK FAILURES

Despite the boom, widespread bank failures occurred during the 1920s. The expansion of banks in the latter nineteenth century started to unravel as an average of 600 banks failed each year between 1921 and 1929. Many were exposed to the property market that had been booming, either through mortgages or mortgage-related securities. The failures exhibited a pattern that John Skelton Williams had reported almost a decade before in his report on loan sharking among national banks; he had been widely derided for his forthright statements.

Bank failures during the 1920s reflected both the size and the geographical location of the bank. In 1920 there were 28,885 active banks in the country, excluding mutual savings banks and private banks. By the end of 1929 the number had declined by 18 percent, to 23,631. Taken as a whole, the figures were daunting, but when broken down by geographic sector they were even more dramatic. Among national banks, 766 had their operations suspended. Banks in the Northeast fared best, recording only a small handful of closings. Banks in the West fared less well; 558 failures occurred in the Western, northern Plains, and Southwestern states. The amounts recorded for state member banks of the Fed (not originally chartered as national banks) were negligible, however. State Fed member banks fared the best because they had direct access to the central bank discount facilities. In the Northeast, no failures were recorded at all. In a testament to the effectiveness of the new central bank, even its critics were quick to point out that the state member banks of the Fed fared much better than others in weathering the banking crisis.

In Florida, especially, the largest number of failures caused by the collapse of the property boom was in small, non-Fed member state banks that failed dramatically after 1926.[26] Fed member banks and national banks fared much better. But the number of closings for non-Fed member banks was startling. During the period, 4,376 banks failed in this group nationwide. Banks in the western north-central region (Kansas, Minnesota, Iowa, Missouri, North Dakota, South Dakota, and Nebraska) fared the worst, with half the closings: 2,189.[27]

During this period, the portfolios of banks began to change. Commercial loans declined as a percentage of their assets and were replaced with call loans (or broker loans; those made to stock market investors and speculators). The stock market boom demonstrated that lending at high rates of interest to margin buyers was profitable and complemented many business operations by producing lucrative, and apparently easy, revenues. Ironically the tables had turned in a relatively short time. In

1920 Senator Robert Owen, a Democrat from Oklahoma, declared that high call money rates were depressing the stock market during the 1920–21 recession, allowing short sellers to make a profit and depressing the economy. "Banks ought to be content with a fair rate and avoid usury," he declared, adding that "they should respect the spirit of the statutes which put a limit of six percent as a fair basis."[28]

Many of the smaller state-chartered banks that failed lost revenue during the consumer boom to the installment loan companies that were attached to manufacturers. Automobile loans and loans for smaller consumer durables and nondurables were extended by credit companies owned by those manufacturers or outlets selling the goods, not by banks. These credit facilities were, as noted earlier, performing banking services for the large portion of the population still without adequate credit facilities of their own. In many cases, these facilities were national in scope, since manufacturers' selling outlets, where the loans were originated, were nationwide. A customer buying a General Motors car visited a dealer that was part of a national distribution network, and the loan also came from the same corporate source. Banks that retained a larger portion of their assets as traditional loans suffered as a result, being exposed mainly to local real estate and local businesses. As in previous financial crises, real estate again led the way to bank failures and personal bankruptcies.

An emphasis on call loans was not new in the New York banking market, but the amount on loan reached record highs during the 1920s. The nineteenth-century assumption that loans backed by securities collateral were safe still prevailed, although stock market declines in 1893 and 1907 offered proof that lenders were at risk during periods of market volatility. This provided a causal link between the stock market and the banks and, indirectly, between the stock market and small borrowers. Allocating credit to intermediaries and institutional customers was profitable for banks and far less costly than making consumption loans or small mortgage loans. The lack of a balanced portfolio made banks vulnerable to the rapidly expanding economy and inflated asset values in ways not previously experienced.

Mortgage Bonds Revisited

The market for bonds backed by farm mortgages continued with some interruptions after the scandals of the nineteenth century. The template for the securities remained the same, although the new Farm Credit System brought confidence to the market, which had been characterized by boom and bust cycles in the past. Securities secured by first mortgages were in demand by investors who had learned from the previous debacle that the nature of the collateral could not be taken for granted. Collateral had not changed materially; some properties were more desirable than others and they were leveraged differently. The real problem lay in how they were held as collateral and in the implications for investors in the case of a large number of defaults.

Ads for bonds appeared throughout the country, placed by banks and brokers. All touted mortgage bonds as safe investments since farmland was considered low risk and vital to the economy. An ad in a local Vermont newspaper described the benefits of investing in mortgages: "People are turning to the farm mortgage. Particularly investors of wartime securities who are now discovering that many of their wartime investments were largely speculation." It continued: "Experience and sound business judgment teach us that it is safer and better and we will have more money in the end, to buy securities that do not depreciate in value—securities that can be depended upon to treat us right and later repay us 100 cents on every dollar."[29] This not-so-oblique reference was to Liberty bonds, which sank to a discount in the market after the war. Yet these sorts of ads did not necessarily strike as responsive a chord among the investing public as might be imagined; a large number of Liberty bonds went unclaimed when redeemed by the Treasury, suggesting that investors did not understand the maturity of the various tranches or the market values of bonds in general.

The basis for the second wave of mortgage-backed securities was the Rural Credits Act. Using it as the rationale for long-term financing for farmers, many states passed laws authorizing state governments to issue bonds to raise funds. But this was sometimes a difficult job. In

Minnesota, an amendment was introduced in the state legislature to allow a constitutional revision so that future borrowing could take place. A newspaper reported the problem by stating that "the constitution of the state which specifically provides that Minnesota's credit shall not be given or lent to any individual, association, or corporation has been an insurmountable obstacle in the path of a state rural credits system."[30] This was a constitutional problem pointed out by William Marshall Bullitt in Kentucky several years before. South Dakota had already implemented the necessary changes and was viewed as a successful model for neighboring states to follow.

The mortgage debenture crisis of the 1880s and 1890s had made eastern investors wary of bonds backed by mortgages, but changes made in the way bonds were guaranteed changed attitudes. In the nineteenth century J. B. Watkins in Kansas packaged mortgage loans to directly back bonds. Later, the mortgages were used as collateral for a debenture to be issued by a mortgage company; the collateral was indirect collateral and depended on the trustee to handle the matter properly and assure investors that the debenture was sound.[31] This second type of debenture was known as a "covered" bond. In the event of default, payments to investors were to be covered by the borrowing (issuing) institution. Opinions differed over whether it was preferable to the older type, which did not have the issuing mortgage company as middleman in the process, but as long as the intermediary performed its trust duties, the obligation was considered less risky than a noncovered obligation. In the new case, the mortgage company guaranteed the bond issue and they became known as guaranteed mortgages. This is why brokers were able to claim they were safe. The model used was a replication of the new farm credit bonds.

The situation surrounding farm mortgages began to change during World War I. Mortgage bankers originating farm mortgages organized into the Farm Mortgage Bankers Association (FMBA), established in 1914. The Rural Credits movement had criticized the role of mortgage bankers in the credit allocation process and the organization responded by joining together to defend its role, especially when it became clear that the Farm Credit System would become law. When the outline of the Rural Credits Act became clear, the group voiced its objections to the long-term mortgages proposed by the act. According to them, the European models upon which the new program was based were not appropriate for the American market. More important, it objected to the idea that the new land bank system would be declared an "instrumentality" of the U.S. government and the interest paid by its bonds would become tax-free.[32] This was a feature that private mortgage bankers could not compete with. Eventually, the new land bank bonds would crowd others out of the market and establish a standard for farm mortgages.

Mortgage bankers no longer were found in the dreaded East, where Populists feared the concentration of financial power resided. They were found mostly, but not exclusively, in the central states, ranging from Texas to Montana. Here they were the principal lenders, along with life insurance companies, in the 1920s. As in the past, mortgage rates were higher farther west, averaging about 1 to 2 percent higher than in New York and New England. That was an improvement on the situation in the nineteenth century, where the interest rate spread was wider, but the spread still reflected distance risk. Commercial banks also charged higher rates in the region.[33] These lenders clearly exploited the situation and offered mortgages higher than the 6 percent that was rapidly becoming the benchmark for residential mortgages and many farm mortgages, but charges of loan sharking were not heard. The more contentious issue was the shorter length of the farm mortgage. New longer-term mortgages meant freedom from rollover fees and penalties that characterized the older mortgages, making them so attractive to lenders.

The new mortgage bonds supported by the land banks and the states helped revolutionize the mortgage problem nationwide and squeezed much of the institutionalized high charges out of the lending system. But embedded costs that contained high interest charges still prevailed in many parts of the economy and would only be uncovered by critics who recognized that the old usury laws were being violated in novel ways in the production and marketing process of goods. The old loan shark was receding from view to an extent, but was being replaced by other, less visible high-interest lenders who relied on more sophisticated ways of charging high interest.

THE NEW YORK CHARGE

The mortgage process was not the only example of high-interest lending that refused to die. In the manufacturing process of buildings and consumer durables and nondurables, high interest charges were often added at different stages of production. There rarely was any mention of it because it was not well understood by many for whom a consumption loan still was their main financial concern. Against this backdrop, a much more sophisticated form of loan sharking developed.

At the same time farm mortgages were undergoing structural changes, many cities faced another problem, a shortage of rental housing. New York City, in particular, was suffering from high rents and lack of sufficient housing to satisfy demand. After World War I, the population of the city rose dramatically and demand far exceeded the supply of available housing. Many workers lived in substandard housing as a result. Reports abounded of apartment seekers moving into dilapidated tenements in or around the city just to be able to get to work. An investigation into the problem produced some unexpected results and reignited the loan sharking debate.

A series of hearings were called in New York City to investigate the construction and housing industries; these were known as the Lockwood hearings, named after state senator Charles Lockwood of Brooklyn. The chief counsel for the committee was Samuel Untermyer, last seen in a similar role at the Pujo Committee hearings into the money trust. Born in Virginia, he moved with his family to New York after the death of his father and earned a law degree from Columbia twenty years later. Prominent in private practice, he also had a strong bent toward public service and had a hand in drafting the Federal Reserve Act and the Federal

Trade Commission. The Lockwood hearings initially were called in 1919 and investigated wholesale lending practices in the commercial real estate business. They went on to investigate other practices deemed in violation of antitrust laws, namely the Clayton Act, the second antitrust law after the Sherman Act of 1890 that prohibited vertical mergers. The seemingly disparate group of investigations all had a common denominator: they involved complicated borrowing and lending relationships that were allegedly corrupting businesses in the city.

The committee adopted a tactic similar to the one employed by the Comptroller of the Currency some years before. Almost 500 questionnaires were sent to lending institutions in New York City, including savings banks, to determine whether they were charging usurious rates or engaging in dubious lending practices. Many complied with the questionnaire, and many later found themselves served with subpoenas based on the quality of their responses. The committee also discovered that many of the institutions could not be taken at their word when describing lending policies. Numerous acknowledged and alleged practices had broader implications for antitrust. Frequently the insurance companies, savings banks, and other small business lenders would not make loans to the construction industry unless builders bought unwanted parcels of land from them. This often included buying tenement buildings or out-of-town properties the lenders no longer wanted. This process of tie-ins and related practices appeared in sharp contrast to the antitrust provisions of the Clayton Act, passed by Congress after the Pujo hearings in 1914. Another practice with implications for the marketing of securitized farm bonds was requiring potential borrowers to take Liberty loans off the books of the insurance companies at par when their market price was close to 95 percent of par, having been marked down 5 percent from the original price.

These practices forced property owners to increase rents in a city already experiencing a housing shortage because of the high effective interest rates caused by those practices in the first place. Equally important, the relationships between the large insurance companies and the building industry were central to the Lockwood committee investigations. Untermyer demonstrated that while loans to builders were made at the standard rate of around 6 percent, lenders then added fees and commissions that raised the rate to 20 percent and, often, to 50 percent. In some cases, borrowers were forced to incorporate themselves before receiving funds so they could not claim usury after the fact, since the laws did not apply to corporations. That usually meant a standard lending rate of 15 percent before fees and commissions were added. A witness at the hearings told Untermyer that "loans at a rate of interest higher than that allowed by law are not made to individuals" but admitted that they were only "made to corporations." The audience and staff members in the hearing room erupted into laughter.[34]

Another favorite was giving borrowers a discounted loan but charging them interest on the full principal amount, similar to the technique employed by salary buyers. When the committee summarized its first two years of activity, it noted that "although these transactions cannot be said to be in contravention to the letter of the law, they are without ethical justification."[35] Unlike earlier denunciations of usury, the Lockwood committee was able to demonstrate the far-reaching effects it could have in specific economic terms, especially at the corporate level where it, technically, did not exist.

During the hearings, Untermyer questioned a local mortgage broker about the practices. He asked him how building could be expected to be stimulated if builders had to go to extreme lengths to please lenders. He then stated that "people who want to borrow money can't get it unless they buy suburban lots they don't want, unless they buy run-down tenements, unless they buy Liberty bonds at par, unless they pay huge discounts—and these exactions are made by persons with respectable sounding names, are they not?" The broker responded by saying, "Some of them are very respectable." To which Untermyer shot back, "I said respectable sounding."[36]

After the first session of the committee ended in 1921, Untermyer shocked New York when he proposed that usury laws no longer apply to real estate transactions of more than $10,000. At the same time, over forty insurance companies located in New York City agreed to abide by

committee recommendations and reform their activities so that usurious rates were no longer charged and the kickback system was eliminated. Untermyer went even further, suggesting that the state organize
a state trade commission to look into industry abuses. He proposed that
a bill be introduced in Albany to establish one but was flatly rejected
twice. After the second attempt, Governor Nathan Lewis Miller, a Republican, said that "it is a very radical departure in state policy."[37] There
was also a strong suggestion that Untermyer was sensationalizing the
findings of the committee, the same criticism leveled against the Pujo
Committee hearings years before.

The New York hearings continued after the housing problem was
addressed and probed other suspect practices, calling a long list of
prominent business people in the process. It began a tradition of state
involvement in business practices that would continue for years; in the
absence of appropriate federal law or the inaction of federal agencies,
when confronted with problems, the state was ready to intervene under
its own powers. More important than headlines or political battles was
the fact that the Lockwood committee had discovered that usurious
rates of interest were imbedded in the production process in the building trade. Similar discoveries would be made in other sectors of the
economy during the 1920s.

The *New York Times* complimented the Lockwood committee for
its work on the housing problem, noting that "since the war the situation has developed into an imminent menace to public health. It is a
credit to the Lockwood committee that the facts have been brought out
and many of the malefactors legally dealt with."[38] In a state with a history of a venal legislature, it was recognized that the committee had
done something to restore Albany's reputation while contributing to
the continuing debate over usury. By exposing institutional usury hidden in the production process, the committee demonstrated that high-
interest lending had moved from storefront operations to banking suites
and other, less familiar, locations. At the same time that loan sharking
opponents were proclaiming victory, the opposite was being proved.

In 1921, Chicago began its own investigation of its building industry under the Dailey Commission, named after State Senator John Dailey. Its findings also included interest of as much as 27 percent being charged builders, adding to corruption in the building industry. Rents were high as a result, and those rates of interest drew funds away from other businesses and farmers. Insurance companies were also named in the commission's final report as being responsible for excessive interest charges, just as they were in New York.

EVIDENCE TO THE CONTRARY

As the consumer boom entered its final stage in the late 1920s, the victory proclaimed by many over loan sharking appeared premature. While many unlicensed lenders had gone legitimate or out of business, many flourished as usual despite the progress of the USLL. The American tradition of declaring war on perceived social evils was proving costly and somewhat unwinnable. Prohibition had proved successful at the legislative level but was a costly failure at the local level, where the number of speakeasies easily overwhelmed the ability of local police forces to cope with them, especially in cities. The war against loan sharks was soon to follow suit.

In 1928 Edward Filene remarked in a radio interview that "the usury investigations in New York and other parts of the country are a compelling challenge that we shall banish this social injustice."[39] This was not a remark suggesting victory in the war against loan sharks. It only reflected the reality of consumer credit in the later 1920s. Unlicensed lenders still were a significant part of everyday financing for individuals. In addition to providing consumption loans, high-interest lenders began appearing in unfamiliar places; loan sharking had become institutionalized. The convenience of manufacturer-provided financing led to high-interest rate charges built in to a product's final price without being divulged. In the past, down-on-their-luck borrowers needed cash to make ends meet and they paid the price. In the 1920s, consumers paid the price for the convenience of time payments many could barely afford. That convenience came with a heavy price tag.

Arguments in favor of high interest charges built into a final sales price usually noted that sellers on the installment plan faced higher risks and associated costs than those that provided no financing and, therefore, the higher prices were justified. New York was one of the few states that actually considered that the high prices contained usurious interest, based upon two court cases in particular. This ran counter to the prevailing trend at the time of adopting a hands-off policy when considering the matter of high interest rates being built into installment prices. One of the major concerns was that if usury ceilings were applied to installment payments, then the state involved could be accused of contributing to price fixing.[40] In other words, the state would appear to be setting prices for goods by applying existing usury laws to buying on credit. While the argument was not convincing, high interest rates continued to be built into prices without much challenge.

By the late 1920s, $4 billion of consumer credit was extended every year, with automobile installment loans accounting for almost 60 percent of the total. The second largest category was household furniture. But the numbers were only best guesstimates by the Twentieth Century Fund, which noted that official statistics were not kept by the federal government or any private group. The influence of loan sharks was felt in the numbers. Over $150 million of the $2.4 billion in auto loans was extended by unlicensed lenders. Of the total $4 billion, $750 million was extended by the same type of lenders. The notion that progress had been made against loan sharks could not be disputed since, prior to the USLL and the introduction of installment buying, the unlicensed percentages, in theory, would have been much higher and, probably, less economic activity would have taken place as a result.

But the level of loan shark activity suggested that the war was far from won. Consumer credit stayed mainly flat after 1926, when the property boom ended.[41] Perceptions were changing on the side of regulators but not on the side of high-interest lenders. Concepts and techniques were becoming more sophisticated, however. As soon as it appeared that the USLL was gaining acceptance in the states, two lenders expanded their businesses significantly. One was experienced at lending, while the other used the occasion to start lending nationwide.

Sharks in Sheep's Clothing?

Two companies that benefited greatly from the USLL were the Household Finance Corporation and the Beneficial Corporation, founded by Clarence Hodson. They became the two top licensed small loan lenders in the country in the 1920s. Both proclaimed themselves as pioneers in the fight against loan sharks but both clearly were interested in the new higher rates tolerated by the USLL.

Household, founded in 1878, became the first consumer credit company to go public in 1928, when it sold its initial public offering through investment bankers Lee Higginson & Company. Beneficial went to the public market for funding later, in 1931, when it issued a debenture. Household's initial public offering was priced at $40 per share. The *Wall Street Journal* noted that its investors were mainly institutions and professional money managers. At the time, Household acknowledged that it would not make loans under $100 because they were too costly to service. It did, however, lower its nominal monthly interest rate. A year later, the company amalgamated with four other small lenders with total assets of $26 million to expand. In 1925 the company had thirty-four offices in nine states with $6.5 million in loans outstanding. The new, expanded company had 114 offices in fourteen states where the USLL was effective. The reason for the expansion was simple: the small loan business was considered safe. Household announced that its losses were only 0.75 percent of all loans outstanding. Beneficial had similar numbers. Household also announced that it estimated the gross national income at $90 billion per year, $40 billion of which was spent in retail stores, of which $4.5 billion was spent on an installment basis. Equally important, it showed that its overall default rate was lower than that for installment loans at department stores.[42]

Although it was a direct product of the USLL, Household claimed to have teamed with the Russell Sage Foundation to write the prototype draft that passed through the states. The foundation itself acknowledged many contributions to the development and implementation of the USLL but never mentioned Household Finance in its own history.[43] On the contrary, past legal proceedings in the District of Columbia and several states were brought against offices of the Household Loan Company. As industrial lenders, both Beneficial and Household Finance were on solid ground legally, although Household was attempting to shed its image as an unlicensed lender that had more recently taken the higher road.

Not all companies involved in installment credit wanted to remain in the business. In 1928, General Electric sold its installment credit subsidiary to the Industrial Acceptance Corporation. Founded only seven years before, the subsidiary provided financing to dealers of GE products. GE claimed that the installment business required the kind of expertise it could not provide and that a sale was the best way to insure its continued existence. The alternative, lending to the call money market, was very profitable and involved much less administrative work than installment loans.

Charges of usury and crippling debt were heard in other quarters, as well. The American banks' fondness for charging high interest rates was on full display after World War I. When German war reparations were negotiated in Paris, a plan to charge Germany the highest amount of reparations ever recorded was accompanied by discussions on the exact amount and repayment schedule. Different amounts were heatedly discussed but the terms troubled John Maynard Keynes, a member of the British delegation. The talks were dominated by bankers from J. P. Morgan & Company, representing the United States, and Keynes felt the details would impoverish the Germans, leading to future troubles. He argued against them at the time and in his *The Economic Consequences of the Peace*. But the mood following the war was punitive and harsh conditions were imposed. The effects of compound interest only exacerbated the problem. Payments were to be made over a period of years. The totals were only approximate at the time and his calculations produced a number that was slightly higher than the Allies own estimates. According to Keynes:

> On the basis if my estimate of $40,000,000,000 for the total liability ... assuming interest at 5 percent, this will raise the annual payment to $2,150,000,000 without allowance for amortization. . . . At 5 percent compound interest, a capital sum doubles itself in fifteen years. On the assumption that Germany cannot pay more than $750,000,000 annually until 1936 ... the $25,000,000,000 on which interest is deferred will have risen to $50,000,000,000, carrying an annual interest charge of $2,500,000,000 ... at the end of any year in which she pays less than this sum she will owe more than she did at the beginning of it.[44]

Keynes resigned his position on the British delegation as a result of the final reparations bill against the Germans that were very close to his calculations.

Renegotiations followed later in the 1920s and by 1929 all sides to the original deal were showing signs of impatience. In 1929, the president of the Reichsbank noted that it was time for more goodwill and less bickering about alleged American motives for imposing such harsh terms on the interest due especially. Hjalmar Schact, also a delegate at the Versailles conference, recognized the American penchant for high interest charges by banks although diplomatically he did not blame them for the troubles they would create. He commented that Germans should not be deluded "into the prevailing European error of finding in American usury and greed the cause of hardships and discomforts," the *Chicago Daily Tribune* reported in an editorial.[45] While 5 percent did not strike many as a usurious rate of interest, it was still 75 basis points higher than the coupon of the last Liberty bond issued by the United States in 1918, which was selling at around 95 percent of par at the time. On that basis, however, the German reparation yield was equivalent to the current yield on the Liberty loan. Arguing for a lower rate was tantamount to providing the Germans with a soft rate, which was not in tenor with the political climate.

SONS OF THE WILD JACKASS

Politics affected the loan sharking debate in the 1920s. Democrats and Progressive Republicans dominated the debate about credit, although their message was not united. After two decades of meaningful reforms on a variety of social and economic fronts, it was assumed that loan sharking was receding, as had been predicted after the war. But unlike reforms in voting, consumer protection, and public health, loan sharking receded and hid behind a corporate veil difficult to penetrate. When individual politicians attempted to expose credit problems, they often resorted to extreme arguments that put them on the fringe of the political debate.

In the later 1920s the loan shark problem continued to be discussed on the state level while Congress was preoccupied with other related matters, namely the continuing role of the Federal Reserve and the problems caused by the land boom. It was at the national level that the Progressives, heirs to the Populists, were able to bring credit issues to the forefront. Lively and often technical debate was waged about banking topics but, unfortunately, the main critics of the status quo often were not taken seriously. Despite that the Progressives often influenced banking legislation substantially.

States' rights in banking was a dominant theme of the 1920s, followed closely by opposition to the Fed. One of the staunchest critics of the Federal Reserve and Wall Street was Representative Louis T. McFadden, a Republican from Pennsylvania. He was joined by a chorus of agrarian legislators from the Midwest, although they often differed on policy. The agrarians criticized the central bank for the farm crisis of 1920 that was caused by a collapse in commodity prices after the heady years of World War I. The old suspicions that the central bank was nothing more than an official but clandestine institution to further Wall Street interests still held sway. The farming states sent a colorful, often irascible contingent of legislators to Washington, D.C. McFadden was not included in the group but his later remarks, in the 1930s, would have made him a prime candidate. His influence on banking was much greater than that of the agrarians, or of Republican insurgents, during the 1920s.

Born in Bradford County, Pennsylvania, in 1876, he attended a commercial college in Elmira, New York. McFadden joined the First National Bank of Canton, Pennsylvania, in 1892, a nationally chartered institution despite its small size. His first job was janitor. Seven years later he was made cashier and rose through the ranks. In 1906, he served as treasurer of the Pennsylvania Bankers' Association, and was made president of the bank in 1916.

McFadden's career changed when he was elected to the House of Representatives in 1915. He served until 1935, in an increasingly turbulent and enigmatic career. Although portraying himself as a prudent banker, he was berated in public by Comptroller John Skelton Williams for running a marginal banking operation in Pennsylvania. A decade later, his name became forever associated with the McFadden Act, a restrictive piece of legislation passed in 1927. Throughout his career, he remained a foe of the Federal Reserve, viewing it as an institution that actually undermined national banks rather than helped them. His vocal opposition to the nomination of Eugene Meyer as its chairman also raised the suggestion of anti-Semitism since Meyer was Jewish. And after the crash of 1929, his views became so radical that he was finally stripped of his important House chairmanship that allowed him to introduce the McFadden Act in the first place.

McFadden's battle with the Comptroller of the Currency began shortly after taking his seat in the House. McFadden sent a letter to Williams calling for abolition of the office and an investigation of Williams's administration. The request came at a delicate moment; Williams was due for reappointment. He responded strongly, accusing McFadden of being motivated by greed. Noting that the congressman

never provided facts to support his allegations, Williams took an unusual step and released a statement that McFadden's bank had been
under constant supervision for the past twenty years for shoddy banking practices. He also claimed that only the comptroller's constant supervision had kept it solvent. He noted that its capital had diminished
over time while other banks in the area had grown.[46]

Most damning was Williams's comment that McFadden and his
family had been recipients of loans far in excess of the bank's capital.
He counterattacked McFadden in strong language. Regarding First
National, he stated that:

> The bank continues to violate the law; and this feature together with
> other unsatisfactory conditions seem largely due to lack of proper man-
> agement. The examiner is of the opinion that the bank will not observe
> the law or regulations of this office as long as President McFadden is
> the Managing Director, because the other directors seem to take no
> personal and active interest in the bank and permit President McFadden
> to use the bank for his personal interest without due regard for safe and
> sound banking.[47]

Despite the countercharge, McFadden remained president of the bank
until 1925, when he finally resigned. He was chairman of the House
Banking and Currency Committee from 1920 to 1931.

McFadden's experiences led him to introduce changes to the National Bank Act. In 1924 he proposed that an amendment be made to
the existing law that would help national banks compete with the state
banks. Unencumbered by the National Bank Act, state banks had wider
powers in the states than national banks, whose expansion was actually
limited. At issue was the matter of branch banking. Many states permitted state banks within their borders to branch, at least partially, within
the state, a power denied to national banks. McFadden wanted them to
compete equally. But in the 1920s the differences between national
and state banks ran deep, and more than one executive at a state bank
claimed they were immune from any sort of federal banking regulation.

The differences between the two chartered banks reflected the overall distrust of things federal.

McFadden's legislation proposed that the two types of banks be put on equal footing by permitting branching by national banks anywhere state laws permitted the branching of state banks. Despite its common-sense proposals, the bill ran into opposition. One Progressive congressman denounced it as a path to a larger and even more powerful money trust that would completely dominate banking at the expense of the state banks. At the time, the idea of banks expanding across state lines was not the issue, but the language of the act effectively prohibited branching within and between states. It did, however, give greater powers sought by McFadden to national banks. Supporters, including Senator Carter Glass of Virginia, an author of the original Federal Reserve Act, applauded its passing.

The McFadden Act was replete with vague and often confusing language but was well summarized by Charles W. Carey of the American Bankers' Association (ABA). He exhorted his members to understand that the McFadden bill "is the first effort of Congress to regulate branch banking. As originally introduced, it would have accomplished that end without amendments attached that were even more restrictive. Without them, it would still limit branch banking."[48] The McFadden Act was remembered by history as prohibiting interstate branching by any bank, regardless of charter, because it deferred to prevailing state laws, all of which were remarkably similar. State bankers did not want the larger institutions, from urban areas in particular, becoming banking carpetbaggers in their states.

The ABA support of the McFadden Act was reiterated less than two years later. Speaking before an ABA gathering two weeks before the October market crash, John Pole, Comptroller of the Currency, suggested that the ban on interstate banking should not extend to intrastate or intra-regional branching. Many states had local laws prohibiting banks from branching outside their local counties. While the local application of the act satisfied small state banks, it created an even more balkanized banking system. He argued that branch banking by national banks should be allowed within certain economic zones but not necessarily those within Fed districts or between states. The idea was to promote economic activity and centralized regulation, which would necessarily fall on his office to provide. But the state banks did not act on his proposal at the convention, prompting *Barron's* to remark that "the failure of the convention to take a definite stand on the question of branch banking was due in part to the opposition of the state bank division, and in part to the feeling that the banking situation is changing so rapidly that just appraisal of the situation is not yet possible."[49]

The branch banking part of the act is the best-remembered part of McFadden's law; its impact on the Federal Reserve was crucial at the time. When the Fed was created in 1913, it was put on a relatively short leash by Congress. The institution was given a twenty-year original life by Congress, a relatively long sunset clause, but a sunset clause, nevertheless. The twenty-year period was similar to the original lives of the first and second Bank of the United States, both chartered during the early nineteenth century. The strong economy and relatively low inflation rates during the 1920s won much praise for the Fed during the decade and its charter was made permanent in 1927 by the McFadden Act.

Another feature of the act gave national banks the ability to make real estate loans for periods longer than one year. Banks had made loans previously, but they were on a one-year rollover basis, meaning they would be automatically renewed at the prevailing interest rate. This was similar to the floating rate mortgage loans made later in the century called adjustable rate mortgages (ARMs), which were later used to avoid usury ceilings on real property loans. But at the time, it allowed banks greater flexibility with their balance sheets and insured that borrowers would be able to lock in a fixed rate for the life of the loan.[50]

Elections in the early 1920s brought a fresh group of Progressive Republicans to the Senate. Their inspirational leader was Robert M. La Follette of Wisconsin, the dean of the Progressives, along with George Norris of Nebraska. Also elected were a small group of unknowns who would make varying impressions upon officials in Washington, D.C. They all hailed from the Midwest and had remarkably similar views on the usual foes of agrarians: the Fed and Wall Street financiers. Most were also strict Prohibitionists, believing that spirits were enslaving the workingman.

Traveling to D.C. for the first time in 1920 was Peter Norbeck, a South Dakota Republican who won his seat after having served a term as governor. An oil driller by occupation, he attended the University of South Dakota and later was instrumental in developing the Mt. Rushmore National Memorial site. Unlike many of his colleagues, Norbeck was not flamboyant, preferring to work within the Senate toward his ends rather than take to the pulpit to gain exposure. But his aggressiveness and sense of humor were well known. In 1927 President Calvin Coolidge was inducted into the Sioux Indian nation in South Dakota. Inductees needed an appropriate Indian name and the Sioux decided upon "Great Sullen Warrior" for the president, noting his taciturn nature. Norbeck, already an honorary member of the tribe known as "Chief Charging Hawk," approved of the name, as was required by custom.

Another of the new members of the Senate became a favorite target of the press because of his homespun language and what were portrayed as his provincial attitudes. Smith Wildman Brookhart, Republican from Iowa, was dedicated to farm causes. He became a thorn in the side of his party; many Republicans wanted him out of office by the end of his first term. Like McFadden, Brookhart seemed intent on making a long-lasting impression. Born in Missouri, he attended a local technical college in Iowa. After graduation, he taught school for five years before studying law, and passed the bar in 1892. He served as an officer in both the Spanish–American War and World War I, attaining the rank of lieutenant colonel before returning to civilian life. He also became an expert marksman. From 1921–25, during his first term in the Senate, he served as president of the National Rifle Association. His major political break came in 1922 when he was elected to fill the vacancy of Iowa Progressive Senator William S. Kenyon, who resigned from office. Brookhart already was labeled a blunderer, fool, uncouth, or a barbarian (a reference to his middle name). There was substantial opposition to his election at the grassroots level in Iowa but he, nevertheless, won the seat. His victory was seen as a result of the economic plight among farmers, his main constituents.[51]

Brookhart was a lifelong foe of big business, inheriting his antipathy from the earlier Progressive tradition. The agrarians already believed that a great Fed plot had been hatched to deflate farm prices in 1920, and falling commodity prices only added fuel to the fire. When the stock market rally began after 1925, they believed that the Fed began diverting funds to the money market in New York at the expense of the rest of the country. When credit to farmers fell dramatically after 1925, the agrarians blamed Wall Street for using funds that, otherwise, could have found their way into the Farm Credit System. The old conspiracy theories of the nineteenth century were alive and well.

When he first went to D.C., Brookhart suggested that the Federal Reserve Board should be reconstituted to include representatives from agriculture and labor. His ideal board had no bankers or Wall Street people sitting on it. More important, he also proposed that the Federal Reserve increase its reserve requirement on member banks so that more reserves would be held in the regional Fed banks. He estimated that 75 percent of Iowa banks' funds were on loan to New York banks. The Fed requirements stated that 25 percent of bank reserves should be on deposit with the local Fed district bank; Brookhart wanted to increase the requirement to 75 percent. The goal was to prevent local funds from finding their way to the call money market through the New York banks. He proposed that member banks, and nonmembers as well, be prohibited from making speculative loans in any form.[52]

Another proposal also concerned reserves. He wanted the Fed to pay 2 percent on reserves on deposit for member banks. That included a prohibition against counting call money loans for reserve purposes. The central bank did not pay interest on reserves at the time and would not for the remainder of the twentieth century. State banks, on the other hand, kept their reserves at larger city banks, where they earned interest on the reserve deposit. As a result, many of the smaller banks avoided becoming associated with the Fed to sidestep red tape and bank examiners, earning interest on reserves in the process.

Brookhart also wanted the discount rate, a major tool of monetary policy at the time, lowered to 3 percent. The proposal was to support this through the force of law, not simply as a dictate of Fed policy. He held that only Congress could dictate interest rates and that the 3 percent level, lower than the 3.5 percent in force at the time, would protect farmers and consumers. The proposal was an attempt to return to the lower interest rates from earlier in the decade, from a time before the Fed raised the discount rate three times in 1928. He said that he detected a "great scheme of credit control to maintain high interest rates in the country at large," further noting that "a study of the financial reviews indicates that a drive will be made immediately after the first of the year to force the Federal Reserve Bank to raise the rediscount rates above the present level of 3½ percent." He added that if "the rediscount rate is three percent then a two percent margin is wide enough under the ordinary interest rate under the usury law."[53] This was a reference to the usury clause in the National Bank Act. Brookhart wanted to lower the 7 percent rate to 5 percent and introduced legislation to do so. He wanted to achieve the same effect by legislating against speculation, not using Federal Reserve policy.

The remarks proved prescient, if a bit premature. Fifteen months later in March 1929 the Federal Reserve Board indicated it was considering raising the discount rate for member banks only, to dissuade speculation in the market. On the surface, that sounded like a viable policy to cut down speculation but did not side with the proposals of the Iowa senator. The New York Fed bank, on the other hand, suggested that it should be raised for all banks, not just members, to prevent bootleg loans. Some months before, Benjamin Strong, president of the New York Fed, appointed Charles Mitchell of National City Bank as a director of the bank. The loquacious Mitchell was an unabashed bull and would prove instrumental in the stock market crash that followed in October 1929 by continuing to keep interest rates low after a market break in March 1929.

Brookhart's proposals were constructed around a dislike of the central bank and its ability to make financial policy since the idea still prevailed that the Fed was firmly in the hands of Wall Street. The idea would gain even greater acceptance after the crash. His proposals were purely protective of smaller banks. If the stock market bubble burst, the local Midwestern banks would be protected from any failures by brokers. When the idea failed to muster interest, Brookhart retreated to the time-proven method of stopping what he considered excessive speculation: he suggested that state banks that failed to adhere to his proposed regulations be denied use of the mail. He declared that "unless something of this kind is done we are now headed for the greatest panic in the history of the world."[54]

Not everyone in the Midwest held this view common about insurgents, the name given to the radical Progressives, and it was considered extreme. In a speech in Illinois the head of a local land bank in the Federal Land Bank system stated clearly that the reason commercial banks were not making many loans to farmers was because of the high numbers of bank failures occurring around the country.[55] The failures had little to do with money being sent to the call money market in New York, in his opinion. Bad loans came back to haunt the banks because of the real estate speculation in the 1920s, along with bad business loans. The call money controversy was part of a much larger problem infecting banks around the country, although the Progressives only attacked the part that directly affected farmers in particular.

Despite his often-divisive public comments, conclusions of that nature made Brookhart look prophetic after the crash. The radicalism of the agrarian Progressives began to ring true. Only a few months before, their conclusions appeared to be nothing more than the ranting of a marginal group. Their complaints never changed: Wall Street was aided and abetted by the Fed and was creating the greatest market bubble ever seen in the United States. Despite his predictions, however, Brookhart was fighting a losing battle. Personality blunted his message. His mannerisms cost him politically. "If Smith Wildman Brookhart of Iowa had a more active capacity for deductive reasoning," remarked a satirical commentary of the day, "he might really be the significant figure he modestly likes to think he is."[56]

As a Prohibitionist, Brookhart took exception to the elite of Wall Street's drinking at social functions. He revealed in a Senate speech that he had attended a party in 1926 in Washington, D.C., attended by what he called the "big men" of Wall Street. Liquor flowed freely. At the dinner party that followed he sat between Otto Kahn of Kuhn, Loeb & Co., the most urbane financier of the period—from the traditionally Jewish investment bank that previously had been identified in the money trust hearings—and Edward E. Loomis of the Lehigh Valley Railroad. He recalled that both tried to influence him on financial policy while drinking copiously. While resisting their advances, he later revealed that he felt somewhat out of place because of the manner in which he was dressed. Brookhart wore a business suit rather than the white tie and tails favored at formal occasions. He remarked, "I was the only one there dressed like an American citizen."[57]

The details of the affair caused a public commotion. *Commonweal* noted that Brookhart suffered from a "gross lapse in good taste" for revealing details of a casual dinner. Both Kahn and Loomis declined comment. Shortly thereafter, Brookhart was invited to New York to debate Prohibition with noted attorney Clarence Darrow, who took the side of the "wets" over the "drys." After a spirited debate, Darrow remarked that his opponent was, "sincere; it's too bad he is uncivilized."[58]

The radical Republicans were quickly becoming marginalized when, suddenly, in 1929, they were given a new lease on life as a group and became renowned around the country. Their celebrity came from a speech given by Senator George Moses of New Hampshire, who coined a term that was to prove enduring. At a speech before a meeting of New England manufacturers, Moses dubbed his western dissident colleagues as the "Sons of the Wild Jackass." The name reverberated throughout the meeting and, later, the country. Moses was president pro tempore of the Senate and chairman of the Republican Senate Campaign Committee, and his acerbic remark was not well received by his colleagues. The speech also referred to Smith Brookhart's revelations about the

D.C. dinner party at which liquor was served. Moses claimed that "all Senators now attend dinners with trepidation." After hearing the remarks, Brookhart replied that it was clear that "we do not need booze at these dinners to lift us to a high plane of eloquence."

The flap did not end quickly. Conjecture swirled around what exactly a "son of the wild jackass" was. Most thought it implied that the radicals were offspring of the Democrats more than members of the Republican Party. The term was so potent that a book appeared several years later with the title *Sons of the Wild Jackass*, written by two experienced Washington, D.C. journalists. To give the group a collective personality, they included over a dozen senators and a former congressman in their list, immediately immortalizing them. Named from the Senate were Brookhart, Henrik Shipstead of Minnesota, and Robert La Follette Jr. of Wisconsin, among others. The lone member of the House was former Representative Fiorello La Guardia of New York.[59] All were well-known thorns in the side of the establishment. There were also some notable exceptions, namely McFadden, omitted for reasons unknown. As their initial anger faded into pride, many of the dissidents welcomed the attention despite the less than flattering name. McFadden, on the other hand, considered his omission to be a slight.

Despite their commonsense proposals, the insurgent Republicans appeared to be fighting a losing battle. The McFadden Act was the exception. It imposed restrictions on bank expansion that lasted for decades; an unusual legislative feat considering it was written during a boom period in the stock market and the economy, not after a financial crisis. Generally the proposals and comments of the group were taken as the ranting of a marginal group of Farm Belt dissidents who did not understand the intricacies of the financial markets. Their real problem was that they proposed traditional methods of dealing with a less-than-perfect banking system. The Federal Reserve had been established to allow its financial policies to govern the markets. The insurgents, on the other hand, proposed legislation to remedy the weaknesses in the system. In the 1920s, at least, until new banking and securities laws were enacted between 1933 and 1935, the older statutory method of dealing with banking and markets (not often used in any event) had been supplanted with a principles-based system that allowed the Fed to guide the markets rather than impose congressional will on them. The market-based policy regime was in full force and would not be stopped by Brookhart's proposals based on a dim view of the very nature of the central bank. In the insurgents' view, the Fed was the handmaiden of Wall Street and would only cater to its interests. Ten years later, after the crash, that view was more widely accepted. In the 1920s, it ran counter to a decade of Republican-inspired policies that allowed business a wide berth.

The Call Money Controversy

The radical Progressives correctly identified the call money market as a source of potential problems. Wall Street bankers also realized the potential threat but remained silent because the market was on an upward trajectory. This left the issue squarely in the hands of the Progressives but no one was taking them seriously outside their own constituencies. Their brief moment finally came in 1928.

Senator Robert M. La Follette Jr., who had just succeeded his father in the Senate, introduced a resolution calling for the Federal Reserve to curb speculation in the call money market by restricting the amount of loans member banks could make to it. Shortly thereafter, a subcommittee began hearings on the matter. La Follette told the subcommittee that making loans to the call market was a violation of the Federal Reserve Act. He noted that between 1921 and 1928 the amount on loan in the market had increased five times, from $778 million to $3.8 billion. This large amount was fueling speculation in the stock market and endangering the financial system as a whole.

The call market was something of a mystery to everyone except Wall Street banks and brokers until the mid-1920s, when it began to gain notoriety. Official rates in the market were around 4.5 percent for most of the 1920s, with peaks of about 5 or sometimes even 6 percent. But the actual rates obtained by many lenders could be much higher depending upon the amount of funds available, the amount called in on any particular day, and the time of day when funds were made available for lending. In these cases intraday rates could be as high as 15 percent or more; substantially higher than banks could obtain by making ordinary commercial and industrial loans, the usual type for business. Equally important, these high rates could be obtained without fear of usury charges, especially in New York, because commercial loans were exempt. The market was controlled by the New York banks, leaving smaller out-of-town banks vulnerable to market fluctuations.

Banks were not the only lenders. They often served as conduits for large corporations that also placed funds in the market, attracted by high returns, especially since stock market loans were assumed to be the least risky type of lending. *The Economist* noted the phenomenon, and remarked that the funds, instead of going to the local Federal Reserve district banks as intended, were, instead, being diverted, and that "has served to call attention afresh to the large part now played in the money market by corporations and institutions having large amounts of cash. During the last year or so these cash resources have grown to very large proportions, and their owners, instead of leaving the money on deposit with their bank, have directed the banks to place the money out on call."[60] In the process, they helped disintermediate the banks. Funds were placed in the market for speculation rather than being loaned to businesses or individuals for productive purposes.

Loans made to the stock market by large corporations were passed through by banks acting as their conduits. These loans were referred to as "bootleg loans," since they were indirect. Many of the largest corporations lent money in this fashion, including E. I. DuPont, Goodyear Tire, Eastman Kodak, Standard Oil of California, General Electric, and Westinghouse. In late 1928 a study was conducted of 1,000 leading industrial companies and it was found that 194 had money on loan, totaling $716 million. That was about 23 percent of the total amount on loan in the call money market at the time.[61] That amount was substantial but still only a fraction of the total money on loan in the equities markets. Other bootleg loans originated with out-of-town banks and foreign lenders.

Lenders not residing in New York City were divided into two groups: out-of-town member banks and out-of-town "others." Member banks were those Fed members who used the larger New York banks as their correspondents when placing money out for lending. This was the money that Brookhart and others wanted to repatriate to their Fed district home banks. The amounts were not insubstantial, as the Progressives realized. In addition to the $716 million from bootleg loans, $1.5 billion was provided by New York banks and $1.65 billion by out-of-town banks, for a total of $3.9 billion at the end of 1928.[62] Funds earmarked for stock market lending reduced the amount of commercial loans made, a fact highlighted by the banking crisis of the decade. "Others" were private banks, trust companies, and foreign institutions.

The incentive for the funds finding their way to market was high lending rates that could sometimes reach 15 to 20 percent on an inter-day basis, although the officially reported average daily report always was lower. This potential for profit drew smaller Fed member banks and foreign institutions as well. In the latter case, they could lend at higher rates without fear of usury laws, the problem that had plagued attempts by some Midwestern cities to raise money in the nineteenth century. The differential between the call money rate and the rate by which banks could make commercial loans favored call money, and funds were diverted on a large scale.

The source of corporate lending, in particular, drew attention to one little-known source that would play a major role in the stock market calamity of 1929. Many companies classified as "others" raised equity in the strong market rise in 1927 and 1928 and then used the funds for loans, lending to the same market from which they had raised funds.[63] Investment bankers also borrowed money to temporarily fund their inventories of new issues of securities. They often borrowed money to finance unsold inventories of new bonds and stocks until they had the opportunity to sell them. This pyramiding effect placed many of them, including lending banks, at risk from a potentially falling stock market.

But that possibility seemed outweighed by the general euphoria of the period when asset prices, based upon what was considered strong collateral, appeared solid. While Florida real estate proved worthless, stock market loans seemed as solid as farm mortgages after the Farm Credit System had been established.

MORE BATTLES

In the late 1920s the prediction of victory over loan sharks proved to be not only wishful thinking but entirely incorrect. Loan sharking had an analogy in stock exchange developments. In 1921, the New York Curb Market previously conducted outdoors, moved indoors when the American Stock Exchange was opened in lower Manhattan. Loan sharks moved from storefront offices to corporate offices, where they plied their trade by building high interest charges into the final prices charged to consumers.

The consumer, upon which the 1920s economy rested, paid the price for high interest. The only question was when the effects would be felt negatively. Large companies had the benefit of borrowing at money market rates and lending at higher call money rates, but that shadow banking activity left the consumer inadequately covered. Rather than being served by small, unlicensed lenders, consumers now were served, if served at all, by licensed lenders who charged the maximum rates allowed by the USLL. Paying 40 percent annual interest was preferable to paying 300 percent or more, but the rates still appeared too high to sustain a prolonged economic boom.

Consumer credit had improved with the number of licensed lenders, but the price was high and did not improve materially with the entry of banks into small loan lending. In 1930, the Twentieth Century Fund remarked that "nine out of ten people one meets in the street cannot even today go to a regular bank and borrow money." It generally was agreed that banks were preferable to loan companies for retail loans but they served mostly wealthier clients and small businesses on the retail side, being committed to company accounts and operations in the markets. Industrial lenders provided the bulk of legitimate loans for small consumers.

Businesses that did not meet bank requirements also were forced into the clutches of loan sharks. In 1928, a small business owner in California sued a lender, claiming that he had to pay $150,000 interest on a $500,000 loan for a period of less than a year. Developments of that sort did not support the contention that loan sharking was defeated. In 1927, the Santa Fe Railroad announced that it was suspending its policy of firing workers who had their wages garnished a second time by loan sharks. They took the position that workers were being charged usurious rates and should not have to suffer as a result, and any rate above 10 percent would be challenged by the company.

The obituaries for loan sharks continued to be written well into the mid-1920s. Because the Russell Sage Foundation was located in New York and its goals were well known, New York commentators were certain that unlicensed lending was moribund. New York had comprehensive usury laws and tolerated higher-rate lending on the corporate level because call loans and other market-based loans were not subject to usury laws. But the optimists began to change their opinion by the later 1920s. While the USLL mandated stricter lending practices and regulation of licensed lenders, many loan sharks still operated nationwide. As Daniel Tolman demonstrated before his jail term, loan sharks proved adept at decamping to friendlier environments or simply closing shop at short notice to avoid unfriendly regulators.

In the late 1920s, there were still 335 offices of unlicensed lenders operating nationwide. Atlanta, Milwaukee, and Chicago were home to seven of the eleven firms that owned most of the offices. None headquartered in New York, although all had offices in the city. The Atlanta lenders, in particular, were the target of a New York campaign to drive loan sharks out of the city, since much of their business was salary buying, still widespread in the city. The unfriendly atmosphere in the city caused many loan sharks to reconsider, and many were said to be planning to leave in search of greener, and safer, pastures. State Attorney

General Albert Ottinger was considering a campaign against unlicensed lenders in 1928 and called a conference to discuss jailing some of them as a warning against further incursions by out-of-state lenders. He also wanted to enlist the United States Attorney General's office to see whether loan sharks were violating postal laws. This prompted many of the lenders to close their books and hastily collect outstanding debts before decamping, prompting many borrowers to complain to the attorney general.

New York State mounted the challenge to loan sharks in 1928 when Ottinger announced that his office was investigating loan sharking. He estimated that $26 million per year was paid to sharks, $20 million from New York City residents alone. Companies that provided loan facilities for their employees reported to him that they had not fired anyone for wage garnishment in years, demonstrating that low-rate loans were successful in the battle against loan sharks. Later in the year, Ottinger announced a concentrated drive against loan sharks who required borrowers to buy certificates from their lending companies as a condition for getting a loan. Once the loan finally was paid, the certificates were impossible to dispose of, raising the effective rate well above usury limits.

The Russell Sage Foundation also was swamped with complaints. It estimated that there were over 2,000 lenders operating in the city without the required licenses that were so highly touted ten years before.[64] Many lenders were found operating in the tenement districts of the city. "The situation is far worse than we had regarded it," acknowledged Leon Henderson, its director.[65] Shortly after, a New York magistrate charged four local men with usury and postal fraud. They were arraigned and held on $500 bail each, a small sum considering the charges. One disappeared and could not be located, adding to suspicions that he escaped across state lines. New Jersey was quick to react because many of those on the financial lam traditionally bolted across the Hudson River. Tolman had established residence there before his arrest twenty years before.

New Jersey began its campaign against loan sharks at the same time. New Jersey had one of the strictest usury laws still on the books, stipulating the maximum rate of interest at the traditional 6 percent for contractual, no-consumption loans. In the face of that law, it was unlikely that out-of-state lenders would take up business residence in the state when they could operate from safer havens, such as Atlanta. The attorney general announced that many lenders were charging interest as high as 36 percent. In 1928, the state legislature began an investigation. Under the USLL, that rate was legal in some states but not New Jersey. The New York tactic of invoking federal postal laws against loan sharks also proved effective in the short-term, much as the Louisiana lottery was constrained a few decades before.

In Illinois in 1927 a Chicago grand jury was convened to investigate widespread salary buying that charged borrowers as much as 240 percent per year for loans of no more than $25. The lenders were national chains of salary buyers charging in excess of 3.5 percent per month, the legal limit, most with headquarters in Atlanta, the same group New York discovered in its investigations. Georgia had all of the necessary laws in place at the time, including a version of the USLL. The great irony was that Georgia, originally, was founded as a colony by James Oglethorpe, with the intention of providing a safe haven for debtors. In the 1920s it was providing a haven for loan sharks.

Mindful of the problems encountered with unlicensed lenders even as the USLL and versions of it made their ways through state legislatures, the Russell Sage Foundation mounted another campaign against loan sharks in 1927. Leon Henderson promised to use its resources in the renewed battle by enlisting the help of employers in protecting their workers against usurers. Several railroads pledged their support. In Kansas City, a local ordinance was used to protect sixty workers who had been forced into bankruptcy by local lenders. In Alabama, less success was achieved when an anti-loan shark bill failed to pass in the state legislature. Passing an anti-loan shark law alone was not enough to defeat unlicensed lenders; victims of sharks and salary buyers needed help from employers in the battle. This was a natural outcome of the slow growth in wages in the 1920s. Those at the bottom of the economic ladder fared the worst. As the *Chicago Tribune* noted, "negroes and poor whites are the greatest victims of the usurist."

The state of usury laws and small loan laws in 1929 demonstrated that the country still was divided, much as it had been before the loan shark drive began twenty years before. States tended to follow neighboring states in passing laws and distance still dictated usury ceilings where they existed. The Middle Atlantic states still conformed to a 6 percent ceiling, along with other small loan laws, while New England followed Massachusetts's lead by abolishing the old ceilings while adopting specific laws for industrial lenders, a USLL, credit union laws, and pawnbroking laws. On the West Coast, higher usury ceilings prevailed while, in the Plains and Mountain West states, there was a paucity of laws despite a long tradition of political unrest and vociferous complaints about usury, especially charged to farmers.

As 1929 approached the lamentations and indignation over usury resurfaced. The *Washington Post* noted that the usurer "negotiates his nefarious transaction when his victim is so bewildered by financial pressure that he does not question the cost of the relief offered."[66] What was not said was that millions of people had relied on the services of loan sharks in the past and continued to do so. Delivering better retail banking was still a policy goal but relied on individual financial institutions to deliver the service rather than originating from Washington, D.C. The USLL, while a constructive beginning to curb excesses in this long-standing problem, too often relied upon state bankers sitting in legislatures to pass a bill inimical to their own interests. And the call money market continued to divert funds better suited for loans for productive purposes. The cost after 1929 would be high.

CHAPTER FOUR
THE CRASH AS A CREDIT EVENT

DURING THE LATTER PART OF THE 1920S, IT WAS CLEAR that loan sharking had not been defeated. The campaign to establish the Uniform Small Loan Law (USLL) had managed to introduce some order and regulation into small, retail lending, but there were no signs of a significant victory over loan sharks. Usury had become embedded in many practices, such as installment buying, and would be difficult to root out by state regulators and legislators, and most had come to realize that lending small amounts at 36 percent interest was no bargain for the borrower.

In the late 1920s the public mood was more jubilant than at any time in the twentieth century. The United States had become a consumer society, and goods of all sorts were on offer to the public. The costs of purchasing on time were not as important to the buyer as accumulating the goods, and the average household was becoming more leveraged than at any time in the past. The stock market continued to rise and was a source of quick riches, or so it was claimed. In a comment published in the *Ladies' Home Journal* in August 1929, John Raskob, the chairman of the Democratic National Committee and a well-known investor, remarked that "everyone ought to be rich," and gave his reasons why the stock market was a sound place to make a fortune. Loan sharking was having an effect on everyday life for the average worker, but easy money was the topic *de jour*. Even without understanding the intricacies of credit and the markets, some commentators were aware that there was a potential for a very unhappy ending.

During the 1920s credit conditions in the United States had improved. Progress had been made in providing small loans and mortgages at more reasonable rates than in the past but, structurally, many of these loans still had onerous conditions attached that left borrowers vulnerable. Repayment terms often were short, with mortgages requiring full repayment, with interest, within five to seven years. When combined with even shorter periods for consumer durables, such as cars, purchased on the installment plan, it became obvious that the average wage earner faced an uphill battle in servicing his debts. Wages grew slowly in the 1920s despite the outward appearances of a boom, so reliance on borrowed money was becoming more prevalent. The 1920s marked the appearance of the American consumer society but it hinged on credit to sustain itself.

Fifty years of combating usury in one manner or other had produced mixed results. The USLL had been passed in a majority of the states in various forms, but the legal rates allowed hardly were encouraging. At 3.5 percent per month maximum, the annualized rate still could amount to 42 percent for a year or around 36 percent if the loan was extended for another six months at a lower, stipulated rate. While certainly better than 100-plus percent, the rate was still extremely high considering that the Fed discount rate ranged from 3.5 to 6 percent between 1925 and 1930.

Franklin D. Roosevelt related his own experience as a lender when he was governor of New York. Speaking to a convention of credit unions in Georgia, he recounted an experience that occurred during one of his visits to Warm Springs, which he frequently visited for his health. Telling the delegates that the biblical prohibitions against usury frequently were violated, he noted, "I am sorry to say that a great many people in the State of Georgia and a great many people in the State of New York are failing to live up to the precept of the bible not to practice usury. They are continually charging usury to their fellow citizens." He was well aware that the major unlicensed lenders in New York during the latter 1920s were headquartered in Atlanta. After praising the work of credit unions for providing low consumer interest rates, he went on to describe a personal experience with lending to a poor but creditworthy borrower. He told the story of a poor local black tenant farmer in Georgia who had scraped together some money to buy a farm. Banks and others were charging 14 percent for a mortgage at the time, so the farmer asked FDR to lend him $300, which the governor agreed to do. When the farmer asked how much the interest would be, he mentioned to the governor that he could not afford more than 10 percent. Roosevelt asked him if 6 percent would be agreeable. "He almost dropped dead," FDR continued. "I let him have the money and it is almost paid off now."[1]

Since New York was at the center of the usury controversy and had suffered from Atlanta loan sharking firms, the comments were dismissed as tendentious. It had already been considered uneconomical to lend at the old 6 percent rate, so the governor was using the occasion to make a point. Someone of his wealth could afford to make a small loan based on a personal judgment of a borrower's character, but those in the money lending business had many other factors to consider, which cost time and money. But the point was valid as far as real estate was concerned.

Opponents of usury and loan sharking included other colorful characters also fighting for a cause that was losing ground. Judge Kennesaw Mountain Landis of the federal bench in Chicago, later a commissioner of baseball, was known admiringly in the press as the "Hellcat of the Federal Court." Originally nominated to the court by Theodore Roosevelt in 1905, he was a long-time foe of loan sharks and made his disdain of them known at every opportunity. Since the earlier part of the century, he wreaked as much havoc as possible on their operations and sent several members of a Chicago loan shark organization to prison. He once remarked that "porch-climbers and burglars are perfect gentlemen compared with loan sharks." His disdain also extended to their lawyers, who were "no better than they are."[2] He threatened to banish lawyers who had represented high-interest lenders from appearing in his court.

Similar experiences were widespread. In 1929 a national business publication recounted the story of a young letter carrier who lost his child to illness and found himself indebted to loan sharks as a result. Luckily, he consulted a local credit union, where the treasurer, knowing that loan sharks rarely pressed their case in the face of stiff opposition, negotiated his debt down to $800 from $3,500. Then the employees of the credit union cosigned the note to guarantee the debt. As the magazine noted, "usury can be eliminated by the creation of [more] credit. It cannot be eliminated by scolding the usurer."[3] The author of the article noted that the highest rate he had personally seen among loan sharks was 3,600 percent. This was in spite of the partial success of the USLL. The story was similar to those from the nineteenth century before any loan sharking laws were passed.

The anti-loan shark movement was widespread and had support from prominent personalities. But loan sharking remained a thorny problem and its economic consequences were not explored beyond relatively superficial analyses of competition and the supply of loanable funds. The support that the Russell Sage Foundation attracted from industrial lenders eager to be associated with it, such as Household Finance, suggested that its program was more acceptable to high-interest lenders than to state legislators or policymakers. The blueprint offered by the USLL was easily circumvented by lenders who could still claim they were adhering to the letter of the law. Advocates of usury ceilings discovered that there were many easily exploited ways to circumvent a well-intentioned law.

FORTIFYING THE FRONT LINE

In 1929 the Russell Sage Foundation went on renewed offensive against loan sharks. The intent was not to continue pressing for the USLL but to save it in its original form. Skepticism was building in some states about the maximum interest rates allowed. Although almost thirty states had adopted the law, many in the Midwest wanted to rescind it because they felt the terms of around 3.5 percent per month were too harsh. A bill was introduced in the Indiana legislature to reduce the rate from 42 percent to 18 percent. Similar measures were introduced in Ohio and Missouri. The Indiana bill drew Leon Henderson, director of the foundation, to Indianapolis to argue for the higher rate on the same grounds that had been argued before: the higher rate would draw more legitimate lenders and discourage loan sharks. The foundation claimed that loan sharks were behind the new Indiana measures, hoping that new lower rates would eliminate competition for their services by forcing legitimate lenders out of business. The argument was not that convincing, however, since it was an admission that the new, higher rates were not working as well as hoped.

By the late 1920s it was becoming clear that unlicensed lenders were not the only loan sharks, only those charging the highest rates. As far as small consumption loans were concerned, loan sharks had effectively been able to circumvent the technicalities of the small loan laws. Increasingly, they refused to make loans under $300. When a potential customer said that a $100 loan was all he needed, the lender suggested he would lend him $301 and the customer could immediately return $201 to him. What was not mentioned was that the original loan required 3.5 percent interest per month on the total, or $10.54. That amount was still owed even though the customer only used $100. The effective rate became 10.54 percent per month, or 126 percent per year.

The loan shark claimed his rates were in line with state laws, but the effective interest paid was outrageously high. With the nominal amount above $300, the loan shark could argue that the loan did not fall under the USLL in any event.

The salary buying business used similar techniques. At the time the USLL was passed, most wages were well under $300 per week and salary buyers changed their documents to note that the advance they offered was a "sale" of notes rather than a loan. Calling this the "loan shark's subterfuge," the Russell Sage Foundation noted that lenders began "purchasing" salaries at a discount that reflected high rates of interest and, "By calling his return discount instead of interest, he sought to get a return far beyond the legal maximum. And he could operate without license and supervision."[4]

Illinois had similar experiences with its version of the USLL. The state declared war against salary buyers operating in its major cities in 1929. At the same time, the state legislature considered lowering the maximum monthly interest rate to as low as 2 percent from its current level of 3.5 percent. Monthly rates below 2 percent were considered uneconomical. Even at that lower level, there was fear that loan sharks would return in force. One prominent businessman was worried about the actions of the legislature. He noted that "if they start tampering with the law, they are liable to take the teeth out of it, and if that happens things will revert to the old conditions where the grasping loan sharks flourished."[5] In that respect, the point made by the Russell Sage Foundation two decades before had become axiomatic but the tolerable upper limit remained under considerable discussion.

New York also provided a confusing example of low rates producing results that could be interpreted differently. The Russell Sage Foundation claimed that the state's lower rates for consumer loans, 2.5 percent per month since 1915, had dissuaded legitimate lenders. They used the $26 million that Albert Ottinger previously claimed was extracted from the local economy as proof that the New York laws needed fixing. State officials did not disagree with the numbers but did disagree about the problem itself. They realized that the problem of loan sharking had never been effectively solved, with or without the foundation's efforts. In 1928, it was estimated that industrial lenders had made $75 million in consumption loans in New York, with the number expected to increase every year. Many commentators thought that the entry of large commercial banks like National City into the field would increase the number to as much as $500 million per year.[6] New York officials saw it differently. Loan shark activities had become deeply ingrained in the public and would not be weeded out easily. New York had been plagued by out-of-state lenders during the 1920s despite its lower than average rates and was suffering as a result. How was it that a moderate level of consumer interest rates could be superseded by loan sharks charging higher rates?

New York officials realized that loan sharking had never been defeated in the one area that plagued urban areas the most, salary buying; the almost invisible weapon of loan sharks. As a result, the state responded with proposed legislation that would have raised the monthly interest charge for legitimate lenders from 2.5 to 3 percent and encouraged other institutions to enter small lending for loans less than $300. But the salary buying problem remained. As the legislation passed the state senate, it became clear that all small loans were being lumped together in one category. The idea was that a higher rate would benefit small one-time borrowers as well as those needing their salaries in advance. The problem was that the salary buying programs were disciplined; the borrower got less in return for the advance and had little option but to continue in the program, being quickly hooked on the plans. And lenders still reported loan problems to employers. By lumping the two types of loans together, New York inadvertently made abolishing salary buying more difficult.

New York had not passed a version of the USLL by 1928. That year, Attorney General Albert Ottinger again stated that his campaign against loan sharks would continue. He made six proposals designed to stamp them out. Five were in accord with the general principles of the small loan laws and one was more controversial. In that case, he proposed that employers pay employees once a week rather than every two weeks, which was the standard at the time. It was the most unpopular of the proposals, widely criticized by employers as too time-consuming and costly to administer. While it was designed to attack salary buyers, employers sided with the salary buyers. Unwittingly or not, they provided a strong argument for allowing salary buyers to remain in business.

Mortgage Market Problems

The building and real estate boom that developed after the First World War continued throughout the 1920s. Until the Florida real estate collapse, the market had remained strong, but after 1926 it began to show signs of weakness nationwide. As with similar problems in the earlier part of the century, the problems appeared outside the largest urban areas of New York City and Chicago and further fueled the arguments of Republican insurgents and Democrats who were critical of the Fed and Wall Street. Strong urban real estate markets and weaker rural ones only reinforced the notion of two Americas that Populists had complained of years before.

Despite the progress made in providing loans for residential mortgages by commercial lenders, many were still made on a private basis between individuals. In one case, a New York couple borrowed $75,000 from Thomas Alva Edison to purchase a property in the Bronx. The terms were stringent. The loan was to be repaid in three installments at 6 percent interest. If a payment was missed, the loan immediately came due. In 1925 the borrowers failed to make a payment and the inventor sued. It took almost four years for the case to reach the courts. Ironically, Edison was a producer of one of the early silent films about usury.

The shifting tide in residential mortgages, in particular, was anticipated by lenders, and new products were developed to help homeowners finance their purchases while charging high rates of interest at the same time. One popular method of augmenting a residential mortgage was for homeowners to take out a second mortgage on their property in an attempt to extend the repayment schedule. The banks that did retail mortgage business did not offer the product, however, and usually steered borrowers to industrial lenders. The interest rate was much higher than the 6 percent common on mortgages and often could reach the 35 to 40 percent level of other loans offered by the same lenders. This put a portion of mortgage payments in the same rate range as consumer loans and caused great difficulties in the mortgage market in the latter 1920s.

The market for securitized mortgages in the 1920s was active and demand for them helped fuel the real estate boom. Many of the collateralized issues were sold in denominations of as little as $100, although nominal values of $500 to $1,000 were more common. One of the more interesting features was that many paid their interest in gold, reminiscent of the exception clause controversy in the nineteenth century, suggesting that many of the bonds were marketed to foreigners. Equally, many of the issues supporting new building projects were eschewed by institutional investors and sold to the retail investing public, who were less familiar with the intricacies of the market than their institutional counterparts.[7] Securities backed by large urban buildings seemed to defy what was becoming a weakening trend. Demand for mortgage-backed securities, known technically as guaranteed mortgage participation certificates, was strong even in the late 1920s. New issues totaled almost $1.2 billion in 1927 and 1928 alone, compared with $2.2 billion issued between 1919 and 1926. By 1929, about 25 percent of those outstanding were in technical default and those outstanding in the secondary market sold for about 75 percent of par.[8] Despite the spotty record of earlier issues, investors were still keen to buy them since they offered a reasonable yield spread over U.S. Treasury issues and had interest paid in gold. They were encouraged by pundits and the press. *Barron's* suggested investors buy mortgage bonds of Armour and Company, the company founded by commodities trader P. D. Armour in the nineteenth century.[9]

Many residential mortgages were provided by life insurance companies. In 1928 $375 million in residential mortgages was recorded, an average of $3,500 each for over 100,000 homes.[10] These were not directly made by the insurance companies but were packaged as mortgage-related securities bought by them as investments. In 1927 the number of first mortgages reached a historic high, with over $1 billion created. New York and Chicago properties accounted for 54 and 37 percent of those mortgages, respectively. Forty percent of the total was for apartment houses, 26 percent for office buildings, and 10 percent for hotels.[11] Not all sections of the country benefited, however. Investors were attracted to real estate in the metropolitan areas or immediately adjacent to them. In 1928 it was estimated that 80 percent of the property in Yonkers, New York, was owned by nonresidents of the city. Investors were interested particularly in apartment buildings that were being built within a short commute from New York City. The city was the great suburb of New York at the time, with a mix of one-family homes and apartment buildings and prided itself on its distinctiveness. A realtor noted, somewhat unkindly, that "the type of apartment which is being built in Westchester County must not be confused with the Bronx type. Westchester is building apartments being patterned after the Park Avenue projects and they attract the highest type of tenants."[12]

The New York boom was shared by Chicago. Of all the mortgage-related securities issued in the early 1920s, 72 percent were backed by buildings in New York and Chicago (46 and 26 percent, respectively). Detroit, the third most popular location, accounted for only 7 percent. The reason for the two top cities dominating the market appears to have been bond investors' fondness for tall buildings and skyscrapers, thought to be excellent collateral backing.[13] Other less exclusive properties outside these favored areas fared less well. Between 1926 and 1929 the number of residential mortgages either in foreclosure or delinquent in payments rose substantially. The number almost doubled from 68,000 to 134,900.[14] The nationwide building boom that began after the war started to slow substantially despite the greater availability of residential, nonfarm mortgages. Homeowners and consumers were becoming extended financially, but investor demand kept the supply of credit available for commercial building.

American mortgage bonds were not the only ones to suffer in the late 1920s. The Federal Reserve had purchased a small amount of the German Central Bank for Agriculture's (*Rentenbank*) 6 percent bonds due in 1960 at a price of 93.50. Within a year they had declined fourteen full points to 79.50. The bonds were secured by direct German agricultural mortgages that were not valued at more than 40 percent of their assessed value. The cloudy political climate in Germany had a deleterious effect on the issue and other similar bond prices, especially the long-term dated, that reflected the long-term nature of German mortgage lending. With a yield to maturity of 7.75 percent, *Barron's* concluded that they "appear attractive as an investment holding for national banks."[15]

The large number of foreclosures prompted many mortgage bankers to call for uniform federal legislation on the foreclosure process. Differences in the foreclosure process in the states and the large-scale securitization that took place in the 1920s militated for uniform procedures, especially in the marketing of new mortgage-backed securities coming to market. "In the matter of foreclosure clauses alone," commented one mortgage banker, "the State laws provide for redemptions in case of default at from a few days to several years." In Connecticut, a large mortgage company was charged with fraud for failing to disclose defaulted loans it held and continuing payments to cover up the problem caused by an overvaluation of its assets. Many of these issues would linger into 1929 and play a significant role in the market crash in October.[16]

"STREET MONEY" AND BANKING

Concerns about consumer interest rates were overshadowed by a powerful discussion in Washington, D.C., about the role of the Federal Reserve and call money in the market boom of 1929. The Republican insurgents continued their pressure on the Fed, insisting that legislation was needed to reform the banking system, not economic policies coming from an institution dominated by Wall Street bankers and their sympathizers.

Henrik Shipstead, a Republican insurgent from Minnesota, introduced a resolution in the Senate in early 1929 requiring the Fed to disclose any discussions it had had since 1924 with foreign central banks regarding the advance notice it gave the Bank of England and others about its plans for changing the discount rate. The intent was to discover what effect such policy tips had, if any, on the level of stock market prices, the value of gold and the dollar, and the amount of money foreign banks had on loan in the New York call market. While the request sounded like a conspiracy theory probe, the relationship between central bankers, especially Benjamin Strong of the New York Fed and Montagu Norman, Governor of the Bank of England, was known to be particularly strong.

In the mid-1920s, the Fed maintained a policy of keeping U.S. interest rates low to help support the British pound and aid agricultural exports at the same time. That move should have appeased Republican insurgents but only tended to reinforce the conspiracy theories in the Midwest and support the real estate boom. Also in 1929 Smith Brookhart went a step further by announcing that he was planning to introduce another bill to stop bank loans from fueling stock market speculation similar to the one he had first announced in 1928. Calling the Federal Reserve Act the most "colossal failure in all legislative history," he noted that the central bank had failed to stop market speculation and had fueled the asset bubble, instead, by its incongruous policies. Noting that banks were making speculative loans to the stock market but the Fed was prohibited from rediscounting such loans, he asserted that "it is preposterous to claim that the Government of the United States or the various states should be called upon to furnish a banking system to sustain an institution of stock gamblers."[17] To partially alleviate the problem, he again suggested that the Fed be allowed to pay 2 percent on reserves it held on behalf of its member banks.

Usury began to assume a more prominent role in the discussion about call money lending after 1926 than it had earlier in the decade.

One indication was a suggestion that a new national usury law be passed. One sponsor of the idea was New York State Senator David Floyd Davis, a businessman who served as president of the National Association for Procuring the Enactment of a National Usury Statute, a group organized for the purpose. The bills introducing the idea would be presented in Congress but would not amend the Federal Reserve Act. Instead, the Treasury would be empowered to coordinate the usury ceiling with the various states, following the National Bank Act of 1864. Davis stated:

> It is the view of those interesting themselves in the enactment of the proposed law that had an adequate call money usury law been in existence there would have been no occasion for the reverberant warning to the Federal Reserve member banks of the New York district . . . those enlisted in this movement consider the necessity of warning the member banks of the New York district as clear evidence that there was disloyalty, and to put it gently, unethical practices existing within their own family circle; and they believe the temptation of high call money rates was the corrupting influence.[18]

The proposed bill gained little support. The corrupting influence he referred to occurred during the winter of 1929. At the beginning of the year, the rising stock market and inflated asset prices began to worry those on Wall Street, who feared that the Federal Reserve would act to curtail speculation and, especially, margin trading. The most obvious tool the Fed could use to stop margin buying and short selling was its discount rate. Raising that rate would send a signal to the market that more expensive money across the board was needed to bring stock prices back into a more normal range. The discount rate was raised on three occasions in 1928. The policy attempted to discourage speculators, not lenders.

At the same time, two Feds existed, for all practical purposes, and an apparent conflict arose between them. The Federal Reserve Board in Washington had the ultimate decision-making power but the New York Fed bank was the most powerful of the twelve regional banks and implemented most of the practical market operations that would spell success or failure for policy. This was the problem the Republican insurgents always feared; that New York bankers dominated the New York Fed and would act in concert to protect their own interests, especially when the board was indecisive or uncertain about the economy. Even the *Wall Street Journal* acknowledged this indirectly. In January 1929 the paper stated:

> The directors of the Federal Reserve Banks and members of the Federal Reserve Board face a situation not only extraordinarily complicated but without precedent. The course of interest rates and credit conditions the balance of this year depend, to an unusual degree, on the Federal Reserve policy . . . there is every reason to believe the Federal Reserve Banks are equally baffled for, after all, reserve bankers are in possession of little more information than Wall Street collectively.[19]

The policy problem was that credit seemed to be expanding faster than the economy in general. The second problem was whether to include broker loans in the overall credit statistics. The *Wall Street Journal* reported that general business activity in 1928 increased by 2 percent over the previous year while bank credit increased by around 6 percent. But if broker loans were added, $2 billion, the increase was 8 percent.[20]

This was the problem faced by the Fed. Controlling the stock market indices, reaching historic highs monthly, was not the primary target of Fed policy. The overvalued market was symptomatic of a larger problem: the expansion of credit. Broker loans had become a form of shadow banking, a term that became widely used eighty years later during another financial crisis. Nonbank organizations were providing credit funds outside the banking system and they were being bootlegged in through large New York City banks. On this basis, it seemed that the Federal Reserve Board would target broker call loans to reduce the supply. That would also help small businesses and individuals by encouraging banks to make potentially productive loans, not those simply for speculation.

The term "bootleg loans" was the banking equivalent of bootleg spirits. They were produced outside regulation and often came from a foreign source; in this case Europe rather than Canada, as in the case of spirit production. In the case of alcohol, the producers were targeted. But in the case of high-interest loans, critics contended that the Federal Reserve actually protected the producers. Both social evils were targeted with what appeared on the surface to be rigorous regulation but, at the end of the day, both were able to operate openly with only sporadic enforcement. The bootleg loan was the Wall Street equivalent of a speakeasy. In the case of call money lending, actual regulation or enforcement did not exist and no one bothered examining it for potential accusations of usury until the latter part of the 1920s.

The unregulated nature of this round-tripping of loanable funds was described succinctly in *The Nation:*

> When the corporations withdrew their funds from banks to make brokers' loans the banks in turn advanced money to the corporations by drawing upon the Federal Reserve Bank. Now the Federal Reserve Board has declared that its funds should not be used to bolster up the speculative system in this way. The ultimate effect of this warning will be important although it is not certain that any action by the Federal Reserve Board can check the present speculative fever.[21]

The remark proved correct within only a few weeks. The New York Fed bank favored raising the discount rate, a move that would apply across the board but would leave the call money rate untouched. Other Fed banks, including Chicago, were also thought to favor the policy but the board in Washington, D.C., and the individual banks remained silent on the issue as rumors and speculation swirled in the press. The uncertainty finally spilled over to the market. In late March 1929 the stock market began to deteriorate over the fears that interest rates would rise soon. Call money lenders nervously refused to extend loans overnight. A large wire house broker, E. A. Pierce and Company, suspended margin trading on the Chicago Stock Exchange, citing the tendency of

Chicago banks to call margin loans at short notice.[22] The move unsettled all the stock markets and many small speculators were forced to the wall by the drop in prices while the Chicago Fed bank and others left the discount rate unchanged at 6 percent.

Two months before the October crash, the rate was allowed to exceed 7 percent on demand call loans, those with a term of sometimes more than one day although still technically callable at any time. The *Chicago Tribune* noted that "this action will bring the rate in line with that charged in New York and will do much to keep the Middle Western funds at home instead of being sent to the East where heretofore higher rates could be obtained."[23]

Several days later, on March 27, the Federal Reserve Board met in D.C. The stock market suffered another bad day, again anticipating a rate rise, but no decision was reached after a two-hour meeting. Call money reached intraday highs of as much as 20 percent as many suppliers of funds began to withdraw their money from the loan market and those that remained were bid up. In light of that, the Fed took no action. Criticisms of the central bank arose from many quarters as a result. Representative Louis McFadden of Pennsylvania proposed that the House Monetary and Banking Committee hold hearings on the Fed and its role in curbing speculation.

The market clearly was looking for official action on rampant speculation and inflated asset prices but the Fed did not provide guidance. Then on March 29 the New York Fed bank, led by Charles Mitchell of National City Bank and a New York Fed director, stepped into the breach with action of its own.

In the last week of March broker call loans dropped $144 million. Many of the withdrawals came from out-of-town banks. The Fed had been quietly discouraging smaller member banks outside the money centers from making bootleg loans, apparently taking notice of proposals made by Smith Brookhart and others but clearly not acknowledging outside pressure. Before the Fed Board could react publicly, the New York bank took matters into its own hands. Mitchell said that National City would add funds regardless of the "attitude of the Federal Reserve

Board." He announced that National City Bank was providing funds to the call money market with the assent of the New York Fed bank to make up the shortage and lower the call money rate. Mitchell stated that "we lent on our own account in the call money market approximately $250 million and that compared with our normal amount of from $100 million to $125 million."

Expanding on the operation, he gave an example of how well leverage worked in the stock market during bull markets. If an investor held $100,000 worth of stocks employing $20,000 on 20 percent margin, then $80,000 worth of credit was employed. If the holdings were sold and the new investor acquired them for $200,000 on 40 percent margin, or $80,000 (at the higher rates charged by brokers during the market fall), then $120,000 worth of credit was employed. He concluded that "the question of stock prices is inextricably bound up with that of the expansion in credit and this is one point that the Federal Reserve authorities apparently do not dare discuss."[24] His solution for investors was simple: maintain less leverage in trading accounts so that a market drop would not trigger a margin call. He did not advocate any official policy action other than supplying the market with funds. This was an example of encouraging the users of funds to dampen their enthusiasm, not openly discouraging the providers of funds.

The New York operation had the desired effect and stock prices resumed their upward trend. Most market commentators were in favor of the action. The *Financial Chronicle* acknowledged that the timing of Mitchell's public pronouncements was unfortunate but, "Mr. Mitchell and his action has saved the day for the financial community. No one can say how great a calamity would have happened had he not stepped into the breach at the right moment."[25] Other comments were less favorable. The New York correspondent of *The Economist* noted that the bulls had won the day over moderates and openly questioned the future of the market. Senator Carter Glass of Virginia called for Mitchell's immediate dismissal from the New York Fed bank. Glass, a former newspaperman who also served as Woodrow Wilson's Treasury Secretary was known to be conservative and irascible at times. He favored the idea of a congressionally regulated money market, not one influenced by Fed policy. Noting his irascibility, the *New York Times* commented that "he is one of the rapid-burners in public life. This is not to deny that a great deal of useful light ordinarily accompanies his heat . . . Senator Glass seems to have confused a temporary emergency with a permanent policy. The banks did not come forward with funds to promote speculation but to prevent what threatened to be a serious crisis in the money market."[26] Most commentators rallied to Mitchell's defense.

Nationally syndicated financial columnist M. S. Rukeyser remarked that:

> although Senator Carter Glass of Virginia asked the Federal Reserve Board to discharge Mr. Mitchell as a Class A director of the Federal Reserve Board of New York, the Board had no criticism to make of his conduct in averting a money crisis . . . members of the Board, however, would have preferred that in his public statement Mr. Mitchell had indicated that such a statement was not inconsistent with Federal Reserve policy instead of letting some people infer that he was defying the Federal Reserve.[27]

But that seemed to be the case, although Mitchell was seen as savior of the markets at the time. After the crash in October, public sentiment turned against him.

Outside New York, opinions varied from the standard criticisms of Mitchell. An Ohio newspaper was concerned that high rates in the broker loan market were dissuading banks and other investors from buying government bonds: "America's recent usury debauch, pleasant for money lenders, worries the national treasury considerably. One result has been a drop of $500,000,000 in the value of government bonds of which more than 11 billions are outstanding . . . Months of profitable usury, stimulated by the Federal Reserve and unchecked by any government agency, have destroyed the bankers' appetite for low rate government bonds."[28]

Before the October crash, Henry Ford joined the discussion. He wrote that government bond borrowing was ineffective and costly.

Instead, he suggested it should be replaced by the issuance of additional currency, which could be retired at any time, at no cost to Washington. If a project cost $30 million, the government should simply print the amount and pay for the costs involved. When the project was finished and began producing revenue, the amount could be retired from circulation at no cost.[29] Ford also called new financial ideas of the period "financial engineering," one of the first times the term was used. The call money problem was encouraging other discussions.

A nagging question about the March incident remained. Money was being withdrawn from the broker loan market but intraday rates were high. While the policy of the Fed as a whole was clear if not slow, the rapid exit of call money from the market was not as evident. Why did the suppliers of funds begin to abandon the stock market when they could receive almost 20 percent on an intraday basis? The only apparent risk they immediately faced was a sharp market downturn that would severely damage margin traders.

When the market resumed its upward climb after the March incident, traders legitimately argued that high margin rates impeded their ability to remain in the market during times of distress, causing them to sell. And that, in turn, could trigger charges of usury since the call money rates greatly exceeded New York's official usury ceiling of 6 percent when they were bid up, although it was legal in New York. But more important, lenders did not want to be blamed for a crash after the fact. Banks, especially, did not want to face accusations of usury, real or implied.

While the market discussed the outflow of funds in March and April 1929, the exit was not as large as it would be later in the year. The upward trajectory of the amount of broker loans resumed in July, reaching its peak in September before declining in October and, particularly, in November. At the same time another measure of leverage in the stock market was being monitored by the New York Stock Exchange (NYSE) that revealed patterns that would link what was called the market "break" in March with the much larger one that occurred in late October. The exchange compared the amount of broker loans outstanding against the total capitalization of stocks listed. It discovered that when the amount was 10 percent or higher, a break occurred. In March 1926 the ratio stood at 10 percent, and it reached around 9.80 to 9.90 percent again in the weeks before Black Friday in October, when the market already was showing signs of weakness. But since it had not actually touched 10 percent, *Barron's* felt that the market was still in reasonable territory. On October 28, 1929, the day before Black Friday, the news-paper commented that "if a 10 percent ratio, or thereabouts, means a breaking point in the stock market, its coming has not been heralded in this case by monthly ratios immediately preceding."[30]

Part of the explanation lay in the market for new securities issues in the months preceding the crash. Many of the new issues of both stocks and bonds were in syndication and dealers borrowed from the broker loan market to finance those inventories until they were sold. The prob-lem puzzled the Fed. Borrowing to fund positions originated from both brokers *and* dealers, although the numbers were lumped together and a clear picture of exactly who or what was responsible for the increase confused even the central bank. Technically, was it broker loans to fund the investment bankers' unsold inventories of new issues or broker loans that went to speculators? On the eve of the crash, the amount of call money on loan remained stable, although the market tenor was far from strong. This was due to the large number of new stock issues currently in syndication. Ten individual issues were in the pipeline, with a total value of $270 million, accounting for demand for term broker loans when secondary market activity was declining. The largest of the issues were Bethlehem Steel and Union Carbide, along with St. Regis Paper and Pacific Gas and Electric.[31] The capital-raising process was different from secondary market operations but the two were lumped together for reporting purposes.

The Federal Reserve's apparent inaction on further increases in the discount rate was noted by Senator William H. King, a Democrat of Utah, who called for an examination of the Fed in May 1929. The focus of the inquiry would be whether the central bank was aiding the market rise through structural deficiencies in its own organization. The term usury reappeared and was mentioned since there was a suspicion that banks were charging too much for their services in term loans to the securities markets; this was among many other lines of inquiry. While the individual charge was not damaging, when combined with many others of a similar nature, it gave the impression that high interest rates were at the heart of the market's rise. Many began to believe that the true and steady profits from the sharp rise in the market index was being made by the banks lending call money as well as speculators cashing in on quick gains once those new issues were released for trading.

Prior to early 1929 the matter of usury often was forgotten in the stock market. That began to change in the spring of 1929, especially after so many smaller investors were severely hurt by the money market problems in March and April, when they received margin calls they could not answer. The New York usury law remained at 6 percent although corporate lending (loans over $5,000) was exempt. But other legal problems remained. Many of the call loans made to speculators were term, or time, loans and were structured differently than an ordinary overnight call loan. If they were for less than $5,000, technically, they were subject to the usury ceiling. Since call money usually was charged at higher rates, the lenders potentially were liable to prosecution under the New York usury statutes.

The *Wall Street Journal* reported the problem in March 1929, stating that "because of the legal question involved most banks are refraining from lending any times funds at all at prevailing rates, which accounts for the dearth of such funds now." The paper quoted a recent bank study that concluded its discussion of the problem by suggesting to bank lenders that "with respect to loans made to individuals or to partnerships you are limited to charging the rate of interest provided for by Section 200 of the Banking Law [of New York], viz. 6 percent." The study was designed to advise banks and suggest ways to avoid further problems in New York. This was central to the issue because many Wall Street firms that catered to investors were organized as partnerships and lending to them and their customers at higher than the usury ceiling exposed the bank lenders to potential litigation. As a result, the study concluded by stating, "We think that in making so-called 'Street loans' for corporations and individuals you should endeavor to make all of these loans demand [overnight] loans, where the rate of interest is more than 6 percent, because so long as they are demand loans the question [of usury] could never arise."[32]

Term call money presented a special problem in the market for new securities issues. When a new issue of stocks or bonds was initially sold in the market, the settlement period for investors to make payment was longer than it would be later in the century. If payment was required in a week, investors could borrow in the term market to cover their costs. This was similar to the account period used in the London Stock market and was standard practice on stock exchanges. If the issue performed poorly and sank in price after payment, investors immediately would dump the stock, adding to market instability. If the money was called by the lender for any reason, the same effect occurred. The $5,000 amount appeared small, but margin requirements at the time were regulated by brokers, not any federal securities or banking regulators. As a result, a $5,000 margin loan could represent as much as a $25,000 stock purchase, a considerable sum since the average nonfarm worker earned less than $2,000 per year. That sort of leverage was behind the market's rise and subsequent collapse.

"INVISIBLE" BANKING AND THE CRASH

When the Federal Reserve was founded, what was known about existing conditions and the influence of commercial banks was put under its regulatory umbrella. Not included or as clear were the activities into which they expanded after World War I as the economy grew and the consumer boom and stock market rally developed. The expansion of banks into the broker loan market and the subsequent participation of nonbank lenders challenged the limits of existing regulation and proved to run ahead of any remedies coming from Washington, D.C.

The problem with the Fed and interest rates was put in a broader perspective by prominent Cleveland banker Leonard P. Ayres. Trained as a statistician, he graduated from Boston University in 1902 and began a career in education teaching in Puerto Rico, quickly becoming superintendent of schools. In 1908 Ayres joined the Russell Sage Foundation to head its education department. During World War I, he organized a department of statistics for the military and, after the war, joined the Cleveland Trust Company. He spent the rest of his career studying economic trends, with a special interest in the stock market. Speaking before the United States Chamber of Commerce in 1929, he described the American financial system as one of "invisible banking," anticipating the shadow banking of the latter twentieth century. Ayres told his audience, "Out of my investigation of the present credit situation I have come to the conclusion that there is going on in this country a very serious degree of a new kind of credit inflation: one that is rapidly impairing the usefulness of our commercial banking system because it is resulting in taking corporation money out of the banks and banking it in the loan markets." The invisible banking system, he continued:

> is quite different from the regular, legal, organized banking system. It is quite untroubled by state laws. It is never bothered by those recurrent visits of bank examiners. It does not have to report details of its operations to the Federal Reserve System. It does not care what the bank reserves are. It has no obligation, legal or implied, for the safeguarding of the credit system and yet it is in the banking business.[33]

The *Washington Post*, after reporting Ayres's remarks, concluded, "When banks lend money on call at rates exceeding 6 percent do they not actually encourage the 'invisible banking' to which Col. Ayres refers? Everybody, visible and invisible, seems to be ignoring the law against usury."[34] Several days later a reader wrote to the newspaper and asked, "What will become of the banking system of this country if the habit spreads?" The warning went unheeded, despite the obvious dangers to both the economy and the reputation of the Fed. Part of the explanation lay in the constant predictions that all would be well, which came from accepted sources closer to Wall Street than a prominent Cleveland banker.

The *Wall Street Journal* reported on credit market conditions in May and concluded that relatively low rates on time and ordinary call money were prevalent at the time because many lenders refused to extend funds because of the usury law. It concluded one market commentary by noting "these figures belie statements of any serious and fundamental credit stringency."[35] As a weekly market commentary, the point was valid, but in a broader context, the lure of high interest rates, fueled by a desire for margin money, had already done its damage.

Irving Fisher, the well known Yale economist, noted that Ayres's comments about invisible banking "aided signally in diagnosing the ailment of the credit situation with relation to Wall Street . . . but Mr. Ayres fails to state precisely what should be done about it."[36] The *New York Times* recognized the enormity of the problem, however. It stated that Ayres suggestion for some form of legislative control was "sufficiently vague yet it states the nature of the problem. The present chairman of the House Banking Committee has formally declared that it may become necessary to place supervision of the future granting of brokers loans under the Federal Reserve system." Without mentioning McFadden by name, the paper acknowledged the sensitive nature of the topic and supported Ayres.[37]

Nothing came from any of the bills introduced by the insurgents or the short-lived organization for a usury statute but it was clear that usury, call money, and the stock market had been linked. The root causes and potential consequences of excessive call money lending were argued on the floor of Congress as well as in statehouses, but the stock market and the banks were too busy making money to take notice. The reputation of the Wild Jackasses did not help the cause, although the technical arguments they presented in favor of curbing the market were among the most cogent of the decade. After fame in the late 1920s they were quickly forgotten by the mid-1930s. Their legacy would be felt later, when the Banking Act of 1933 and the Securities Exchange Act of 1934 were passed.

Pessimistic views on the impending market crisis were not confined to the insurgents. Even well-known market operators expressed serious misgivings about the market frenzy. William J. Durant, the ex-president of General Motors, Bernard Baruch, the already-legendary Wall Street trader, and Joseph Kennedy, another well-known trader and future chairman of the Securities Exchange Commission, among others, made it known publicly that they were out of the market, at least on the "long" side. Durant was particularly critical of the Fed for creating the speculative binge and called for congressional action to reform it.

The usual pundits in the financial press took note but continued to express guarded optimism, and the mainstream financial press was not alone in their views about the market. Two weeks before the crash, the Harvard Economic Society noted that present conditions were difficult but confidently stated that "we believe that such a decline will not inaugurate a period of prolonged liquidation but will prove intermediate like all other recessions in stock prices since 1921."[38]

In the general euphoria of the period, naysayers outside the financial community were ignored in favor of those who believed the bubble would continue. Three years before the crash, syndicated financial columnist M. S. Rukeyser commented that "in the United States the commentator on market events can be optimistic (or bullish) and with it, and can be wrong and get away and be pessimistic (or bearish) and right and yet be subjected to intense criticism."[39] The comment proved as germane for the future as it was in the 1920s.

The reason for these comments was that the months leading to the crash were not as exuberant as those preceding them. Shortly before the crash, the *Wall Street Journal* reported an optimistic view for the near future, however. "The consensus is that after the current period of adjustment is over, stocks again will rebound and make new highs," the paper claimed in its daily column.[40]

That view was widely held among many companies and bankers. Their reasons were based on their interpretations of the economy. The economy appeared to be on good footing in the last quarter of 1929. Agricultural production was steady and prices were strong, the automobile industry reported a robust order book, and the railroads reported solid earnings. The one questionable spot on the horizon was the building industry, reporting sluggish conditions reflecting the problems in the mortgage market and the overbuilding of the decade. While the *New York Times* was sanguine about the strong outlook, especially in New York and Chicago, it was much less optimistic about broker loans. "The continued expansion of broker loans remains the principal disturbing factor in the general money situation," it commented.[41]

The Fed unexpectedly raised the discount rates from 5 percent to 6 percent in early August as the stock market was heading higher. On August 8, the market took a severe tumble and an estimated $2 billion was shaved off share values. Margin calls were behind the sharp fall. At the same time, the amount of call money in circulation increased by $60 million as lenders responded and supplied the market with funds. These "other" lenders were becoming more identifiable and included individuals as well as corporations and foreigners. Many wealthy individuals were suspected of liquidating stocks and lending the cash to the call money market rather than reinvesting. They took a less risky method of making above-average returns at the expense of smaller investors. And in this instance, they could withdraw their money at any time.

The general mortgage malaise continued and extended to the commercial real estate sector as well as the residential. About a week before the October 24 crash, the American Bond and Mortgage Company, one of the largest sellers of mortgage-backed bonds, fell into financial difficulty. Most of the bonds sold by the company were secured by commercial mortgages, including those on hotels, shopping areas, and apartment buildings. A committee of investors met with the company to determine the fate of fifty-three individual bond issues, totaling $153 million, that were in default or poised to default shortly. The major investors in these securities were insurance companies, and the defaults made them uneasy at a time when asset values were in bubble-like proportions. The company's bond operations finally were assumed by its trustee, the Chicago Title and Trust Company. At the time, the restructuring of the company was portrayed as nothing more than a consolidation of an overextended industry that had become bloated over the preceding decade. Mergers would occur among other companies; the Bankers Bond and Mortgage Company of America would be created from three smaller companies in December 1929.[42]

The late summer of 1929 proved to be the beginning of the overall market decline that was greatly accelerated by the October crash. The market index reached its peak in September before beginning to slip later in the month and continuing to fall into October. Call money available then declined significantly between October and the end of November. Between September 1 and October 1, the ratio of stocks purchased using margin money increased by 13 percent, while the Dow Jones market averages declined by 10 percent. The ratio remained unchanged between October 1 and November 1 as the index dropped 20 percent but then brokers' loans dropped 19 percent although the ratio remained essentially the same. By December the picture was clearer. The value of all stocks dropped 39 percent between October 1 and December 1, brokers' loans declined 51 percent, and the index fell 30 percent.

The collapse in the outstanding amount of broker loans in late 1929, extending into the bear market years that followed, gave further credence to the Fed conspiracy theories of the Republican insurgents. Loans from corporations and foreign entities dropped more significantly than those from New York or regional banks, adding to the sharp drop in the market indices across the board. In each case, when the market dropped, the amount of call money on loan receded. This occurred in March and October 1926; January, February, and June 1928; and March and May 1929.

During the same period, other, briefer, market declines were not accompanied by a drop in broker loans; time loans helped soften the blow until the index recovered in the following days and weeks. But by 1929 the anti-loan sharking campaign of the attorney general in New York began to make some lenders nervous that they could be charged with usury. While prosecution for violating New York statutes was not an immediate concern, charges alone could be a public relations problem, especially considering the more strident anti-loan sharking tone in the latter part of the 1920s. Now that term broker loans had fallen under the usury discussion, many lenders began to withdraw their funds in times of market distress rather than risk poor publicity and potential legal costs for charges against which there was scant defense. Lending above 6 percent was the attraction for those with funds to lend and little could be said to prove otherwise. But now that attraction was shifting to traditional call money, not just term call money.

A sharp decline in broker loans was noticeable just days before the crash. On October 23 *Barron's* noted that broker loans declined for the week by $167 million. The bulk of that was attributable to declines from out-of-town banks ($98 million) and others ($52 million). Call money ended the same week at 6 percent, up 1 percent from the week earlier.[43] But the shift from term call loans to ordinary call loans because of the continuing fear of usury charges was noticeable. The day before the crash Charles Mitchell of National City Bank spoke optimistically about the market. "The whole issue, as I see, is a shifting in the form of credit from long time to short time and not necessarily in the amount of credit," he commented upon his return from a trip to Europe.[44] The shift benefited bankers because regular call money was slightly more liquid than term.

The market began to crash on October 24, dubbed "Black Thursday." Winston Churchill, until recently the Chancellor of the Exchequer in Britain, witnessed the chaos on the floor of the New York Stock Exchange from the visitors' gallery. His presence only exacerbated the suspicions of the Republican insurgents that his policies and those of the Bank of England contributed to the market decline. Suspected collusion between the Fed and the Bank of England over interest rates and gold still was strong. The sharp drop in the market only fueled suspicions. When the market began its steep decline, however, critics and professional traders shared a common sentiment; they all saw it coming but had no means to prevent it.

By late afternoon, the ticker tape was half a day behind and the back offices of the brokerage firms and the exchange itself were having a difficult time keeping their heads above the avalanche of sell orders. After the close, it was announced that the day's volume was more than 12 million shares, a record. By mid-morning of Black Thursday, two groups met in an attempt to cope with the crisis. The Federal Reserve Board met in D.C., and a bankers' group met in New York City at J. P. Morgan's headquarters at Broad and Wall. Of the two, the bankers' group had more experience with market crises. Included were Thomas Lamont of Morgan, Albert Wiggin of Chase National, Charles Mitchell, and George F. Baker Jr. of First National Bank. As in the past, they sought ways to bring the market out of its tailspin. Using a time-proven method, they committed a substantial amount of funds to the market in the hope that their buying power would be matched by the investment community. But things did not work as well as they had in the past.

The bankers committed an estimated $130 million to stabilize the market. The press reported the amount to be substantially higher, recalling at the same time the rescue operation Morgan had performed in 1907. The first buy order was entered on the floor of the exchange by Richard Whitney, president of the NYSE, known as Morgan's broker. The first stock he put in a buy order for was U. S. Steel, a company created by Pierpont Morgan thirty years before, several points above the market price of $200 per share. Steel was the most actively purchased stock by the pool, accounting for some $27 million in stabilization alone. Other stocks supported were AT&T, Anaconda Copper, General Electric, and the New York Central, many with historically strong Morgan connections. The action partially stabilized the market, which remained orderly for the next two days. Within another few days the slide began again, however. On Monday, October 28, the market fell heavily again. More than 9 million shares were traded, and significant losses were seen in some major blue chips, including U. S. Steel, which led the most active list, losing about 15 percent of its value. More than $14 billion had been wiped off the markets' value, according to estimates.

The bankers tried to put on a brave face by stating that their actions were intended only to ensure an orderly market and that they had no other control over actual prices. Tuesday, October 29, proved more disastrous for the market than the preceding days. More than 16 million shares changed hands, and the bankers' pool was already exhausted from the previous week's intervention. The newspapers, which had been quick to point out five days earlier that the crash in prices was the result of inefficiencies in the back rooms of the brokerage firms, finally realized that a significant event had occurred. The *Minneapolis Star* reported that "the reaction came with the same abruptness as the one yesterday in which billions of dollars in value were lost." Clearly, this was not simply a back office problem.

Many margin calls could not be met, and the positions were sold by brokers following standard market practice, inducing even more selling. Other investors recognized the magnitude of the market rout and entered sell orders to exit their stocks at any price. All of this caused a change in the call money market. In Chicago, Continental Illinois Bank, the largest outside New York City, lowered its call loan rate to 6 percent from 8 percent, the level to which it had been raised only two months before. By the end of 1929, *Barron's* noted that "recently when the [term] call money rates were so high, practically all of the lending was done on day-to-day rates as there is a 6 percent usury law limit on time money in New York State."[45] With the market down so sharply, brokers and bankers wanted to avoid any suggestion of usury.

Recriminations over Usury

Critics maintained that the Federal Reserve banks, especially the New York Fed, were to blame for the crash. Most prominent among them was H. Parker Willis, the first secretary of the Federal Reserve Board, banking adviser to several foreign central banks, and professor at George Washington University and Columbia, who put the blame squarely on directors of the twelve district banks: "They have sat tight and said nothing while the 'small man' from Maine to California has gradually been led to invest his savings in the stock market with the result that the constantly rising tide of speculation at higher and higher prices has swept over the business of the country."

Willis's criticism was not confined to the regional Fed banks alone. He also laid blame on the Federal Reserve Board. Beginning in 1925, he charged that the Fed's plan to keep U.S. interest rates low to prevent an outflow of funds from Britain had driven the American stock market rally that the banks further fueled with broker loans.[46] The Fed also came under heavy criticism for failing to control bootleg loans. Ironically, some of those loans came from abroad, despite the slightly higher interest rates in Britain. He noted that the 1925 policy did not serve Britain well because the resulting high value of the pound caused a general strike in Britain in 1926 when Winston Churchill was Chancellor of the Exchequer under Stanley Baldwin. As he calculated blame, however, he also created a policy problem for regulators and legislators; if everyone was to blame then how could effective regulation prevent the problem from occurring again? The stream of criticism concerning broker loans that began in the mid-1920s and continued after the crash proved valuable several years later when reforms were introduced during the early years of the New Deal.

Bankers and politicians laid most of the blame for the crash on more nebulous factors, such as investor expectations and greed. Outside New York, however, criticism continued to focus on lending rates, especially for call money. A West Virginia newspaper remarked that the crash was a blessing: "it was an effect, not a cause . . . there was at work the infection of rational usury." The complacency of the Fed created a:

> whoopee for Wall Street. Why moralize about the sin and illegality, or reason, over the economics of usury when the Federal Reserve Board was playing with eight and ten percent to accommodate member banks and the National City Bank was doing the good Samaritan at 16, 17, 18, and 19, and 20 percent? . . . the people want security against a condition in which usury is the rule and the craze.[47]

Two months after the crash, the same newspaper echoed similar conclusions. It was convinced that the "Federal Reserve Board aided and
abetted—either in ignorance of the facts or the principle involved—by
the mere recognition of the theory that the Federal Reserve rate should
control stock gambling, private usury, bootlegging or any other im-
moral practice." Several months after the crash, when broker loan rates
had dropped, the *Gazette* noted that "the country is responding to the
temporary change from the government's abandonment of usury. It
awaits the definite assurance from the executive or congress that there is
a reasonable rate beyond which the nerves of the board may not yield
the rights of those who do not gamble in stocks."[48] The great debate of
the 1930s quickly was taking shape. Bankers had diverted other people's
money to call loans that effectively bankrupted many in the October
market rout.

The sentiment was echoed many times late in 1929. While many responses were originals written by local newspaper staff, others were re-
prints of syndicated columns written by Arthur Brisbane, a writer for
the Hearst newspapers. Brisbane worked for Joseph Pulitzer as editor at
the *New York World* before being hired by William Randolph Hearst to
be editor of the *New York Journal*. He was known as the "patron saint
of yellow journalism" for his simple, populist style. He was famous for
stating that if a journalist did not hit his readers hard with the first sentence, there was no need for another. His columns were the most widely
syndicated in the country, reprinted in over one thousand newspapers a
week with an estimated readership of 20 million. Hearst also paid him
a reputed $250,000 per year, an amount greater than the salary of many
bankers at the time.

His syndicated column, "Today," became a nationwide critique of
bankers. During the April 1929 interest rate controversy between the
Fed and the banks, he wrote that "the worst of it is that 'outsiders' pour
in money eager for the usury debauch, and no effective plan for shutting
out these bootleg loans is offered. Even if the Federal Reserve planned
to encourage usury and increase bank profits, it seems unable to suggest

anything . . . there ought, however, to be some limit to usury, even when sanctified by Federal Reserve approval."[49] After the crash, he concluded that "A maximum interest rate which should not go above 7 percent for private or corporation loans, would be a good start. No need to worry about bankers not lending their money. A banker with money idle is like a broody hen with no place to sit. They will lend for lending is their life."[50] The ideas became widely accepted in the 1930s as distrust of banks, combined with thousands of bank failures, caused many savers to withdraw their deposits and hoard cash rather than entrust it to anyone associated with Wall Street.

CREDIT AFTER THE CRASH

The amount of consumer credit outstanding began to decline dramatically after 1929. From a peak of $6.44 billion in 1929, it fell to $3.48 billion in 1933, a decline of 48 percent.[51] It did not reach its 1929 level again until 1937. The decline in consumer credit was more than an expected result of a deteriorating economy. It contributed to the worst economic crisis in American history. The point was quickly made by the Twentieth Century Fund. Noting the proliferation of mass lending to individuals with no standard collateral, the fund acknowledged that "only in recent years has it been recognized that consumption must also be financed by the extension of reasonable loans."[52] But high-interest lenders were not providing a service to the producers of goods or to society by charging rates that drained the consumers' ability to repay; future demand required reasonable rates so buyers could repay and buy again.

Evans Clark, director of the fund, provided a summary of the sources of consumer credit in the 1920s. Noting that the banks were not the major source, he listed the lenders and the amounts contributed to the total. The results were somewhat surprising, especially in light of the claims made by the Russell Sage Foundation about the victory over loan sharks.

Of the approximate $2.60 billion in small consumer loans made per year (excluding autos and other durables), the breakdown was:

—Unlicensed lenders: $750 million
—Pawnbrokers: $600 million
—Personal finance companies: $500 million
—Co-maker loan companies: $360 million
—Commercial banks: $150 million
—Credit unions: $63 million
—Remedial loan societies: $60 million
—Axias: $50 million
—Employer loan funds: $20 million

The estimated amount was about one half the total outstanding, underlining the short-term nature of the loans. Surprisingly, loan sharks accounted for 29 percent of the total. Putting a less negative spin on that number, the report noted that unlicensed lenders who charged reasonable rates also were included. Quickly acknowledging that the numbers were not much more than guesswork, the fund referred to the lenders as "agencies" of mass finance.

Equally important was the fund's comments on the social usefulness of mass credit. In addition to providing demand for mass production, "the public now begins to see the broader human and social usefulness of financing the working man and woman to get the essential services of life—medical care, education, recreation and other tangible necessities." Without government assistance to provide education, health care, or other social infrastructure, borrowing was the only method for the average worker to attain some of these benefits. Even more important was the conclusion reached by the fund concerning the report itself: "It is astonishing that a business [consumer lending] that is now as large as some of the leading industries of the country could have grown up without any general public knowledge of its size—and in many quarters even of its existence. More incredible yet is the fact that no comprehensive study of it has ever been published."[53]

One of the leading consumer finance companies thought the crash would not have much of an impact on its future revenues. Household Finance's president remained firmly optimistic. "The stock market crash will neither increase the number of small loans nor cause them to decrease," said L. C. Harbison in late November 1929, adding that "eighty five percent of the people will not visibly be affected in any way." He assumed the 15 percent who would be negatively affected were the highest earners, not the majority, a conjecture that proved contradictory to most suppositions about the average borrower. The *Wall Street Journal* noted that active accounts at Household more than doubled the year following its reduction in the lending rate and that it had 235,000 accounts representing $30 million in loans. By the third quarter of 1929, it already had earned more than it did in 1928. The paper also noted that the company was the only stand-alone consumer lender listed on the New York Stock Exchange.[54] Business was good but the reasons for it were not discussed.

Despite all of the events and diversions of the late 1920s, loan sharking continued unabated. Although declared victorious before World War I, the campaign against loan sharks continued in many cities after the crash. In the District of Columbia, it became particularly nasty. The *Washington Post* began a campaign after the crash, pointing out the high rates that lenders exacted with impunity on borrowers. The affair was reminiscent of many conducted by newspapers in the district and other large cities twenty years before, which apparently met with only limited, if any, success. The investigation revealed that many unlicensed moneylenders were referred to potential customers by other reputable lenders who, for whatever reason, refused to do business with them. This was the case throughout most of the 1920s and picked up steam after the crash. In some cases, the legitimate lender owned the loan shark operation but remained silent while an "operator" conducted business for him. The most common practice was for a borrower to sign a note for a loan amount. The operator would then sell the note to another party, often the silent partner, at a discount, who would then present it for payment at maturity. While it had always been clear that the discount note scheme was simply another method of charging high interest, the procedure still was successful and the purchaser of the note claimed that he was just buying a note as an investment to be paid at a future date.

Bootleggers were among these silent partners who would advance cash and gain a 50 percent return on their portion of the transaction. Other silent lenders included businessmen as well as racketeers who were joining the ranks of loan sharks. In addition, fellow employees often lent to other workers, collecting interest ranging from 25 to 100 percent. The oldest cottage industry was in full gear and gaining due to the rapidly developing Depression.

The campaign hit a sensitive nerve. The *Washington Post* journalist spearheading the campaign received much hate mail, including one that read, "If you know when your [sic] healthy and want to stay that way, lay off the loan companies." The newspaper proudly published it on page one.[55]

A month later, the first arrest was made following the campaign. A Baltimore lender was arrested under the 1913 District of Columbia usury law, which stipulated that anyone lending money above 6 percent had to be registered, which he was not. Amid much fanfare, he was released on $500 bond, with the prosecutor claiming that further charges could follow. The original charge did not carry much of a penalty, however. The fine was not less than $25 nor more than $200 and a possible imprisonment of not less than five days or more than thirty. Neither the money nor the prison sentence provided much of a deterrent.

The early months of the Depression placed severe hardships on Chicago, among other cities. In the winter of 1930, the Chicago police announced that they would not assist loan sharks in collecting unpaid loans made to policemen. Only requests from legitimate businesses would be considered. Chicago was suffering from another bout of financial distress and many city workers were not being paid on time. Back salaries finally were paid in March when the city comptroller found enough cash to pay teachers and police, among others. One newspaper noted, almost jubilantly, that employees happily marched away from city hall after receiving their checks, even though they held their cash "only for the distance from the city hall to the pawnshop or loan shark and almost all of them had creditors waiting."[56]

Loan sharks thrived in Chicago and other large cities, and the early years of the Depression proved that business was profitable. One well-known loan shark was interviewed by the Chicago state attorney on allegations of usury. As an unlicensed lender, his activities were confined to charging a nominal 7 percent interest, but he was accused of charging as much as 240 percent in his salary buying business. A notable complaint charged that he exacted $42 in interest on a salary loan of $15. When the borrower could not pay, the loan shark sued him for $75. The same defendant had been through the Chicago courts numerous times before. Judge Kennesaw Mountain Landis once told the defendant that he was prying open the door to his own prison cell, but his lending activities continued. The problem was that the maximum penalty for violating the small loan law in Illinois was six months in prison and a $500 fine. Even the remote possibility of a prison sentence did not serve as an adequate deterrent, although the penalties were harsher in Illinois than those in Washington, D.C.

Financial services in D.C. came under a withering attack from Senator John J. Blaine, a Republican of Wisconsin, who was being urged by Smith Brookhart to investigate securities fraud in the district. Securities dealing, real estate, and lending at high interest were all widely practiced in the city, with fewer protections for the residents than those found in the states. Blaine noted that a homeowner who had been foreclosed had no legal notice to appear in court to present a defense. Foreclosure was accomplished by the lender simply publishing notice, without giving the borrower the right to respond. Brookhart noted that "the laws relating to the question of usury in the District of Columbia are so defective that some of these financial operators may take from a widow 20 percent of the loan she obtains upon her little home as a commission."[57] Despite the wide publicity surrounding the passing of anti-loan sharking laws in the district twenty years before and the *Washington Post* campaign, little had been accomplished to control lending after the war.[58]

The D.C. campaign met with limited success. A year later, Representative Fiorello La Guardia of New York, one of the designated Wild Jackasses, wrote to the U.S. attorney general asking him to look into the loan sharking business in the district. He contended that the law allowing 12 percent interest at the time was more than generous to loan sharks. The attorney general responded that it was not his job to administer to the district and that usury was the business of the district corporation counsel.

In what became known as the hometown of loan sharking in the 1920s, the Twentieth Century Fund reported that an Atlanta borrower paid $1,550 on an original loan of $76 before it finally was settled. It also discovered that many of the loan sharks operated from one-man offices despite the growth of unlicensed lending chains. Although the foundation could not substantiate the size of the average loan made by loan sharks, it assumed that their total volume of business was about $750 million on loans of $50 each, suggesting 15 million transactions. Of the total, 70 percent came from salary purchases or chattel mortgages and 20 percent from automobile loans.[59]

California had one of the stricter usury laws in the country for small loans, limiting the amount of interest to 12 percent per year. In 1930, a change to the law named Proposition 10 was proposed that would have left the legal limit untouched but have effectively raised it through many exemptions and loopholes. It provided no relief for borrowers who paid back their loans early. It also would have exempted corporations from the usury law, something the existing law did not countenance. The *Los Angeles Times* supported the old law and the defeat of the proposition, using language often heard in the loan sharking debate. "It is entirely in the interests of the lender, it is dangerous, it is unnecessary, it is discriminatory," the paper stated emphatically.[60] The proposition was defeated.

Part of the problem with the resurgence in loan sharking had to do with record-keeping. Compiling economic statistics only began seriously in the mid-1920s, so many of the assumptions made about lending, call money, and other forms of credit until then were based mostly on hearsay or intuition. Once statistics were compiled, it became apparent that loan sharking had never been defeated. At the same time, earlier defenses of call money as an essential ingredient in market mechanics faded as the extent of call money lending, especially from nonbank sources, became clear. Only after the crash did the full extent of the credit binge of the decade become clear, as opinion was refuted by hard facts.

Post-Crash Reactions

The call money problem was not forgotten in the wake of the crash. It became the center of discussion in early attempts to reform the banks and the markets. The House Banking and Currency Committee met several months after the crash with broker loan rates and their relation to the Fed the main topic of discussion. Roy Young, governor of the Federal Reserve Board, was one of its main witnesses.

When interviewed by the committee, Young remarked that the current method of setting broker loan rates, by a committee of three loan brokers on the floor of the New York Stock Exchange, remained the best method of determining the rate. He also noted that the discount rate was a laggard when compared to call money and that the two rates could become disconnected in point of time since the call rate was a market rate while the discount rate was set by the Fed and remained unchanged until further notice. At the time, it was not clear that many members of the House understood the distinction.

Young admitted that the 20 percent rate charged on broker loans did have a direct, dampening effect on the economy after the crash. He also noted that the banks were prepared for the crash; if they had not been, the damage from October 1929 would have been much greater. His attitude toward banks and lending to the call money market, among other activities, was already on record. Two years earlier, he had told a bankers' convention in Gary, Indiana, that those who did not heed the principles of sound banking practice had little room to complain. "Many people in America seem to be more concerned about the present situation than the Federal Reserve System is. If unsound credit practices have developed, these practices will in time correct themselves, and if some of the over-indulgent get 'burnt' during the period of correction, they will have to shoulder the blame themselves and not attempt to shift it to someone else." This was not the message many bankers outside New York necessarily wanted to hear. He continued, adding, "Dissatisfaction is expressed because the Federal Reserve System refrains from prediction and cannot always anticipate. I have stated to you that conditions, to a large extent, bring about Federal Reserve policies rather than Federal Reserve policies bring about conditions. That is just the position of the System at the moment."[61]

His main interrogator on the committee, Representative Francis Seiberling of Ohio, asked him whether a national usury law should be passed rather than entrust the matter of rate setting to a stock exchange committee. Young demurred but did state that rates were best left to market forces rather than to Congress. A different view was offered by J. W. Pole, the Comptroller of the Currency. When asked whether a national usury law was feasible, he said that it would be possible among the national banks and member banks of the Fed. The National Bank Act of 1864 still applied to the national banks, but Fed members were another matter. Pole added that the siphoning of funds by banks from local economies to the call money market was bad for credit generally and should be avoided in the future. It was becoming clear that the dynamics of the call money market were well understood by regulators but little had been done until it was too late.

Another matter of concern in the post-crash months was the matter of national bank branching. Although expressly forbidden by the McFadden Act, the large banks were exploring the possibility of acquiring state banks in an attempt to cross state lines. The act forbade banks from opening new (*de novo*) branches in other states by acquisition rather than building them from scratch. Pole suggested that Congress was capable of preventing that type of expansion. A year later, however, he changed direction by strongly supporting the idea of allowing banks to expand. But at the time, there was a fear among bankers outside New York that the large banks would encroach on their territories, especially after many had quickly withdrawn from the call money market. The McFadden Act, designed in part to protect small banks from their out-of-state New York rivals, was not thought to be airtight enough to dissuade the money center banks from planning incursions into the states.

Another strong supporter of the status quo was Charles Mitchell of National City Bank. Appearing before the House Committee, he told committee members that he was opposed to putting restrictions on call money and favored branching. He described the organization of the National City Bank parent company that separated investment, commercial, and trust banking. The idea that the parent could use affiliates to do business with each other was not in its business model. As he noted, the trust affiliate could not purchase securities from the investment affiliate without authorization of the person making the trust. He was referring to a model becoming popular at the time called chain banking. In this arrangement, banks would expand, offering services that fell short of traditional banking but clearly were owned by the same parent. The term was taken from the retail chain store phenomenon that was spreading quickly across the country. In chain banking, the ownership and management of the banks or affiliates was similar, so they could complement each other without outside interference.

The worsening economic climate made the irascible even more irascible. In the midterm congressional election of 1930, Democrats gained fifty-two seats at the expense of Republicans, although they still lacked the upper hand in the House by two seats. After the election, a delegation of seven Democratic congressmen met at the White House with President Hoover to tell him that the Democratic victory would not mean that they would not hinder him in the drive to restore the economy. The meeting drew the ire of Carter Glass, a Democratic senator from Virginia, who openly questioned who appointed them emissaries to the party that had presided over the boom and the crash. He stated that the Republicans were discredited on economic and historical grounds and should not be consulted on future economic policy because of past failures.

Representative Louis McFadden also made headlines in the latter part of 1930 when a speech he made in Congress deploring the bankers and their international connections was widely reported. Concerned that Wall Street bankers and the Fed had developed strong, secretive international relationships with their counterparts at the Bank of France and the Reichsbank, he was worried about the uses to which the new Bank for International Settlements could be employed, especially as they related to gold. He also strongly opposed the nomination of Eugene Meyer to be the next governor of the Federal Reserve, succeeding Roy Young. Many of McFadden's remarks were considered offensive by Herbert Hoover and members of Congress, who quickly distanced themselves from him.

McFadden couched his remarks in banking organization terms, well aware that the large banks were trying to avoid the restrictions of his namesake act, passed three years before. Concerning the crash, he remarked:

> Banks have not been content to do a legitimate banking business but they have organized affiliated companies under State laws that have permitted them to do those things which are prohibited directly under the law . . . they have been the sources from which hundreds of millions of dollars' worth of these fancy securities have been unloaded on the innocent public. This resulted in the wide speculation of last year; in fact the very thing that caused the crash of last October was the fact that early in the summer these reorganization and financing houses . . . became aware of the fact that pressure was on from the Federal Reserve to reduce credit lines and that an economic depression was imminent and they all tried to get rid of their securities at one and the same time.[62]

His remarks reflected the growing sentiment that the failure of many new issues contributed significantly to the crash. Within a short time, however, his comments would become even more outrageous as his frustration grew over the lack of an economic recovery.

After his implied criticism of Herbert Hoover, McFadden again went on the attack a year later, excoriating the president for a proposed moratorium on German war reparations. In a speech in Congress, he declared that, in arranging for a moratorium, Hoover behaved in a manner that "savored more of the ways of an oriental potentate drunk with power than of conduct proper for the President of the United States. . . . If the German international bankers of Wall Street and their satellites had not had this job waiting to be done, Herbert Hoover would never have been elected President of the United States. They helped select him. They helped elect him."[63] McFadden clearly was using the hyperbolic style of communication that had become increasingly strident as the economic crisis continued.

The response to the comment was swift. McFadden's hometown newspaper remarked, "A double-barreled recoil from his shot at President Hoover today struck Representative McFadden, irreconcilable Republican from Pennsylvania."[64] Pennsylvania Republicans moved to strip him of his congressional patronage, normally conferred upon members of Congress to appoint postmasters in their home states. The action was a clear indication of how much the party had come to dislike him. Some members accused him of treason. But their reactions did not affect McFadden.

A year later, in 1932, he introduced three impeachment proceedings in the House, two against Hoover and the other against members of the Federal Reserve Board. It was the first time a president had impeachment proceedings introduced in the House since Andrew Johnson's presidency. In the two separate impeachment charges, McFadden never garnered more than eleven votes in his favor, including his own. Both were dismissed by roll call vote and were never referred to committee. One congressman described the lack of support "on the roll call vote as hard a spanking as a grown man could get." A local New York newspaper quickly dismissed McFadden as a disgruntled legislator, still smarting from the reprimand a year before. "That not all legislators elected by the people are shining examples of tolerance and breadth was shown in [McFadden's] recent asinine attempt," it wrote two days after the affair.

"The shafts of the chagrined Pennsylvania legislator rebounded only to his own utter defacement."[65]

Sentiment remained strong against Wall Street and the Fed after the crash. Almost two years after the event, Congressional hearings were organized by McFadden and Carter Glass, in their roles as chairs of the House and Senate Committees on Banking and Currency. Advance notice of the sort of questions they wanted answered by Wall Street was distributed among the top securities houses. Many bankers and brokers simply wanted to stonewall any questions, while others seemed more agreeable to answer to prevent further problems with Congress. The questions centered on two problems, in the eyes of Congress. Was the Fed lending to foreign governments at a time the domestic economy was drastically contracting, and why were there so many bank failures in the wake of the crash? Both suggested the Fed was preoccupied with international finance, a familiar refrain of McFadden as well as the Republican insurgents. Another implication was that commercial banks in the major money centers had hastened the demise of so many smaller banks by their actions internationally and in the call money market. The issue was given more immediacy after the failure of the Bank of United States, the largest to date.

On the Fed lending to foreign governments, Louis McFadden proposed an unorthodox solution that stunned Washington. Britain and France both owed the United States money and a solution he floated proved controversial, to say the least. He suggested that if Britain and France could not repay then they should cede some of their colonies in the Western hemisphere to the United States. The idea was met with stunned disbelief. One member of the UK government remarked that "the time is long past when loyal British subjects can be ceded to a foreign power for a monetary consideration." A French journal was less diplomatic. "Never before," said *Des Debats*, "have Americans been so badly informed on Europe and so badly disposed toward their former associates. It would be imprudent therefore to count on their spirit of justice and their sense of realities. It is regrettable, but that is the way it is."[66]

MORE BANK FAILURES AND "INVISIBLE" RESERVES

Uncertain conditions among the banks and the money market contributed to more bank failures in 1929 and 1930. The trend in closings, beginning in the early 1920s, accelerated, but after the crash new reasons were offered for them. There were still 24,000 banks in the United States despite the massive failures of the preceding years, but only 8,000 belonged to the Fed system. In 1930, twice as many banks failed as in 1929.

The failure problem clearly worsened after the crash. In 1930 and 1931, 1,350 and 2,203 banks, respectively, failed nationwide. The hardest hit regions of the country were, again, the central northeastern states (Ohio, Indiana, Illinois, Michigan, and Wisconsin) with 282 failures, and the central northwestern states (Minnesota, Iowa, Missouri, North Dakota, South Dakota, Nebraska, and Kansas) with 415. Of the total, only thirty national banks failed in 1931 and eighty-five failed in the central northeastern region in 1931. In the north central region, thirty-eight and eighty-four failed in those two years. State non-Fed members were even smaller, with only five and forty-five in the central northeastern area and four and five in central northern states in the same years.[67]

The deteriorating banking situation turned what was a severe recession into the Great Depression. The main trigger was the matter of bank reserves. Because of the network of correspondent banks holding reserves for smaller banks outside the Fed system, the actual reserve levels of banks were double counted. When a bank wrote a check to another bank for a reserve balance, the amount was counted twice for reporting purposes; as a result, the amount of reserves in the banking system was overstated. In times of crisis, this meant that fewer reserves existed than could actually be converted to cash for immediate depositor demands on a bank.[68] As a result, many banks appeared healthy but would not be able to withstand cash demands.

The main culprit in this process was an old banking practice used in American banking since the early nineteenth century. The time lag between when a check was written and cashed was (and is) referred to as "float." The technique can be practiced by either party, the check writer on either end of the transaction. The bank writing the check ordinarily wanted to slow its clearing so the amount remains in its accounts as long as possible. If asked to send reserves back to the original bank, the correspondent could drag its feet or otherwise be slow in returning the balance, creating an actual cash crisis for the original bank that may have been facing immediate demands for cash from its depositors because of a bank run, common during the Depression. Thus, the amount of reserves being reported by the banks was not accurate. During the 1920s, this amount was referred to as "invisible reserves."[69] This was part of the phenomenon that Ayres referred to in his speech, although he did not specifically mention double counting reserves.

Reserves were an important issue at the time, although the potential problems they posed to the financial system were understated. The *Wall Street Journal* cited Fed statistics to demonstrate that "so far as the 'visible' part of the country's credit mechanism is concerned—apart from the newer loan elements that constitute an 'invisible banking system'— the situation is notably strong." Citing sturdy reported reserves and an abundance of gold flowing into the country, the paper commented that "the banking situation had been strengthened, at least superficially, of late at an unprecedented rate—even more rapidly than in 1921."[70] Ayres's previous remarks were acknowledged but no one was sure how the invisible system actually fit into the larger market mosaic and what dangers it presented beyond inflated stock prices.

Reserves needed to be kept in banks closer to home, whether in a regional Fed bank or in a larger nonmember correspondent. The farther from home the reserves wandered, the greater the risks to which they became exposed, especially from a potentially declining stock market. But runs on banks also were partly emotional. When depositors heard of banking problems elsewhere, they sometimes formed lines outside their own banks to withdraw funds. This domino effect could place a bank under severe strain even if it possessed adequate liquid assets.

Negative publicity nationwide was generated by bank failures. The largest banking failure to date occurred when the Bank of United

States, located in New York City, failed in 1930, and the event became national news. The bank was purposely named after the long-defunct Bank of the United States, omitting "the" from its name. Over the years, it developed a retail business and had several subsidiary companies doing other business, such as securities dealing. Many of its branches were decorated with flags, giving the impression that it somehow was an official, government institution. The bank was located in Manhattan, with branches located mostly in working class and immigrant neighborhoods. Finally, word of its problems leaked to the public and a run on the bank began. One commentator described the scenes: "from all over the Bronx, the East Side, Brooklyn, and the upper West Side, people rushed frantically to get their money. Wild-eyed with wonderment and bewilderment, they stood in long lines and worried or pushed . . . armored trucks brought more money, but the demand was greater than the supply."[71]

After police and troops were called in to restore order, the bank was placed in receivership. The bank had about sixty branches that served 400,000 depositors, and depositors eventually recovered some of their funds from a settlement. The management of the bank had used the deposits to help purchase its stock in the market. When the market crashed, the stock price of the bank fell substantially. Since the purchases were funded with customer deposits, it wiped them out as well.

Although the bank was a member of the Federal Reserve Bank of New York, the collapse came too suddenly for an effective bailout. Many of the large New York City banks refused to help stabilize it, adding to the resentment of the large banks in general. Initially, over $300 million in deposits was lost, representing the savings of many working class and first generation Americans. The New York banking authorities attempted a rescue but they were too late to prevent runs on its branches. Newspapers around the country published photographs of lines that formed outside the branches as anxious depositors lined up to withdraw their funds. The publicity led many depositors in other parts of the country to withdraw their funds from other banks, adding to a widespread liquidity problem. The banking superintendent in New

York was indicted for not acting quickly enough to prevent the problem. Eventually, he was exonerated and some of the deposits were partially reimbursed, but the crisis spread rapidly, exacerbating the invisible reserves problem.

Bank runs developed in many cities, with St. Louis and Chicago particularly hard hit several months later. The growing problem caused many banks to request extra cash from the Fed to meet withdrawal demand. Small businesses began to fail and the economic outlook deteriorated quickly. Six months after the crash, most commentators realized that the situation was more serious than the recession experienced in 1920–21 and that it was still deteriorating rather than rebounding as had originally been expected.

The Chicago rash of bank failures that began in the summer of 1932 hit the city particularly hard. In June forty-nine failures occurred in the state, with forty registered in Chicago. Although failures in various cities could have been based upon different factors, the rash of Chicago failures was not caused by a mass panic but by certain banks' weak financial positions witnessed some months before the crash occurred.[72]

In 1930, interest rates began to drop as economic activity declined. The call money rate fell from to 1.5 percent in the summer, the lowest rate since 1917, and the Fed lowered its discount rate to 2 percent in December, the lowest rate ever recorded. The amount of bank credit outstanding in 1930 fell by $3 billion and broker loans made by nonbank lenders fell by $5.5 billion as foreign and corporate lenders abandoned stock market lending.[73] Outstanding broker loans fell to their lowest level since they first were examined in aggregate in 1926.

The year following the crash saw intense criticism of the Fed and Wall Street. That criticism was widespread but it was clear on all sides that the economic difficulties were the result of a significant credit market event. The *Chicago Tribune* noted that there were many "who are convinced that everything could have been kept straight by expanding credit at certain times and contracting it at others." But the paper also recognized that "all proposals involving the quantity theory of money and more interference therewith than we have at present with the gold standard, inelastic as it is, bear the objection that we don't know what the results will be. We do know that they are uncertain."[74] That uncertainty at official levels enabled a new breed of loan shark to emerge who would give the old profession the back alley image for which it subsequently became known. Official interest rates declined during the Depression unless the debt was owed to a private lender. The back alley rates were poised to set new records.

CHAPTER FIVE

THE GREAT DEPRESSION

DESPITE THE GUARDEDLY OPTIMISTIC ECONOMIC OUTLOOK
bankers, business people, and politicians offered, the Depression in
1930 proved to be unprecedented. The stock market index fell to new
lows. A traders' bear pool dedicated to short selling was detected on the
New York Stock Exchange and ruled a fraud under New York law. Call
money dropped to 1.5 percent, the lowest level since World War I, and
brokers' loans dropped to less than $2 billion outstanding, the lowest
level since the stock market boom began in 1925. Commodity prices
fell dramatically and had to be supported by the Federal Farm Board.

The Great Depression also brought out the soothsayers and science
fiction writers. H. G. Wells wrote a book in 1933 titled *The Shape of
Things to Come*, which became popular on both sides of the Atlantic. In
it, he predicted a terrible world war would occur in 1940 that would

devastate civilization. In the wake of that war, he predicted, would come a total collapse of social and economic structures. Replacing them would be a world where "there remains no way of becoming passively wealthy. Gambling is ruthlessly eradicated. Usury ranks with forgery as a monetary offense. . . . [T]here are no speculators, shareholders, private usurers or rent lords."

The Depression would prove profitable to loan sharks; it would provide equal success to wets, who wanted to see the Prohibition amendment repealed. Pressure built to return to the production of alcoholic beverages because the ban was ineffective and strengthened organized crime at the same time. An organization named the Association Against the Prohibition Amendment (AAPA) was formed in 1925 with the express intent of returning the United States to legal production of alcohol, pressing Congress for a federal excise tax on spirits at the same time. The organization was sponsored by members of the duPont family and John Raskob, a former chair of the Democratic National Committee who opposed Franklin Roosevelt. The organization assumed that the excise tax would replace the income tax, freeing those in the top tax bracket from paying taxes. The idea had some merit. When visiting the United States in 1929, Winston Churchill was asked his thoughts on Prohibition. He responded by saying, "We raise over £100 million a year from our liquor taxes, an amount I understand you give to your bootleggers."

The repeal of Prohibition in March 1933 reversed the most ignored Constitutional amendment ever passed. Once the matter was settled, the AAPA transformed itself into the American Liberty League, an organization claiming over 100,000 members. In reality, it was a lobbying group determined to undermine the New Deal. Its influence began to wane after Roosevelt was re-elected in 1936, but it produced a torrent of anti-New Deal booklets and pamphlets that would become a model for similar groups in the future. The active membership of both the AAPA and the Liberty League, despite their claims of large numbers, was confined to a small group of prominent businessmen opposed to income tax and liberal politics. Their elitist nature also demonstrated why it was so difficult to repeal usury laws, since the league included among its members many bankers and financiers, all of whom recognized the value of the pro-business propaganda the league produced.

The grassroots movement fostered by the Russell Sage Foundation and others had much more difficulty passing state reforms on usury ceilings than the AAPA did in removing Prohibition in a relatively short period of time, mainly because of the stature and resources of its members. The AAPA mounted a large propaganda campaign against Prohibition. It employed many of the propaganda methods used during World War I against the Germans. The association estimated that over 4 million copies of books, brochures, and pamphlets were distributed in favor of repeal in 1930 alone.[1] That number was ten times the number of Sarah Emery's booklet, *Seven Financial Conspiracies,* distributed in the Midwest fifty years before.

One book, *Roosevelt Revealed*, which critically examined the first years of the New Deal, sounded a familiar if somewhat old theme. The author claimed that the Roosevelt administration accomplished the same depreciation of the dollar that the introduction of greenbacks had done seventy years before, with Roosevelt's bank holiday, closing the banks for a week in March 1933 to protect the U.S. gold reserves and the passage of the Glass–Steagall Act weeks later. It claimed that "abroad, our money no longer is worth 100 cents on the dollar, but a bare 81.7 cents." Furthermore, any attempt to raise commodity prices to help farmers regain lost income was impossible because "what magician could readjust the value of one year's dollar to that of another year?"[2] Skeptics were plentiful, but the depth of the Depression was unmatched; many solutions were proposals without precedent or merit.

While the AAPA was having an impact on national policy, the economic situation deteriorated for farmers in an already unenviable position. The collapse in commodity and agricultural prices greatly diminished farm revenues to the point where it was cheaper to let crops rot in the field than harvest them at a loss. Reduced farm incomes were unable to cover farming costs or pay the mortgages on farm properties that had expanded greatly between 1918 and 1921. The large number of bank failures during the 1920s made the farm problem more acute. Before the 1932 presidential election, it became a crisis.

A previous crisis in farm mortgages was a distant memory but it was not forgotten. The *Wall Street Journal* commented:

> Anyone living in one of the Midwestern state capitals during the '90s will read this week's dispatches from Bismarck, N.D., with a stirring of dim memories of things long forgotten. The North Dakota Senate voted to 'publish,' but not adopt, a resolution which invites 39 of the states to secede from the Union, leaving New England, New York, Pennsylvania, and New Jersey to constitute a new political entity reeking with wealth and corruption.

The old Populist rallying cry was being heard again but the newspaper did not take sides. The *Journal* recognized that all areas of the country had complaints about the economy and the wide divisions in wealth before Roosevelt's inauguration. Noting that Congress had not yet done enough about the Depression, the paper concluded that "there is no help for it unless all of us, whether we still dwell within the United States or have involuntarily become citizens of the Disunited States of America, will manage to bear with each other's emotions. If there is any better way to save the Union the North Dakota Senate will let us know—if it cares to save the Union."[3]

Farmers organized into local groups throughout the Midwest to protect themselves as best they could, given the state of the economy. Many attempted to stop trucks transporting livestock or crops from delivering their loads, under the assumption that shortages would help lift prices. In most cases, local police refrained from using force because many protestors carried American flags with them. Declining incomes began to be felt beyond the Farm Belt, however, as the purchasing power of farmers was cut from $16 billion per year to around $5 billion. The *New York Times* commented that "the Laodician [lukewarm] attitude of the city man to the farmer has been rudely shaken because it is now suspected that the industrial depression has its roots in the agricultural debacle."⁴ The idea that the economy was the product of internal links between different sectors was recognized, if a bit late.

Eɴᴛᴇʀ ᴏʀɢᴀɴɪᴢᴇᴅ ᴄʀɪᴍᴇ

The poor economy made credit conditions even more difficult. As the credit markets retracted and unemployment rose, credit for small borrowers began to diminish from its 1929 level as little consumer debt was being rolled over and small borrowers were having difficulties meeting their debt repayments. Many of the unlicensed lenders that entered the market for small loans in the 1920s also retreated, leaving borrowers to their own devices. Banks did not take up the slack.

The extreme conditions helped give rise to a new type of loan shark, one who had been seen previously only on the margins. Organized crime quickly became attracted to lending in urban areas as workers became more impoverished. Unemployment reached 23 percent in 1932 and remained over 20 percent in 1933. For his part, Louis McFadden knew what was at the heart of the problem. "Unemployment was caused by J. P. Morgan and Co., which seeks to control the world," he claimed, as he was pushed farther to the fringes of political power. The gloom and desperation that appeared so quickly after the 1920s boom inauspiciously pushed Herbert Hoover out of office in the 1932 election. The elections of 1932 also saw more incumbents voted out of office. One hundred twenty-three sitting senators and congressmen were replaced, thirteen from the Senate and 110 from the House.

Although the new Congress had a Democratic majority, it was unable to pass any meaningful legislation while waiting for Roosevelt to be inaugurated in March 1933. During this time it picked up the nickname "debating body," which would be difficult to shed in the years ahead. All the social chaos produced a natural result, as some commentators began publicly questioning whether the United States could not use a bit of dictatorship to set it straight. *Barron's* remarked that a "lighthearted dictator might be a relief from the pompous futility of such a Congress as we have recently had."

As the Depression deepened, money lending fell increasingly into the hands of gangsters who quickly recognized the workingman's need for small consumption loans. When Arthur Flegenheimer, a notorious racketeer also known as Dutch Schultz, was shot by an unknown assailant in Newark in 1935, some light was shed on the growing, shadowy business. Schultz was the target of a wide criminal investigation in New York; he later died of his gunshot wounds. The *New York Times* remarked that "the ancient racket of usury, refurbished with the strongarm methods of modern gangsters, was said yesterday to have been an important contributing factor which brought about the shooting." Schultz was a loan shark, among other pursuits, and New York authorities revealed that his racket charged vulnerable borrowers a rate of interest of 1,040 percent per year. The rate was obtained easily; for every $5 Schultz lent in small amounts, interest was charged at $1 per week, or 20 percent.

The presence of gangsters in the loan shark business instigated new campaigns against unlicensed lending, especially in New York. Loan sharks with clear links to organized crime were brought to court in Manhattan and Brooklyn. In one case, a lender had a book with 450 accounts, loans made mainly to taxi drivers and clerks. He employed collection agents with names like "The Mug," "Monkey," and "Bugsy." This shark received a six-month sentence. The public's attitude toward loan sharking became more strident as gangster involvement became clear.

The police commissioner in New York placed Charles "Lucky" Luciano on a special list as a priority arrest. Promotions were offered for those apprehending him and demotions for those who missed a chance to do so. Luciano, ostensibly a cabaret owner in Manhattan, was suspected in the murder of Schultz and became his successor in Newark and New York. He ran an organization known as *Unione Siciliano*. Loan sharking, the most profitable of Schultz's businesses, was believed to be the prime motive behind his murder. But obtaining evidence against Luciano proved to be a serious problem for the police because few complainants came forward. The list of mobsters that New York authorities wanted to interview included Meyer Lansky and Charles "Bugsy" Siegel who, along with three others, were thought to control most of the rackets in New York.

The lending business was so profitable that the mobsters named it their "Shylock racket," adding a Shakespearean touch. It was given additional impetus when many federal government employees were not paid for several months in 1935, forcing them to the loan sharks until the checks began again. Even when mobsters were sent to prison, their old habits continued. In one case, it was discovered that some inmates in New York's Welfare Island prison were charging 50 percent per week to other inmates and their families for small loans. The term of the loans extended to the next official visiting day at the prison.[5]

The presence of mobsters and the spread of loan sharking resulted in a new, vigorous campaign against unlicensed lenders in New York. The effort was led by Thomas Dewey, a graduate of the Columbia University Law School and Assistant U.S. Attorney for the Southern District of New York. He was named special prosecutor in 1935 to investigate organized crime. The appointment was made because there were complaints that the sitting district attorney failed to bring convincing evidence against racketeers. Dewey was chosen for the job by Governor Herbert Lehman.

Dewey had an operating budget of $20,000 per month and began a long series of prosecutions against all sorts of racketeers. His conviction rate—seventy-two of seventy-three cases prosecuted—made him a feared adversary. Over one-third of the convictions were against loan sharks. In 1935, he prosecuted twenty-two cases of loan sharking within a three-week period and won twenty-one cases. Many of the convictions resulted in prison terms of as much as five years. The longer sentences were given to those who used violence against borrowers when collecting payments.

Government employees were a primary target of loan sharks, especially those of the Works Progress Administration (WPA) in New York. Their steady, but often low pay, was tailor made for salary buyers and small-loan lenders. In one case, the wife of an employee, several months pregnant, was abducted from their home in Brooklyn and taken to Jersey City, where she escaped. She told of a $50 loan she had taken and still owed although she had paid $100 back to the loan shark.

Loan sharking was so rampant among WPA employees that, after receiving more than 14,000 complaints of loan sharking in the ranks, Dewey launched a major investigation at that agency. Dewey led a charge of forty agents, who conducted lightning raids around New York. Most of the raids were targeted against small bands of unlicensed lenders rather than larger, better known loan sharks because the small lenders were doing the most damage to the workingman with their terms and tactics.

Dewey's methods were effective, at least in the short-term. The *New York Times* commented that "if Thomas Dewey went no further with his silent investigation of the crime syndicates that levy an unofficial sales tax on the city's millions every day, he would still be a savior and a hero to the thousands who were freed from the moneylenders last week."[6] The raids had captured mostly small loan sharks, since the principals behind them remained invisible to the public. The campaign made him extremely popular and he later became Governor of New York and a two-time Republican presidential candidate.

The Dewey campaign was highly successful at the time. He convicted more loan sharks than anyone before him. He successfully prosecuted 130 people by October 1936, and the Russell Sage Foundation claimed that "the racket was virtually destroyed in that locality." The foundation turned over many of its files to Dewey as evidence, and its director was advised to arm himself after receiving many threatening phone calls.[7] But the claims of victory were again premature since it was clear that the Uniform Small Loan Law rates on loans were too high during the Depression and, in many cases, the unemployed could not obtain loans from licensed lenders.

Nᴇw AGENCIES, OLD PROBLEM

With the Depression, the nature of debt began to change, as well, reflecting the harsh economic conditions. Between 1929 and 1934, Treasury borrowing increased, and the short-term debts of individuals declined, the latter reflecting the commensurate sharp decline in consumer credit. The long-term debt of individuals also suffered; mortgage foreclosures accounted for an estimated one-third to one-half of the $40 billion in outstanding mortgages by 1933. The federal agencies, notably the Federal Housing Agency and the Reconstruction Finance Corporation, refinanced about $5 billion of these mortgages to keep the banks and other lenders from absorbing too great a loss, but a similar amount eventually was written off as a loss.[8]

The Depression threatened the residential mortgage market and all the businesses that derived income from it. Most important, it threatened the savings and loan associations that sprang up during the 1920s. Thousands of these small institutions operated on a simple business model: they accepted savings deposits and made home loans. But they were not full-service commercial banks and, as a result, were not Fed members.

Because of these complications, at the behest of Herbert Hoover, Congress created the Federal Home Loan Bank in 1932 to buy performing mortgages from savings banks to provide liquidity in time of crisis. The new agency was modeled after the Farm Credit System, which had proved successful in stabilizing the farm mortgage rate. Twelve regional banks were put in place, presided over by the Federal Home Loan Bank Board in Washington. The idea was to create a Federal Reserve type institution for residential mortgage lenders. These banks could buy mortgages from the lenders, providing the sector with cash at a time when credit was scarce. The idea was less controversial than the Farm Credit System, especially since the Depression was deepening and ideological and legal objections were set aside in favor of economic stability. A major stumbling block, however, was encountered when the question of who the new banks were intended to service was raised: homeowners or financial institutions.

For his part, Republican Representative Fiorello La Guardia of New York thought he knew the answer. Homeowners could apply directly to the new agency, avoiding banks and savings institutions that could add extra costs to the process. He claimed this was the intent of the act but if it were not administered properly, institutional lenders could add charges amounting to usury. Speaking in a radio address in New York City, La Guardia claimed: "I predict now that if there is no direct assistance to the homeowners, that if this law does not abolish usury and unconscionable interest charges, the law will be repealed."[9] But the Federal Home Loan Banks did not lend directly to individuals; they only purchased qualified mortgages from lenders. That provided liquidity to the lenders, enabling them to continue creating mortgages.

Thousands of homeowners in New England discovered this the hard way. After the agency was created, 5,000 potential borrowers suddenly appeared at a Home Loan bank office in Cambridge, Massachusetts. The *Boston Globe* described the scene, reporting that "it looked like a World Series crowd that besieged the new bank . . . they came from all over New England. Some had borrowed money to come. They were home owners in difficulty and they heard that the government would lend them money if no bank would grant them a mortgage."[10] One borrower needed only $31 to pay his mortgage and had run out of alternatives. They were soon disappointed. The bank did not lend directly to homeowners and it did not intermediate distressed loans, even if presented by banks; it only bought performing loans. Individuals had to deal with a bank. If no other source would lend them money, they would fall prey to foreclosure or a loan shark. The word soon spread and the crowds dissipated.

Although the Home Loan Banks did not deal with the public, Congress created two other agencies that came closer to that ideal. Continuing to respond to the crisis, it created the Home Owners' Loan Act, which, in turn, created the Home Owners' Loan Corporation. The corporation was able to support delinquent mortgages by replacing them with its own bonds with lenders and then changing the terms on them to be more favorable to the homeowners. That ability made it a resounding success. Within three years of its founding, the agency purchased 1.8 million delinquent mortgages in this manner, spending a total of $6.2 billion. The agency then exceeded its mandate by buying too many mortgages and had to stop operations as a result.

A year later, in 1934, Congress created the Federal Housing Administration (FHA), designed to support consumer loans in relation to housing. This agency was mandated by a recently passed National Housing Act that offered home improvement loans to homeowners. The improvement part was mostly confined to financing indoor plumbing and lavatories, features that were not universal at the time. The FHA would become better known for making insured mortgage loans, but at the time, it provided several billion in loans that greatly aided the housing market and public health in general. Another benefit of the FHA was in providing consumer credit. When the agency insured loans at the level of lenders, it helped introduce the savings and loans and small banks to consumer loans for the first time. With consumer credit in short supply, banks were attracted to the loans because they were insured so they had little to lose by making them. The FHA administrator, George McDonald, remarked that "I think the local banks which went into this business will never get out of it . . . and they will be enough to furnish competition to the finance companies."[11]

Another newly created agency also intervened in the mortgage market. The Reconstruction Finance Corporation (RFC) came into existence in 1932 to provide funds for a variety of industries during the economic crisis. It provided loans to businesses when credit was extremely tight or nonexistent. The mortgage business was in dire need of funds at the time. Jesse Jones, the RFC's first director, recalled that urban mortgages alone totaled $35 billion. In Chicago, $2.5 billion in mortgages and bonds were in default after the crash and $1 billion were in default by

1932. In New York, $2 billion of mortgages and bonds were in default immediately after the crash. He also noted that many of the bond houses that sold the bonds had "sold more bonds against a business property than the cost of the property . . . rates customarily charged by these mortgage bond houses were 6, 6.5, and 7 percent and they would buy the bonds from the mortgagor at 85 to 90 cents on the dollar."[12]

Urban and suburban homeowners shared their misery with farmers whose problems grew steadily worse after the crash. The foreclosure problem reached crisis proportions, prompting many calls for reform of the farm mortgage system and a moratorium on foreclosures. The governor of North Dakota in 1933 ordered the state militia to prevent foreclosures by sheriffs, removing the legal liability for not performing their duties. He later followed the order with another, prohibiting the forced sale of farm real estate when the farmer was residing on the property. In Iowa, the governor imposed martial law in several counties after farmers had threatened to execute a judge who would not stop foreclosures.

The immediate response came from the life insurance companies, the largest investors in mortgage securities. In January 1933 New York Life Insurance Company acted to prevent foreclosures of mortgages in Iowa, realizing that foreclosure meant an official end to any cash flows they might have received. Other companies soon followed. Then Prudential announced it was suspending foreclosures against resident farmer-owners throughout the country and Canada. Prudential was the largest of the life insurer investors, holding around $210 million worth of mortgage securities of all kinds. The second largest holder, the Equitable Life Company, stopped short of making a public statement but indicated that, along with Metropolitan Life, it was not pressing the foreclosure issue unless the farmer was unwilling to comply with new terms. Metropolitan was the largest holder of farm mortgages in the country, holding about $1.5 billion in its portfolio.[13] By taking the lead with a public announcement, Prudential potentially had less to lose than some of its competitors, but its general amnesty resounded well in the press and among mortgagees.

New Loan Shark Campaigns

After his election in 1932, President Franklin D. Roosevelt began using the rhetoric of anti-usury reformers. Roosevelt's general views on banking were already known when he was inaugurated on March 4, 1933. In his inaugural address he stated, "The money changers have fled from their high seats in the temple of our civilization. We may now restore that temple to the ancient truths. The measure of the restoration lies in the extent to which we apply social values more noble than mere monetary profit." Those lines, along with his comment that "we have nothing to fear but fear itself," remain among the most quoted of his era.

Already known for his views on high interest charges, the president-elect met with Louisiana senator Huey Long in Washington, D.C., in January 1933. At issue was an early version of a banking bill introduced into the Senate by Carter Glass that Long had filibustered when he sat in the Senate after becoming governor because he considered it too favorable to bankers. Long insisted he was going to meet with FDR to "talk turkey" about national and international affairs. Among the topics, the "Kingfish," as Long was known, claimed they discussed was war debts, which was still an issue despite the years that had passed since John Maynard Keynes openly complained about charging the Germans compound interest. Long proclaimed that "Mr. Roosevelt referred to the Scriptures, which he said, says that interest is usury. He knows more about the Bible than I do. You know the Bible says that interest is usury. It deals very strong with usury."[14]

Roosevelt made more memorable headlines when he spoke to the American Bankers Association a year later, discussing what he called the American profit system. He described the American ethic as one that rewarded hard work, both of mind and body. The two combined created the American profit system. The remarks appeared to be the sort of typical political rhetoric used to create a sense of pride but he was immediately criticized for failing to acknowledge the financial sector. He had not mentioned making profits through banking, and Wall

Street quickly seized on the omission to suggest that the Democratic administration was hostile to finance.

The president followed through on his comments on mortgage interest when he ordered the FHA to set the rate on the agency's supported mortgages at 5 percent, claiming that usury in the real estate market was retarding building projects nationwide; he overruled the head of the FHA, who had suggested 6 percent as the appropriate rate. Since Treasury bonds were yielding around 3 percent at the time, the 5 percent rate was generous to investors but also economical to homeowners who often paid over 6 percent despite the presence of the agency in the lender market.[15] The lower rates prompted the head of the FHA, James Moffett, to proclaim that the death knell had sounded for loan sharks. It was a claim that had been made before.

One prominent loan shark became the subject of a lengthy investigation by North Carolina authorities in 1933. As a result, a bench warrant was issued for Harry L. Drake, a salary buyer who did extensive business in North Carolina and the south through thirty-four lending offices in seventeen states. Drake was accused of charging 30 percent per month for his services. He was a veteran of World War I and had previously been in the real estate business, although he was only thirty-six years old at the time of the warrant. He also supplied a Chicago friend, Foster McGaw, with venture capital and went on to become a founding partner of the American Hospital Supply Corporation. He maintained an expensive home in Asheville, but jumped the border to Tennessee when he learned of the warrant. Eventually, the North Carolina authorities discovered his permanent home was in Chicago and issued an extradition request. He was not charged with violating a small loan law but of evading the usury laws in North Carolina, a more serious offense.

When he voluntarily surrendered in Illinois, newspapers quickly dubbed him "the King of the Loan Sharks." By surrendering, he avoided being fingerprinted since he had not been apprehended by authorities. The maximum sentence was ten years if convicted.[16] Drake eventually pleaded guilty in Charlotte in 1933 for violating North Carolina's law and was fined $11,500 with the agreement that he would abandon his lending activities. He sold his loan offices and returned to Chicago. Later that year, he was ignominiously stopped while driving his car in Chicago and detained for a short time by robbers, who released him after stealing $10.

At the same time, a campaign was conducted in Denver against small lenders and convictions were handed down against many loan sharks for operating without a license. But the penalties were not stiff and never amounted to more than six months in prison as the maximum.

That lack of stiffer penalties caused states to consider lowering consumer interest rates during the Depression. A new proposal to introduce credit unions in the District of Columbia was made in 1932. Thirty-five states already had credit unions when the District proposal was introduced. Despite years of waging war on loans sharks in the D.C. press, this particular proposal came very late. In the interim, many other state officials gave residents advice on how to deal with loan shark demands since most of their earlier laws were ineffective. In Illinois, the head of the Chicago Better Business Bureau told loan shark victims to refuse any more payments of principal or interest on loans exceeding 7 percent. The approach was based more on past experience well reported in the national press. It was already common for loan sharks to flee jurisdictions rather than face court battles where their loan terms could be put on full display, but whether a court would actually forgive the principal amount of the debt itself was more contentious. In the past, many courts threw out the interest or the amount charged over the usury ceiling but let the borrowed amount stand as a legitimate debt. Most loan sharks knew this but still opted for flight rather than a court confrontation. Their profitability could suffer the occasional loss through concession.

In 1932 the principals of the Chicago public school system did a study of their teachers' finances to determine how well they were faring during the Depression. Payday furloughs were common and teachers were sometimes paid in municipal tax anticipation notes instead of cash, which naturally could lead them to loan sharks, who would buy the notes at such a sharp discount that the effective interest rate amounted to usury. The results of the survey were revealing. Of a total of $3.47 million borrowed, $1.12 million was borrowed against insurance policies and $1.3 million against personal notes. An estimated 7 percent of the amount borrowed was believed to have been borrowed at loan shark terms (unspecified rates but exceeding the state usury ceiling). What was notable was that if a teacher did not have an insurance policy to borrow against, then the alternatives were limited.[17]

During the Depression, life insurance companies became a major source of credit, along with banks and the other traditional depository institutions. Although not usually thought of as credit providers, insurance companies made loans against outstanding policies or surrendered cash for those who liquidated policies, as the Chicago teachers demonstrated when paychecks fell into arrears.[18]

On the opposite side of the coin, the discount note scheme also was used for fraudulent purposes, not only for tax anticipation notes. Investors sometimes bought discounted notes issued against homes with much higher mortgage amounts. If interest was not received by the bank on the mortgage, the mortgage would be declared in default. Often the homeowner or someone claiming to represent him would offer to purchase the note from investors at a very sharp discount, hoping they would take some cash for the note rather than force a foreclosure and risk getting nothing at all for a long period. The questionable process was difficult to detect. The bank involved often passed information inappropriately to the party offering the discount in much the same way first mortgage lenders often passed requests for second mortgages to known loan sharks. Because of the frequent transactions in discounted notes, it was difficult to follow the trail of the parties involved or detect their true intent.

The *Chicago Tribune* continued its own war against loan sharks and adopted a recommendation originally made by the Russell Sage Foundation. The newspaper urged the Illinois legislature to pass reform legislation to make the existing small loan law more effective. The idea was to provide stricter licensing for lenders, with $20,000 in capital necessary to receive a state lending license. The paper stated that the proposal "would eliminate the loan shark entirely and would make the supervision of reputable agencies more effective." What was overlooked was the fact that the average loan shark in New York City had half that amount invested in the business thirty-five years before, at the turn of the century. The amount seemed small, although the effective rates of interest charged did vary considerably. The suggestion underscored a larger problem.

Despite the battle against loan sharks, the Russell Sage Foundation continued to assert that rates of around 3 percent for the first amount borrowed and 2.0 to 2.5 percent on unpaid balances was the most effective tool to attract legitimate lenders to small loans. The USLL continued to wind its way through the states, with some adopting it for the first time and others modifying existing laws because loan sharking continued to be widespread even in the face of prevailing laws. By January 1, 1935, the law in Illinois had undergone six revised drafts, with a rate of 3.5 percent adopted for the first $100 loan and 2.5 percent on remaining balances of more than $100.[19] Many states adopted it in due course. The plan to providing competition for loan sharks again settled on annual rates of interest that were too low for the sharks and too high for the consumer, as had been the case since the First World War.

Congress Reacts

The elections of 1932 displayed wide discontent with Republicans and ushered in a Democratic Congress. The new faces that came with a new president brought a new attitude toward economic conditions and an even harsher view of Wall Street than existed before. Many of the Republican radicals in the Senate and the House who survived the election lost their committee jobs as the Democrats swept control of both houses. Peter Norbeck was replaced by Duncan Fletcher, a long-sitting Democrat from Florida, on the Senate Banking and Currency Committee, while Louis McFadden was replaced by Henry Steagall of Alabama as chairman of the same committee in the House.

The new faces helped institute the greatest number of reforms in banking and finance ever experienced, and they did so in a short period of time. There was a growing feeling among reformers that a concentration of financial power existed among the elite banks and securities firms and that they actively sought to break the hold bankers had on the credit and securities markets. Several of the votes that would be cast in Congress were done on a voice basis, designed in part to show near unanimity and also protect members of Congress from retaliation at the same time.

The first item on the agenda of the new administration and Congress was emergency banking legislation. The gold issue was finally resolved in early March 1933, as soon as FDR took office. The Emergency Banking Act passed on March 9, five days after the new administration was sworn in, took the country off the gold standard. As part of the act, no individual could own gold or transport it, in an attempt to ensure that capital did not flow out of the country. Anyone violating the law was subject to a $10,000 fine and up to ten years in prison. Small savers and investors had been hoarding their savings as the banking crisis deepened and the U.S. money supply had contracted as a result. If ordinary citizens started demanding gold for their cash then the crisis would only deepen. The country never returned to the gold standard after 1933. The week-long March banking holiday ended and the country's stock and futures exchanges, which had been closed since March 3, all fully opened again by March 15.

The stock market collapse came under close scrutiny in 1932 when a Senate committee began examining the market mechanics that had led to the crisis. After a slow start and losing two chief counsels, the committee was given impetus when Ferdinand Pecora, a New York lawyer, was named its counsel early in 1933. Pecora at first seemed an unlikely candidate for the job of interrogating the top echelon of Wall Street. Previous counsels had quarreled with Peter Norbeck, claiming they did not have a free hand to proceed.

Highly recommended for the job because of his interrogative skills, Pecora was the opposite of many of the bankers and brokers he examined.

Born in Sicily, he was brought to the United States by his parents and went to work in a law office in his teens. After saving money, he attended law school at night. He then served on several New York banking commissions. His new job with the banking committee paid him $255 per month, a fraction of what lawyers on Wall Street earned. When asked by Norbeck whether he would work for that amount, Pecora indicated that money was not the primary motive in his life. One newspaper in Montana later noted that "Pecora means sheep in Italian, which probably explains why he has been such a champion of the lambs shorn in Wall Street."[20] As a result of his appointment, Wall Street was outflanked by Progressives and Democrats, all intent on reform.

Although the hearings became known as the Pecora hearings, the report that followed was named the *Fletcher Report*, after Senator Duncan Fletcher. The hearings may have been named for Pecora but Fletcher was firmly in charge. Much to Wall Street's distress, Fletcher was a close confidant of FDR. With Fletcher assuming the reins, the role of the Wild Jackasses began to diminish. Reformers in Congress, less flamboyant than the Republican insurgents, now were in the mainstream.

Brokers' loans were among the first topics examined by the committee once Pecora assumed his role. The link between their availability and prices in the stock market became clear when a representative of the Standard Oil Company testified about his company providing loans. Pecora questioned the executive, whose company was one of the large nonbank lenders to the call money market during the 1920s, concerning the circumstances surrounding the heavy borrowings by brokers until October 1929. His response was straightforward. "I can tell you why we loaned so much money," he stated. "Because there was a demand for it at excessively high rates, over and above what we could get from what we would normally invest in, which are government securities, municipals, and things of that sort." An executive from another oil company, the Cities Service Company, admitted what many observers already suspected. His company was selling securities and then lending the proceeds to the call money market. The committee report concluded from these testimonies: "The consequence of such financial operations was the creation of a vicious cycle which hastened the financial collapse of October 1929."[21]

Similar sentiments were echoed by the Twentieth Century Fund when it examined the broker loan phenomenon. It stressed the link between commercial banks and the stock market because of the tendency of banks to provide broker loans rather than sound commercial loans. Between 1927 and 1929 broker loans increased $5.3 billion. The fund noted that, during that period, the New York Stock Exchange-listed companies indicated they received $3.9 billion from the sales of new securities and it claimed that a sizeable portion of that amount was bootlegged into the call money market. Maintaining that commercial banks should avoid lending to companies for capital purposes, the fund stated: "It is far worse when they do so indirectly, especially when the uninformed judgment of security traders is substituted for the presumably sounder judgment of bank executives in the allocation of the funds. Increasing brokers' loans and rising stock prices out of proportion to productive activity and earnings are inflationary in nature and effect."[22]

The committee named some of the other corporations, in addition to Standard Oil and Cities Service, that made loans to the call money market. They included Electric Bond and Share, Sinclair Consolidated Oil, American Can Company, International Nickel Company, General Motors, the Radio Corporation of America, and twelve others. When added to those already known, they formed a formidable group of lenders who had considerable muscle in the securities markets. None were primarily in the financial services business, however.

Another major topic examined by the committee was that of branch banking, group banking, and chain banking. Group and chain banking, essentially, were similar except for the manner in which stock was held.[23] Branch banking across state lines was forbidden by the McFadden Act but chain banking was another issue that arose almost immediately after the act was passed. In chain banking, an affiliate of a parent, operating as a unit of the parent holding company, would open offices in other states or counties, and do a limited but not full banking service. Although looking like a separate entity in an organizational chart, the unit shared officers and management with other units, suggesting to the Pecora committee that the parent bank was exercising its power in proscribed areas while claiming that the unit was independent. A legal loophole around the McFadden Act had been found that allowed bank expansion across state lines.

The committee cited Ohio and Michigan bank holding companies as examples of this type of banking. Its conclusions about the practice revealed its fears that group banking, in particular, had certain deficiencies that led to the financial crisis. The committee stated that "the most patent deficiency in group banking is that the group is only as strong as its weakest unit." The issue during crises was one of confidence. The report continued: "Unit banks which might otherwise have survived are doomed because of their affiliation in the public mind with the weaker units."[24] The banking problems in the Midwest could clearly be seen in the report, as well as the problems that the Bank of United States caused in 1930 when it collapsed after runs on its branches.

The Pecora committee had harsh words for Charles Mitchell. When subpoenas were issued in February 1933 after Pecora assumed the job of chief counsel, Mitchell was one of the first to be called. In addition to presiding over the stock market boom, his public duty was also questioned openly. His part-time job as a director of the Federal Reserve Bank of New York came under scrutiny. The New York Fed had already been blamed for reigniting the fires that fueled the bubble by adding funds to the market when the Federal Reserve Board equivocated about raising interest rates. Peter Norbeck commented: "When the stock market boom went wild, the Federal Reserve Board at Washington made an effort to slow it down and sought the cooperation of Mr. Mitchell who was then director in the New York Federal Reserve Bank . . . he defied the board and speeded up the boom. He took a 'go-to-hell' attitude toward the board and got away with it."[25]

Sentiment was firmly against Mitchell. He previously had defended bank expansion across state lines to the House currency committee two years before and was viewed as being on the wrong side of the new regulatory fence being constructed. As a result, he resigned his job at

National City Bank and the New York Fed after strong pressure and became chair of a Wall Street securities firm. He was the apotheosis of a securities salesman more than a serious banker and bore the brunt of the growing distaste of salesmen on Wall Street among even investment bankers who considered stock salesmen not worthy of the title "investment banker." The *New York Times* remarked that "the resignation of Charles E. Mitchell was inevitable. No banking institution, not even the next-to-largest in the world, could afford even to appear to approve or condone the transactions of which he was a guiding spirit and one of the beneficiaries."[26] A partner at a well-known investment bank that did not employ stock salesmen remarked, "We have sat back for 12 years and watched the dragging down of the name of what has been called an investment banker because of some who should never have been in the business," further stating that the policy at his firm "never employed a high pressure sales campaign."[27] The resignation of Mitchell was a signal that the old order of sales-driven banking and securities executives was coming to an end for the foreseeable future.

THE WALL OF SEPARATION

While the Pecora hearings continued, Congress moved quickly to pass new legislation to remedy the problems that the banking system and Wall Street had created prior to the crash. Many of the problems were attributed to bank organization; they were using affiliates for activities not associated with commercial banking. Samuel Untermyer remarked about a new bill before Congress: "After twenty-one years during which inconceivable havoc was created by these unlawful affiliates, the Glass bill, which I hope is about to be enacted, at least severs these affiliates from the banks. It is about to lock the stable door after the horse has escaped and to do what should have been done two decades ago."[28]

The final version of the Glass bill, passed in 1933, addressed among other things the rate of interest that could be charged on loans by banks. The law allowed banks to charge 100 basis points more than the discount rate on ninety-day commercial paper, but not to exceed the usury ceiling in the states in which they were located (Section 25). If there was no state ceiling, the 7 percent maximum allowed by the National Bank Act of 1864 became the ceiling. There was no overt attempt to impose a national usury ceiling on the states although the new law effectively established a rate of between 6 and 7 percent, which would last for several decades.

The matter of bank runs also was addressed, although indirectly. The new law created Regulation Q of the Federal Reserve. This regulation allowed the Fed to set the maximum rate of interest that could be paid on savings accounts at banks, along with establishing Federal Deposit Insurance Corporation (FDIC) insurance for those deposits. This regulation over banks' cost of funds leveled the playing field among them so they could not compete for deposits by offering higher interest rates than their competitors. Equally, it provided a disincentive for depositors to pull funds from one bank and take them elsewhere. In doing so, the amount that banks charged for loans effectively was limited. If the deposit rate were 4 percent, the lending rate would be perhaps 7 percent or slightly less, making the bank spread around 300 basis points over the cost of interest on deposits. Any lending rate higher than that sort of acceptable spread would draw immediate attention to the bank involved and would cost it business as a result.

The limits on interest on the cost and use of funds effectively gave the United States a usury ceiling in all but name. State usury ceilings governed the rate charged on loans while Regulation Q governed the rate on deposits. Since the Glass bill also mandated the separation of commercial and investment banking, banks did not have the option of shifting operations to a securities affiliate to avoid the new law. Deposits were provided by banking institutions, and other financial services institutions provided specialized services. But the latter could not infringe on the former and the basic banking equation of lending at a reasonable spread over the deposit rate could not be violated.

The Glass bill, which became known as the Glass–Steagall Act, passed both houses of Congress quickly. The House vote was 191–6 in favor. Louis McFadden was one of the few dissenters. The Senate passed it by voice vote. At the time, the most controversial part of the Glass–Steagall Act was not the separation of investment banking from commercial banking but the introduction of deposit insurance. To shore up the banking system, the bill created insurance on accounts in a clear attempt to win back the confidence of depositors. Although deposit insurance had been used in some states before, it was, nevertheless, controversial; some critics maintained that it smacked of socialism on a national level. It was as important politically as it was financially, since the vast majority of deposits in national banks were small, less than $2,500.[29] The president of the American Bankers Association called the deposit insurance provision "a drift toward Socialistic theories and government control of, and the interference in, business will affect our whole course." Not all bankers agreed, however. The president of the state bankers' association said the act marked "the greatest revolution in banking since the passage of the Federal Reserve Act in 1913 and perhaps the greatest in the history of bank legislation."[30] His position clearly reflected state bankers' relief that the new law constrained the national banks from expanding.

Franklin Roosevelt was very pleased with the new banking act and commended Carter Glass for his efforts in drafting it. Other politicians followed suit. Frederic Walcott stated that it was a rare privilege to work with Glass on the bill, other while congressmen requested that Steagall's name should be included with that of Glass for posterity, which it was. The Glass–Steagall Act would endure for almost seventy years before being substantially liberalized by new banking regulations in 1999 that gave banks freer rein in merging and conducting securities businesses once again.

Another major cause behind the stock market crash found a remedy in the Securities Exchange Act, passed a year later, in 1934. The law, through Regulation T, gave the Fed the ability to set margin rates; not the amount of interest charged on margin money but the percent an investor or speculator had to deposit against the dollar value of the position. Before the crash, around 20 percent normally was required by the brokerage houses. The act placed the power to set margin rates squarely in the hands of the central bank, which now had some control over the amount of leverage investors used in trading. The standard self-regulation that Wall Street claimed to exercise over itself clearly was no longer sufficient to protect investors and the market itself.

After the securities and banking acts were passed, and in the wake of the revelations of the Pecora hearings, Wall Street bankers' reputations sank to an all-time low. In some quarters, financiers and bankers were viewed as little better than organized crime figures. A Montana newspaper remarked, "Shocked as we are by the crimes of underworld gangs and their allies higher in the social scale, they are but the natural product of the times . . . the moral fabric of the American people has been determined by economic sappers . . . there is no place in American society for gangsters, whether they work with a sub-machine gun or a rigged market."[31]

Gangsters and bankers had more in common than their desire for gain. They were being described in the press as major but invisible forces behind the newsworthy headlines made by their subordinates, especially in the lending business. During the Dewey investigations in New York, it was commonly believed that fifteen unnamed mobsters ruled the New York rackets. None was named in public, partly because evidence was difficult to obtain. The grand juries established by Thomas Dewey claimed that the people indicted were separated from the street crime they were investigating by at least one other layer of intermediary who ensured that the top crime syndicate management went totally unnoticed. They also concluded that most small businessmen were entirely unwilling to identify those extorting usury from them for fear of reprisal. Most of the complaints they heard were from individuals who could no longer afford to pay loan sharks.

The "power behind the throne" notion was given added credence in 1937 in a book titled *America's Sixty Families*. Wall Street reporter Ferdinand Lundberg, who wrote for the New York *Herald Tribune,* examined the wealth and power acquired by the sixty wealthiest families in the country. Writing in the tradition of Gustavus Myers, one of the original muckrakers who had written a similar tome a generation before, Lundberg took a special interest in those who provided broker loans to the market in the months leading to October, 1929. He named many of the corporations that made loans to the market but also named the families behind those companies, who were major stockholders. The Rockefellers and J. P. Morgan stood behind more than half of the seventeen corporations named. Pierre duPont had $32 million on loan to the call money market, while J. P. Morgan & Company had $110 million. Lundberg's conclusion was straightforward: "In short, the wealthy families stood united behind the disastrous policies, political and corporate, of the 1920s."[32]

ONE MORE ADJUSTMENT

The drive to fix the Fed began indirectly in early 1934 when FDR appointed Marriner S. Eccles, a Utah businessman, to be special assistant to Treasury Secretary Henry Morgenthau. Born in Logan, Utah, Eccles was the oldest of nine children. After attending Brigham Young College, he established an investment company. In 1924, he and his brother joined with a prominent banking family in Utah to form the Eccles–Browning Affiliated Banks, which rapidly began to expand by acquiring banks in Utah and Wyoming. In 1928, he and several partners organized the First Security Corporation, a holding company that managed the banks that had been acquired. The company was one of the first multibank holding companies in the United States.

Eccles nominally was a Republican but his ideas did not endear him to his party. Upon being named to the post, he revealed that he favored a special tax on the wealthy to help spread the wealth during the Depression. He favored tapping the rich through a higher tax rate and a stiff inheritance tax. Despite his own wealth, he saw the nation's problem as a decline in spending. Believing that the rich were hoarding their wealth in the face of a national catastrophe, he remarked that "we need no further capital accumulation for the present," although he acknowledged that "this may frighten people who possess wealth."[33] He was correct, as a similar campaign conducted by Huey Long in Louisiana had many in Washington worried about an outburst of violent populism against the rich.

Of even more concern to Eccles's opponents was his nomination by FDR in the fall of 1934 to be chair of the Federal Reserve. When he was nominated, he commented on his transformation from a progressive Republican to a New Dealer: "Previous to the last national election, I had always supported the Republican national ticket but was not satisfied with their policies, which were not sufficiently liberal and progressive to meet changed conditions. Mr. Roosevelt's idea of what to do appealed to me and since then I have been a strong supporter of Mr. Roosevelt."[34] In his new position, he advocated further reform of the Fed to consolidate its power and prevent future debacles, like the interest rate indecision of 1929, from occurring.

Eccles was the author of a reform banking act that became known as the Eccles Act. Throughout the summer of 1935, many amendments were made to it and several riders were attached that favored the investment banking industry. The bill that passed Congress was a compromise with Eccles's original ideas but provided a sound act in the opinion of even its detractors, like Carter Glass, who believed the Fed was not broken and did not need fixing. The law signed by FDR in August created the Fed open market committee, which would decide on the Federal Reserve Board's operations in the Treasury market and provided for salaried members to the board, appointed by the president. Once the open market committee decided on appropriate actions in the market on behalf of the entire board, it would order the New York bank to carry them out on behalf of the entire system. Individual Fed banks were no longer permitted to act in the money market independent of the system, as the New York Fed had done under Mitchell in 1929.

Institutional reform of the Fed and regulation of the banks and securities markets were much needed after 1929 and the reforms proved resilient for decades to come. With so many issues requiring legislative attention during the early days of the New Deal, the usury discussion receded into the background. A common assumption was that so much banking regulation and reform would undoubtedly defeat loan sharking and high-interest lending once and for all. But that did not prove to be the case. The problems persisted but were becoming more and more institutionalized, so charging a lender with usury ceiling violations became a much more complicated matter. Charging an individual with a misdemeanor or a felony was much easier than leveling the same charges at a bank.

Despite these circumstances, the discussion about usury was not falling out of fashion. As a social malaise, it still ranked at the top. During the early days of the New Deal, the *Chicago Tribune* remarked that by banning usury for centuries, theological laws made the providers of credit nothing more than outlaws, relegating three-quarters of humanity "to the gutter" by leaving them without credit of any sort. But the outlaws endured and grew wealthier at the expense of those who could least afford their rates. The moral problems that usury and loan sharking presented were still prevalent and would not fade away simply because new definitions had been found for an old problem. "Old laws have not been annulled merely because new ones have been found," the paper concluded.

The discussion and the battles continue.

POSTSCRIPT

THE UNEASY EVOLUTION OF LOAN SHARKING AND USURY laws has remained remarkably consistent over the years. Since the original colonies first adopted usury laws and interest ceilings at rates drawn from English usage, the maximum rate always was fixed, typically at 6 or 7 percent. And those rates always were abused. The idea of consumer borrower protection from high-interest rate charges seemed doomed almost from the beginning, yet the usury discussion has persisted for over 200 years in the United States.

Charging low rates of interest to borrowers always was equated with a sense of justice and fairness, yet even the rates allowed under the USLL hardly were fair or just. It is difficult to imagine a borrower realistically being able to repay debts when the legal borrowing rate ranged from 30 to 40 percent per year. Despite the general condemnations of loan

sharking throughout the 1920s and numerous attempts at reform during that decade, the practice simply mutated and continued to plague
consumers and the poor.

Public discussions about high-interest, unlicensed lending continued in the late 1930s and during World War II. Advocacy groups
kept the fires burning. Their arguments sound familiar today; essentially they made the same points that were originally made decades
before. They maintained that even the loan sharks themselves lobbied for a return to the old fixed statutory state ceilings, recognizing
that no one would lend at those levels and that would clear the way
for them to expand while legitimate lenders were discouraged. Apparently, the sharks felt some competition from the reform movement,
especially in the 1920s. The high rates allowed by the USLL became
accepted and were not seen as excessive; they were considered reasonable, allowing lenders to make a decent profit while keeping loan
sharks at bay.

One pubic advocacy group revealed that loan sharks actually disguised
themselves as lobbyists in some states, operating out of empty rented offices, pressuring state legislatures to return to the old 6 and 7 percent levels. While the tactic never succeeded, it did cast long shadows over consumer lending in general and dissuaded many states from passing any sort
of law at all. During World War II, seven states had no consumer law of
any sort of their books, while another twelve had only partially opera-
tive laws. Ironically, those with the least protection were the Plains and
Southern states, where the anti-loan shark movement began after the
Civil War.

After the war ended, high-interest lending became more complicated
with the large-scale introduction of credit cards. Once lenders began
charging interest on unpaid balances, the rates were confusing and
evasive. As a result, Congress passed the Truth in Lending Act in 1968
requiring lenders to state clearly the annual percentage rate charged to
borrowers. The move was welcomed at the time, although lenders soon
found ways to obscure the stated rate on customers' statements by using
highly technical language designed to obscure the required disclosure.

And interest that was compounded daily on unpaid debt balances was able to accomplish predatory rates that looked tame on the surface.

Usury issues continued to arise but were considered settled with regard to credit cards with the *Marquette National Bank v. First of Omaha Corporation* case that was heard by the Supreme Court in 1978. Marquette, a Minnesota bank, claimed that the Nebraska bank, First of Omaha, was charging credit card interest in the state in excess of the Minnesota usury ceiling and should be restrained. Recalling the National Bank Act of 1864, the court ruled that the law of the state in which the lender resided prevailed, not the state of the borrower, since a state usury law did not apply to a national bank residing in another state. As a result of this ruling a new migration of consumer lenders would soon begin, searching for locales friendly for lending. Not surprisingly, South Dakota became the new home of Citibank's credit card subsidiary several years later since New York's rate was capped at 18 percent. Chase Manhattan moved its operations from New York to Delaware to take advantage of a higher rate environment unrestricted by inconvenient lending rate ceilings.

At the same time, the old 6 percent and 7 percent ceilings on mortgages were dealt a blow with the introduction of the adjustable rate mortgage that charged interest at a spread over a standard base rate, using a money market rate such as commercial paper or the London Interbank Offered Rate (LIBOR). With rates linked to a short-term rate, it became arguable whether this, technically, was a long-term mortgage loan or a short-term consumer loan. While it clearly was a mortgage, the technical and legal argument was avoided because the new market-oriented rate conformed to prevailing finance theory that fixed rates of interest slowly were being replaced in some cases by adjustable ones, a move that protected lenders' balance sheets in a period of quickly changing interest rates. Lenders could always be assured of earning the spread over the base rate regardless of interest rate levels as long as the borrower did not default.

While Truth in Lending laws and adjustable rates may have contributed to a decline in the usury discussion when it came to the middle class, loan sharking was still alive and well among the poor. The old practice of salary buying was renamed "payday lending." During the Depression, the rate became standard at around 240 percent (20 percent per month), and that rate has persisted for decades. The customers have remained the same, as well. The Federal Deposit Insurance Corporation estimated that as much as 30 percent of the population is under-banked or unbanked, pointing directly at this large segment as being the primary focus of contemporary loan sharks. They are mostly the poor and recent immigrants.

By the late 1990s a mortgage boom developed during a period of low interest rates. Although it was generally assumed that the usury discussion finally was dead, a relic of the past, the boom and the stock market advance of the 2000s were fueled in part by high-interest lending in the form of novel mortgages, most on an adjustable basis, that had exotic features like lengthy grace periods from principal repayments or artificially low sweetener rates that ultimately left many subprime borrowers (those with less than stellar credit) unable to repay when they were reset higher. The crisis that followed in the credit markets, where many of those mortgages had been packaged into bonds and sold to investors, quickly spilled into the stock markets, very similar to the phenomenon in 1929, and becoming known as the Great Recession.

During the entire period of lending reform attempts in the various states, fixed rates of interest were used until the shift to adjustable rates began in the early 1980s. This older practice is still associated with usury laws today. No single fixed rate is (or was) agreeable as a usury ceiling, and that casts a long shadow over the intellectual basis of usury ceilings because critics maintain that any rate is arbitrary and political. Why 36 percent rather than 42 percent or 18 percent? The discussion becomes fruitless and never-ending.

The idea of usury ceilings is not moribund but requires the same sort of financial innovation that gave rise to adjustable rates on certain types of loans in the first place. Several unsuccessful attempts at reinvigorating a national usury law were introduced at the time of the Dodd–Frank Act in 2010 but were unsuccessful. That compendious law, like many of its banking reform predecessors, did not attack high-interest lending, but concentrated on the activities of banks in performing acceptable functions that did not endanger the financial system. Loan sharks were not its immediate targets. High "emergency" interest rates established by the credit card lenders were the main culprits. Interest charges surged as high as 40 percent at a time when money market rates were near zero and the Federal Reserve was committed to purchasing commercial paper in the money market to ensure the flow of short- and medium-term credit. The lenders' defense was that they needed the higher rates to adjust for new risks in the markets.

Arguments change substantially if adjustable usury ceilings are used instead of the slavish insistence on fixed rates. Lenders have always contended that interest rates are market-oriented and need to be allowed to find their own levels without regulatory interference. Using an adjustable rate would allow lending rates to adjust to market conditions while still protecting borrowers from the vagaries of the market. Regulators could stipulate the size of the spread that lenders can charge over their own bond or swap rates. If a lender, by law, could only charge borrowers a fixed spread above its own swap rate or bond rate then a basic consumer lending rate could be established that would have the benefit of being able to change with market conditions while potentially lowering the high levels allowed by the old USLL at the same time.

Albert Einstein reputedly once remarked that compound interest was the eighth wonder of the world. He also reportedly said that doing the same thing over and over while expecting different results was the definition of insanity. Loan sharks recognize the truth in both comments. The former has been one source of their profits. The latter has been the unsuccessful method used by advocates of regulation constantly using fixed borrowing levels over and over in a vain attempt to control high-interest lending. The anti-loan shark and usury discussions need to employ more contemporary concepts, like adjustable lending rates, to succeed. If that were the case, lenders could be compensated for risky lending while borrowers would stand a fighting chance of being able to pay their debts in timely fashion without becoming mired in a perpetual cycle of debt.

NOTES

CHAPTER ONE

1. *New York Times*, January 8, 1873.

2. *Joshua Balme v. Henry Wornbough*, 1862.

3. The exclusion of "natural persons" from the bank usury constraints was open to different interpretations, but it is generally agreed that it provided a loophole to the usury laws. One early interpretation held that if individuals could agree on a contractual rate above the usury ceilings, then so could national banks within the boundaries of a state. See H. Rozier Dulany Jr., "The Interest and Usury Provisions of the National Bank Act," *Virginia Law Review*, 5 (1918), 266.

4. *The Economist*, September 6, 1894.

5. Cited in John Whipple, *Stringent Usury Laws: The Best Defense Against Hard Times* (Boston: Dayton & Wentworth, 1855), 2–4.

6. Clarence Hodson, *Money-Lenders: Anti-Loan Shark License Laws and Economics of the Small-Loan Business* (New York: Legal Reform Bureau to Eliminate the Loan Shark Evil, 1919), 6.

7. *New York Times*, May 20, 1870.

8. S. E. V. Emery, *Seven Financial Conspiracies Which Have Enslaved the American People* (Lansing, Mich.: Robert Smith & Co., 1894), 37.

9. W. D. Vincent, "Government Loans to the People: A Speech on the Subject Delivered before the Clay Debating Club, Clay Center Kansas, February 19, 1886," Kansas Historical Society, Document 200130.

10. *New York Times*, October 21, 1889.

11. Quoted in the *New York Times*, March 15, 1863.

12. Quoted in Freeman Otis Willey, *The Dawn of a New Era in Finance* (New York: Howard Publishing Company, 1887), 113. A similar interpretation was offered earlier in W. A. Berkey, *The Money Question* (Grand Rapids, Mich.: W. A. Hart, 1876), 76–79.

13. Emery, *Seven Financial Conspiracies*, 22.

14. *Burlington Hawkeye* (Iowa), November 8, 1891, later reprinted in the *Iola Register* (Kansas), May 6, 1892.

15. Wesley Clair Mitchell, *A History of the Greenbacks* (University of Chicago Press, 1903), 423.

16. *Logansport Reporter* (Indiana), October 20, 1894.

17. *New York Times*, August 17, 1865.

18. *New York Times*, May 13, 1852.

19. Larry McFarlane, "Nativism or Not? Perceptions of British Investments in Kansas, 1882–1901," *Great Plains Quarterly* (1987), 233.

20. A. J. Christopher, "Patterns of British Overseas Investment in Land, 1885–1913," *Transactions of the Institute of British Geographers,* 10 (1985), 452.

21. *The Economist*, July 6, 1889.

22. Mira Wilkins, *The History of Foreign Investment in the United States to 1914* (Harvard University Press, 1989), 229–36; Christopher, "Patterns of British Overseas Investment," 456.

23. James Schouler, *A Treatise on the Law of Personal Property* (Boston: Little, Brown and Company, 1873), 28–32.

24. Kenneth A. Snowdon, *Mortgage Banking in the United States, 1870–1940* (Washington, D.C.: Research Institute for Housing America, 2013), 22.

25. *The Economist*, December 30, 1905.

26. Allan G. Bogue, *Money at Interest: The Farm Mortgage on the Middle Border* (University of Nebraska Press, 1955), 128.

27. Kenneth A. Snowden, "Covered Farm Mortgage Bonds in the Late Nineteenth Century U.S.," Working Paper 16242 (National Bureau of Economic Research: July 2010), 2–6; Bogue, *Money at Interest*, 134.

28. *Historical Statistics of the United States*, edited by Susan Carter, Scott Gartner, Michael Haines, Alan Olmstead, and Richard Sutch (Cambridge University Press, 2006), Table Cj203–11.

29. *Historical Statistics*, Table Da 14–27.

30. *Extra Census Bulletin* (Washington, D.C., U.S. Department of the Interior, United States Census Office: June 30, 1894).

31. *New York Times*, October 22, 1896.

32. *Western Kansas World*, July 5, 1890.

33. *The Advocate* (Topeka), March 13, 1890.

34. *Populist Hand-Book for Kansas: A Compilation from Official Sources of Some Facts for Use in Succeeding Political Campaigns* (Indianapolis, Ind.: Vincent Brothers Publishing Company, 1891), 268. Most of the U.S. Census of 1890 was lost in a fire in Washington, D.C. in 1921 and only the *Extra Census Bulletin* of 1891–94 census remains for the period.

35. December wheat means that the contracts were due for December delivery, expiring on a specific day in that month. Futures contracts traded on a quarterly basis, so a contract would be coming due at every season; namely December, March, June, and September or a different quarterly cycle of every year.

36. *New York Times*, January 28, 1900.

37. *Washington Herald*, March 23, 1911.

38. John F. Witte, *The Politics and Development of the Federal Income Tax* (University of Wisconsin Press, 1985), 73.

39. Pollock successfully argued that the tax imposed in 1894 was a direct federal tax on property itself, something prohibited by the Constitution. The Supreme Court agreed and struck down the tax by a 5–4 margin.

40. David Kinley, *The Independent Treasury of the United States and Its Relations to the Banks of the Country,* Document 587 (National Monetary Commission, U.S. Senate, 61st Congress, 2nd session, 1910), 252.

41. *The World*, September 1, 1893, evening edition; *Boston Globe*, September 2, 1893.

42. *Financial Times*, February 21, 1891.

43. *The Investors Review*, Vol IV, edited by A. J. Wilson (London: Wilsons & Milne, July–December 1894), 345.

44. Bogue, *Mortgage at Interest*, 202.

45. *Thomas County Cat*, April 3, 1890.

46. See Jonathan R. Macey and Geoffrey P. Miller, "Double Liability of Bank Shareholders: History and Implications," Faculty Scholarship Series, Paper 1642 (Yale Law School: 1992). Extended or double liability was seen in Britain and some American states as a way of reducing moral hazard at banks because lending policies were assumed to be more conservative as a result.

CHAPTER TWO

1. Herbert Myrick, *The Federal Farm Loan System* (New York: Orange Judd Company, 1916), 11.

2. Clarence Wycliffe Wassam, "Salary Loan Buying in New York City," Ph.D. thesis, Columbia University, 1908, 41.

3. Wassam, "Salary Loan Buying," 42.

4. Wassam, "Salary Loan Buying," 23ff.

5. *New York Times*, July 16, 1911.

6. See Wendy Woloson, *In Hock: Pawning in America from Independence through the Great Depression* (University of Chicago Press, 2010), especially chapter 6.

7. *New York Times*, May 10, 1896.

8. M. R. Neifield, "Credit Unions in the United States," *Journal of Business of the University of Chicago*, 4 (1931), 321–23.

9. *Historical Statistics of the United States*, Table Cj 364.

10. *The World*, January 27, 1896.

11. *Annual Report of the Postmaster-General of the United States*, June 30, 1891 (Washington, D.C.: Government Printing Office, 1891), 85.

12. Wilbur C. Plummer, "Social and Economic Consequences of Buying on the Installment Plan," *Annals of the American Academy*, Vol. CXXIX (January 1927), 30.

13. Quoted in Gustavus Myers, *History of the Great American Fortunes* (Chicago: Charles H. Kerr and Co.), 624.

14. Paul Warburg, *The Federal Reserve System* (New York: Macmillan, 1930), 16–19.

15. *New York Times*, September 15, 1909.

16. *The Economist*, April 13, 1912.

17. Carter Glass, *An Adventure in Constructive Finance* (Garden City, N.Y.: Doubleday Page, 1927), 116.

18. The twelve Fed districts were Boston, New York, Philadelphia, Richmond, Atlanta, St. Louis, Chicago, Minneapolis, Kansas City, San Francisco, Dallas, and Cleveland.

19. *Boston Daily Globe*, August 9, 1915.

20. Charles A. Lindbergh, *Banking and Currency and the Money Trust* (Privately published, 1913), 314.

21. Lindbergh, *Banking and Currency*, 291.

22. House Report, 62nd Congress, 3rd session, 2ff.

23. J. P. Morgan and Co., "Letter from Messrs. J. P. Morgan & Co. in Response to the Invitation of the Sub-Committee of the Committee on Banking and Currency of the House of Representatives" (Privately published: New York City, February 25, 1913), 6.

24. *New York Sun*, January 11, 1913.

25. *Tacoma Times*, November 15, 1912.

26. *New York Times*, February 14, 1918.

27. Ibid.

28. *Commerce and Finance*, October 2, 1918, 1065. Even more ironic was the fact that the fortune was left to a grandson who was found when Tolman's attorney placed ads in the national newspapers seeking an heir. He was a sailor stationed in the Great Lakes who was subsequently besieged with offers of marriage when the discovery was made public. Spending the money would prove a problem since

he reportedly was being held in the brig as a deserter at the time. Eventually it was discovered that the alleged nephew had concocted the story about being related to Tolman to collect the money.

29. Quoted in Jonathan R. Macey and Geoffrey P. Miller, "Origin of the Blue Sky Laws," Faculty Scholarship Series, Paper 1641 (Yale Law School), 357. The individual state blue sky laws led to the passage of the first federal securities legislation with the Securities Act of 1933. The federal law did not supersede the state laws but existed side-by-side with them.

30. Macey and Miller, "Origin of the Blue Sky Laws," 362.

31. *New York Times*, July 16, 1911.

32. *New York Times*, June 27, 1911.

33. Arthur H. Ham, "Remedial Loans: A Constructive Program," Proceedings of the Academy of Political Science in the City of New York, Vol. 2, No. 2 (January 1912), 111. Ham repeated this statistic in many speeches around the country. The amount reported today for 1911 annual income is $587 for all U.S. workers. Non-farm income for workers was reported as $644. See *Historical Statistics of the United States*, Table Ba 4280–82.

34. Arthur H. Ham, *The Chattel Loan Business: A Report* (New York: Russell Sage Foundation, 1909), 15.

35. "Greater New York," *Bulletin of the Merchants Association of New York* (January 5, 1914).

36. *The Sun*, August 17, 1913.

37. Franklin G. Ryan, *Usury and Usury Laws* (Boston: Houghton Mifflin Company, 1924), 110–11.

38. *New York Times*, July 14, 1911.

39. Earle Edward Eubank, "The Loan Shark in Chicago," *Bulletin of the Department of Public Welfare of the City of Chicago*, 4 (November 1916), 22.

40. Eubank, "The Loan Shark in Chicago," 9.

41. Eubank, "The Loan Shark in Chicago," 12.

42. *The Commoner* (Lincoln, Nebraska), January 2, 1914. The industrial bank survived into the twenty-first century, still limited in its banking functions overall but used primarily to cater to the low-income retail customer. Its unique character was that it was a limited banking company that could be owned by nonbanking interests, unlike other banks before financial deregulation in 1999.

43. Louis Robinson, "The Morris Plan," *American Economic Review,* 21 (June 1931), 222.

44. Arthur H. Ham, "People's Banks, An Address Delivered before the National Conference of Charities and Correction," Indianapolis, Indiana, May 15, 1916.

45. Evans Clark, *Financing the Consumer* (New York: Harper & Brothers, 1930), 109–10.

46. Quoted in the *New York Times*, May 13, 1928.

47. Clark, *Financing the Consumer*, 75–81.

48. *New York Times*, December 3, 1928.

49. *New York Times,* October 14, 1912.

50. *New York Times*, March 10, 1912.

51. Ibid.

52. Quoted in the *New York Times*, December 8, 1912.

53. *New York Times*, December 8, 1912.

54. *New York Times*, January 16, 1916.

55. The cities named as homes to the land banks were Springfield (Massachusetts), Wichita (Kansas), Berkeley (California), Baltimore (Maryland), Columbia (South Carolina), Louisville (Kentucky), St. Louis (Missouri), St. Paul (Minnesota), Omaha (Nebraska), New Orleans (Louisiana), Houston (Texas), and Spokane (Washington). Only St. Louis was also the home of a Federal Reserve district bank.

56. *Washington Times,* December 27, 1916.

57. A. C. Wiprud, *The Federal Farm Loan System in Operation* (New York: Harper & Brothers, 1921), 39.

58. Wiprud, *The Federal Farm Loan System*, 103–04.

59. *Northwest Worker* (Everett, Washington), February 17, 1916.

60. William Marshall Bullitt, "The Validity of the Federal Farm Loan Act: An Address before the Farm Mortgage Bankers Association," Kansas City, September 19, 1918.

61. Comptroller of the Currency, *Annual Report* (December 6, 1915), 25.

62. *Otis v. Parker*, 187 US 606, 1903.

CHAPTER THREE

1. David J. Gallert, Walter S. Hilborn, and Geoffrey May, *Small Loans Legislation: A History of the Regulation of the Business of Lending Small Sums* (New York: Russell Sage Foundation, 1932), 53–54.

2. Gustav Cassel, *The Nature and Necessity of Interest* (London: Macmillan, 1903), 181.

3. Gallert and others, *Small Loans Legislation,* 132–35.

4. Franklin W. Ryan, *Usury and Usury Laws: A Juristic-Economic Study of the Effects of State Statutory Maximums for Loan Charges upon Lending Operations in the United States* (Boston: Houghton Mifflin, 1924), 112.

5. Allan Meltzer, *A History of the Federal Reserve*, vol. 1, 1913–51 (University of Chicago Press, 2003), 114.

6. Lee Alston, "Farm Foreclosures in the United States during the Interwar Period," *The Journal of Economic History*, 43, 4 (December 1983), 888.

7. John M. Glenn, Lillian Brandt, and F. Emerson Andrews, *Russell Sage Foundation, 1907–1946* (New York: Russell Sage Foundation, 1947), 143.

8. Ryan, *Usury and Usury Laws*, 180–85.

9. *Bismarck Daily Tribune*, November 8, 1920.

10. *New York Times*, July 12, 1923.

11. Rolf Nugent, "Small Loan Debt in the United States," *Journal of Business of the University of Chicago*, 7 (1934), 1–21.

12. *New York Times*, July 29, 1924.

13. *New York Times*, March 25, 1917.

14. Clarence Hodson, *Money-Lenders: Anti-Loan Shark License Laws and Economics of the Small Loan Business* (New York: Legal Reform Bureau to Eliminate the Loan Shark Evil, 1919), 5.

15. Evans Clark, *Financing the Consumer* (New York: Harper & Brothers, 1930), 219.

16. 251 U.S. 108; 40 S. Ct. 58; 64 L. Ed. 171.

17. *Wall Street Journal*, March 29, 1920.

18. *Chicago Daily Tribune*, October 6, 1928.

19. Clark, *Financing the Consumer,* 10.

20. Wilbur C. Plummer, "Social and Economic Consequences of Buying on the Installment Plan," *Annals of the American Academy*, CXXIX (1927); Edwin R. A. Seligman, *The Economics of Installment Selling: A Study in Consumer's Credit with Special Reference to the Automobile* (New York: Harper & Brothers, 1927). The Seligman study was commissioned by General Motors.

21. *Chicago Commerce*, 18 (September 30, 1922), 10.

22. Franklin W. Ryan, "Installment Buying Now Reaches Billions," *New York Times*, August 2, 1925.

23. These methods were discussed at length in the only detailed study of installment credit done in the 1920s. See Seligman, *The Economics of Installment Selling*, 286–87.

24. Homer B. Vanderblue, "The Florida Land Boom," *The Journal of Land & Public Utility Economics* 3 (1927), 272.

25. Ibid., 261.

26. Federal Reserve *Bulletin*, September 1937.

27. Ibid.

28. *New York Times*, January 23, 1920.

29. The *Vermont Phoenix*, August 19, 1921. The ad was placed by the Brattleboro Trust Company.

30. *New Ulm Review*, October 25, 1922.

31. Kenneth A. Snowden, *Mortgage Banking in the United States, 1870–1940* (Washington, D.C.: Research Institute for Housing America, 2013), 18.

32. Snowden, *Mortgage Banking*, 32ff.

33. Ibid., 40ff.

34. *The Evening World*, June 7, 1921.

35. Joint Legislative Committee on Housing, *Intermediate Report* (Albany, N.Y.: J. B. Lyon, 1922), 194.

36. *New York Times,* June 3, 1921.

37. *Oneonta Daily Star,* March 21, 1922.

38. *New York Times,* February 4, 1922.

39. *New York Times,* April 2, 1928.

40. "Usury Statutes and Installment Sales," *Yale Law Journal,* 48 (1939), 1102.

41. Clark, *Financing the Consumer,* 15, 37. The statistics from the Twentieth Century Fund were also reported by the Federal Reserve and remain the only reliable consumer credit statistic of the 1920s.

42. *New York Times,* August 23, 1929. Household Finance may have overestimated the amount of credit extended on an installment basis; the $4.5 billion, presumably for 1928 was the total for all consumer credit.

43. See Glenn and others, *Russell Sage Foundation.*

44. John Maynard Keynes, *The Economic Consequences of the Peace* (New York: Harcourt Brace & Howe, 1920), 165–66.

45. *Chicago Daily Tribune,* July 3, 1929.

46. According to an article in the *Canton Sentinel* published some years later, the original capital of the bank was $50,000 in 1882 when it was founded, and increased to $100,000 in 1907. In 1901, the bank paid $48,000 in dividends to its shareholders, a sizeable amount given the limited size of its capital. The amount was almost equal to the capital at the time. See *Canton Sentinel,* November 30, 1950. Many of the *Sentinel's* records later were lost in a fire during the 1940s.

47. *New York Times,* March 2, 1919.

48. *New York Times,* January 9, 1927.

49. *Barron's,* October 7, 1929.

50. See Allan H. Meltzer, *A History of the Federal Reserve, 1913–1951* (University of Chicago Press, 2003), 216–17; H. H. Preston, "The McFadden Banking Act," *American Economic Review,* 17 (June 1927): 201–18; Raghuram G. Rajan and Rodney Ramcharan, "Constituencies and Legislation: The Fight over the McFadden Act of 1927" Finance and Economics Discussion Series 2012–61 (Washington, D.C.: Divisions of Research & Statistics and Monetary Affairs, Federal Reserve Board, 2012).

51. Jerry A. Neprash, *The Brookhart Campaigns in Iowa 1920–1926* (Columbia University Press, 1932), 30.

52. Cedric Cowling, "Sons of the Wild Jackass and the Stock Market," *The Business History Review,* 33 (Summer 1959), 143.

53. *New York Times,* January 3, 1928.

54. Quoted in Joseph Stagg Lawrence, *Wall Street and Washington* (Princeton University Press, 1929), 310.

55. Speech by Frank Godfrey, quoted in the *Edwardsville Intelligencer,* March 13, 1929.

56. Anonymous, *Washington Merry-Go-Round* (New York: Blue Ribbon Books, 1931), 200.

57. Ray Tucker and Frederick R. Barkley, *Sons of the Wild Jackass* (Boston: L. G. Page & Co., 1932).

58. George William McDaniel, *Smith Wildman Brookhart, Iowa's Renegade Republican* (Iowa State University Press, 1995), 251.

59. Also named in the list from the senate were William Borah of Idaho, Burton Wheeler of Montana, Hiram Johnson of California, Thomas J. Walsh of Montana, Bronson Cutting of New Mexico, James Couzens of Michigan, Clarence Cleveland Dill of Washington, Gerald Nye of North Dakota, George Norris of Nebraska, and Edward Costigan of Colorado. Fiorello La Guardia of New York was included for being a constant thorn in the side of Republicans while serving in the House of Representatives.

60. *The Economist*, July 14, 1928.

61. Lewis H. Haney, Lyman S. Logan, and Henry S. Gavens, *Brokers' Loans: A Study in the Relation between Speculative Credits and the Stock Market, Business, and Banking* (New York: Harper & Brothers, 1932), 153.

62. Haney and others, *Brokers' Loans*, 155.

63. Ibid., 156.

64. *New York Times*, May 19, 1928 and October 28, 1928.

65. *New York Times*, March 15, 1928.

66. *Washington Post,* September 22, 1927.

CHAPTER FOUR

1. *New York Times*, May 27, 1929.

2. *Boston Daily Globe*, March 5, 1922.

3. *Nation's Business*, October 1929.

4. David J. Gallert, Walter S. Hilborn, and Geoffrey May, *Small Loan Legislation: A History of the Regulation of the Business of Lending Small Sums* (New York: Russell Sage Foundation, 1932), 218.

5. *Chicago Daily Tribune*, April 30, 1929.

6. *New York Times*, January 13, 1929.

7. See William N. Goetzmann and Frank Newman, "Securitization in the 1920s," Working Paper 15650 (National Bureau of Economic Research, January 2010), 5–7.

8. Ernest A. Johnson, "The Record of Long-Term Real Estate Securities," *The Journal of Land and Public Utility Economics*, 12 (1936), 46–48.

9. Any bond collateralized by real property was considered a mortgage bond at the time, whether it was secured by a company's property of some sort or by a pool of commercial or residential mortgages as a participation certificate.

10. *New York Times*, March 31, 1929; statistics supplied by the Los Angeles Realty Board.

11. Statistics reported by the American Bond and Mortgage Company; reported in the *Wall Street Journal*, June 16, 1928.

12. *New York Times*, March 18, 1928.

13. Goetzmann and Newman, "Securitization in the 1920s," 8.

14. *Historical Statistics of the United States*, 2006 edition.

15. *Barron's*, September 9, 1929.

16. See Eugene N. White, "Lessons from the Great American Real Estate Boom and Bust of the 1920s," Working Paper 15573 (National Bureau of Economic Research: December 2009).

17. *New York Times*, February 13, 1929.

18. Ibid.

19. *Wall Street Journal*, January 28, 1929.

20. Ibid.

21. *The Nation*, February 20, 1929.

22. Call money came in two varieties: ordinary call money and renewal money. When a broker did not repay his call money, he was automatically renewed for another day at the same rate. If he considered the rate excessive, he could then replace it with a loan at the market rate if it was lower. *Barron's* estimated that 95 percent of call loans were automatically renewed. See *Barron's,* December 16, 1929.

23. *Chicago Tribune*, August 15, 1929.

24. *New York Times*, March 29, 1929.

25. *Financial Chronicle*, March 31, 1929.

26. *New York Times*, March 30, 1929.

27. *Nation's Business*, June 1929.

28. *The Register* (Sandusky, Ohio), April 25, 1929.

29. Henry Ford, *My Philosophy of Industry* (New York: Coward McCann, 1929), 22.

30. *Barron's*, October 28, 1929.

31. *Wall Street Journal*, October 23, 1929.

32. *Wall Street Journal*, March 8, 1929.

33. Quoted in the *New York Times*, May 4, 1929.

34. *Washington Post*, May 4, 1929. See also Wilford J. Eiteman, "The Relation of Call Money Rates to Stock Market Speculation," *Quarterly Journal of Economics*, 47 (May 1933), 462.

35. *Wall Street Journal*, May 27, 1929.

36. *Daily Boston Globe*, May 27, 1929.

37. *New York Times*, May 4, 1929.

38. Quoted in *Barron's*, October 14, 1929.

39. *Collier's*, November 13, 1926.

40. *Wall Street Journal*, September 27, 1929 as reported in the "Broad Street Gossip" column.

41. *New York Times*, September 15, 1929.

42. The Bankers Bond and Mortgage Company was created when the United States Mortgage and Title Company and the Guardian Title and Mortgage Company, both of Newark, New Jersey, merged. In December 1929, the United States Bond and Mortgage Corporation was, in turn, acquired by the American Home Foundation.

43. *Barron's*, October 28, 1929.

44. *Wall Street Journal*, October 23, 1929.

45. *Barron's*, December 16, 1929.

46. See H. Parker Willis, "Who Caused the Panic of 1929?" *North American Review*, 229 (February 1930), 174–83.

47. *The Charleston Gazette*, December 4, 1929.

48. *The Charleston Gazette*, February 19, 1930.

49. Quoted in the *Wisconsin Rapids Daily Tribune*, May 18, 1929.

50. Quoted in the *Logansport Pharos-Tribune* (Indiana), November 18, 1929.

51. *Historical Statistics of the United States: Colonial Times to 1957* (U.S. Bureau of the Census: Washington, D.C., 1960).

52. Evans Clark, "Mass Financing Comes to Aid Mass Production," *New York Times*, April 27, 1930. See also Evans Clark, *Financing the Consumer* (New York: Harper & Brothers, 1930).

53. Clark, "Mass Financing." There was no estimate made for installment lenders in this report. They were included in other categories.

54. *Wall Street Journal*, November 21, 1929.

55. *Washington Post*, September 18, 1930.

56. *Washington Post*, March 5, 1930.

57. *Washington Post*, May 21, 1929.

58. In a case decided in 1930, *Van Rosen v. Dean*, the District of Columbia Court of Appeals heard a case where the plaintiff purchased real estate with a loan of $177,500 and later claimed the interest charged was usurious. The court threw the case out, stating, "We also agree with the court below in holding that the Loan Shark Law can have no application to a case of this sort, since the act was intended to apply only to persons making small loans upon personal security, as shown by the fact that the amount of such loans is limited by the act to $200.

59. Clark, *Financing the Consumer*, 38–40.

60. *Los Angeles Times*, October 27, 1930.

61. Roy A. Young, *The Present Credit Situation* (Philadelphia: Federal Reserve Bank of Philadelphia, 1928), 10–11.

62. Speech in the House of Representatives, December 16, 1930. Quoted in Louis T. McFadden, *Collective Speeches of Congressman Louis T. McFadden* (Hawthorne, Calif.: Omni Publications, 1970), 76.

63. Louis T. McFadden, *Collective Speeches of Congressman Louis T. McFadden* (Hawthorne, Calif: Omni Publications, 1970). The speech was recorded on December 15, 1931.

64. *The Bradford Era*, December 23, 1931.

65. *Salamanca* (N.Y.) *Republican-Press*, December 15, 1932.

66. Quoted in the *Chicago Daily Tribune*, December 29, 1931.

67. *Federal Reserve Bulletin*, September 1937, 868–71.

68. Gary Richardson, "The Check is in the Mail: Correspondent Clearing and the Collapse of the Banking System, 1930 to 1933," *Journal of Economic History*, 67 (2007), 644.

69. Richardson, "The Check is in the Mail," 645.

70. *Wall Street Journal*, June 26, 1929.

71. M. R. Werner, *Little Napoleons and Dummy Directors: Being the Narrative of the Bank of United States* (New York, Harper & Brothers, 1933), 203.

72. Charles W. Calomiris and Joseph R. Mason, "Contagion and Bank Failures During the Great Depression: The June 1932 Chicago Banking Panic," Working Paper 3904 (National Bureau of Economic Research: November 1934).

73. *Federal Reserve Bulletin*, February 1931.

74. *Chicago Daily Tribune*, January 19, 1931.

CHAPTER FIVE

1. Fletcher Dobyns, *The Amazing Story of Repeal: An Exposé of the Power of Propaganda* (Chicago: Willett, Clark & Co.), 16.

2. James C. Young, *Roosevelt Revealed* (New York: Farrar and Rinehart, 1936), 50.

3. *Wall Street Journal*, January 19, 1933.

4. *New York Times*, September 25, 1932.

5. *New York Times*, January 30, 1934.

6. *New York Times*, November 3, 1935.

7. John M. Glenn, Lillian Brandt, and F. Emerson Andrews, *Russell Sage Foundation, 1907–1944* (New York: Russell Sage Foundation, 1947), 538.

8. Albert Gailord Hart and Evans Clark, *Debts and Recovery: A Study of Changes in the Internal Debt Structure from 1929 to 1937 and a Program for the Future* (New York: Twentieth Century Fund, 1938), 5.

9. *New York Times*, August 19, 1932.

10. *Daily Boston Globe*, November 13, 1932.

11. Joseph D. Coppock, *Government Agencies of Consumer Installment Credit* (New York: National Bureau of Economic Research, 1940), 5.

12. Jesse Jones, with Edward Angly, *Fifty Billion Dollars: My Thirteen Years with the RFC* (New York: Macmillan, 1952), 148.

13. *New York Times*, February 1, 1933.

14. *New York Times*, January 20, 1933.

15. Mortgages guaranteed by the FHA required buyers to put 20 percent down on a mortgage and included amortization payments of 3 percent of the amount borrowed on a twenty-year mortgage, making the annual payments 8 percent, including the 5 percent interest.

16. *Chicago Daily Tribune*, July 20, 1933.

17. *Chicago Daily Tribune*, May 23, 1932.

18. Hart and Clark, *Debts and Recovery*, 21.

19. Glenn and others, *Russell Sage Foundation*, 539.

20. *Helena* (Montana) *Daily Independent*, June 16, 1933.

21. United States Senate, *Stock Exchange Practices: Report of the Committee on Banking and Currency Pursuant to S. Res. 84*. (Washington, D.C.: Government Printing Office, 1934), 13–14.

22. Twentieth Century Fund, *Stock Market Control* (New York: D. Appleton-Century Co., 1934), 95.

23. In chain banking, stock in the enterprise was closely held by a group of individuals while, in group banking, the stock was publicly held, and more widely distributed as a result.

24. United States Senate, *Stock Exchange Practices: Report of the Committee on Banking and Currency*, 73rd Congress, 2nd session (Washington, D.C.: Government Printing Office, June 6, 1934), 294.

25. *New York Times*, February 1, 1933.

26. *New York Times*, February 28, 1933.

27. *New York Times*, April 1, 1933.

28. *New York Times*, May 29, 1933.

29. The original deposit insurance provided by Glass–Steagall was for accounts of $2,500 until July 1, 1934, when it was increased to $10,000. For these accounts, all of the deposits were insured. On larger amounts, the percentage dropped to less than 100 percent.

30. *New York Times*, June 22, 1933.

31. *Helena* (Montana) *Daily Independent*, August 3, 1933.

32. Ferdinand Lundberg, *America's Sixty Families* (New York: Vanguard Press, 1937), 221, 224.

33. *New York Times*, January 30, 1934.

34. *New York Times*, November 11, 1934.

INDEX